Study Group No. 4

MENTAL RETARDATION
AND BEHAVIOURAL RESEARCH

IRMR STUDY GROUPS

1. Infantile Autism: Concepts, Characteristics and Treatment
2. Cellular Organelles and Membranes in Mental Retardation
3. The Brain in unclassified Mental Retardation
4. Mental Retardation and Behavioural Research
5. Assessment for Learning in the Mentally Handicapped

Mental Retardation
and Behavioural Research

STUDY GROUP NO. 4

Study Group held at the University of Hull,
under the auspices of the
Institute for Research into Mental Retardation and with
assistance from The Department of Education and Science

EDITORS

A. D. B. CLARKE, Ph.D.
Professor of Psychology,
University of Hull

and

A. M. CLARKE, Ph.D.
Honorary Research Fellow,
Department of Psychology,
University of Hull

Churchill Livingstone
Edinburgh and London 1973

First Published 1973

International Standard Book Number
0 443 00952 X

Printed in Great Britain by
The Whitefriars Press Ltd., London and Tonbridge

Preface

This book records the Proceedings of a Study Group which was convened by the Institute for Research into Mental Retardation, and which met at the University of Hull on September 14th, 15th and 16th, 1971.

During the last two decades there has been a rapidly accelerating impetus in research into various aspects of mental subnormality. Some of the best, most intellectually brilliant and exciting research has been carried out in the spheres of biochemistry and genetics, with a concentration on the study of chromosome aberrations and congenital errors of metabolism, which have great added to our knowledge of the aetiology of certain kinds of mental defect. However, as Belmont[1] points out, retardation is a behavioural deficiency, and the majority of these research workers have nothing to say about behaviour, other than to describe it as retarded. Research in the behavioural sciences has also been continuing, and, particularly in the U.S.A., much of it has been of sufficiently good quality to indicate, if nothing else, the complexities of the many problems which face the scientist within this area of endeavour. Meanwhile in this country, and many others, those concerned on a day-to-day basis with subnormal behaviour—parents and teachers predominantly, but also paediatricians, educational and clinical psychologists, and social workers—often find themselves working virtually without knowledge of the outcome of recent research or how it might be applied. Many people have become aware that this situation was less than satisfactory, and there are none who have been more persistent in the search for soundly based scientific knowledge to be available to the practising teacher than some of the members of this Study Group such as Mrs W. Curzon and Mr Cave, who have for years been in close touch with members of both camps. They have, in a sense, tried to bridge a gulf separating two groups of people who should have a lot in common, but rarely meet, and often have no idea how to go about communicating with each other.

---

[1] J. M. Belmont (1971) 'Medical-Behavioural Research in Retardation'. In *International Research in Mental Retardation* (Ed. N. Ellis), Vol. 5, New York: Academic Press.

The original title for discussion was *The Application of Fundamental Research in the Behavioural Sciences to Practical Problems in Mental Retardation* and in due course the shortened title of this book was adopted. The need for such a Study Group had been in our minds for a number of years. With the vast increase in research into mental retardation, and particularly in the behavioural sciences, it seemed that too little attention had been devoted to an overview of the whole field in terms particularly of practical applications. Previous attempts at discussing such issues had taken place at international conferences in two-hour symposia, involving no more than four speakers and with little time for discussion. It seemed that the time was now ripe to bring together a small group of research workers, practitioners and administrators who were sufficiently well known to at least some other members of the group to establish fairly rapidly a viable discussion. Some of those invited were unfortunately unable to attend, but even so, despite their absence we were able to achieve a better 'mix' of professions than ever before and a lively discussion of a very wide range of problems related to the behaviour of the mentally handicapped, took place. In the overview at the end of this book we have attempted to highlight most of these.

One matter, however, was so fundamental to much of the discussion that it seems worth mentioning in the Introduction. It relates to the question of regarding all mentally subnormal children or adults as 'retarded', that is, as going through essentially normal developmental sequences at a slower rate and with lower limits, or of perceiving that some at least are in important ways qualitatively different from the normal. The problem can best be illustrated by reference to the interpretation of psychological tests.

An exceptional three-year-old with a mental age of four has spontaneously developed and acquired from his environment sufficient to solve intellectual problems which the normal child will not do for a further year. His development is accelerated, and this has implications for the way he should be handled. The normal or average child of four has a mental age of four, and this, too, has implications for him. The really acute problem confronting parents, teachers and psychologists is how best to help a 12- or 14- or 20-year-old with a mental age of four. In what way, if at all, does he resemble the three-year-old with an exactly similar M.A. or the normal four-year-old? Is he to be treated as a pre-school child, or is he to be afforded the dignity of an adolescent or adult?

Related to this is the problem of whether, particularly in the severely subnormal, parents and teachers should be encouraged to follow a normal developmental approach, or alternatively assume that this in the last logical analysis may not be as helpful to the child as outlining a limited range of social, linguistic and perceptuo-motor skills which he will need and which he could achieve if actively instructed. In other words, is the mentally handicapped child or adolescent to be regarded as a retarded normal and treated as such, or is he to be regarded as handicapped (like the blind or deaf) and taught differently? Or are both ways of looking at him important, as suggested by many people, including Dr. Herriot in Session Five?

Discussion of this question is a constantly recurring theme throughout the book, but for particularly strong accounts of the arguments the reader is referred to Session Three on teacher training and Session Six on language.

Twelve papers formed the basis for discussion and these were circulated in advance. At each session, two speakers each offered an overview of his paper in no more than ten minutes, and the Chairman of Session opened the discussion with a short statement. The former were not recorded, and are therefore not included, unlike the Chairman's remarks which are. In editing the subsequent contributions, an attempt has been made to retain the flavour of the discussion, omitting only the repetitious and redundancies. We believe that the authors of the 12 papers would agree that the discussion was quite as important as the papers themselves, and can be read in its own right, without detailed reference to them.

Behavioural research began with the work of Itard in 1800, and indeed his study is of monumental stature. Through Séguin on the one hand, and less directly through Montessori, his findings exerted a tremendous influence on attitudes to the handicapped in the nineteenth and early twentieth centuries. Binet's studies, abruptly terminated by his premature death in 1911, possessed the same towering quality and from his final little-known writings, one can infer that his survival would have altered the history of Psychology in general and of mental retardation in particular. Cyril Burt's appointment in 1913 by the London County Council as the first educational psychologist in the world brought him rapidly into contact with problems of mental retardation. His careful surveys and studies played a large part in casting doubt on the growing mythology concerning the retarded. The list of early workers in the behavioural sciences relating to handicap is a short if distinguished one and even until the end of the 1930's it lengthened but little. From then on, however, and particularly in the post-war period, the amount of research in this field augmented and a number of (predominantly American) psychologists have received public acknowledgement of their contribution at the hands of the Kennedy committee for international awards. One is, however, entitled to ask what it all adds up to and what it is yielding in practice. Is the research being conducted in areas which practitioners might find useful; are some important areas being neglected? Why are the important findings of well-controlled studies not being implemented? These and many other questions are examples of the ones which the Group tried to tackle.

It should be noted that the views expressed in papers or discussions by those members of the Study Group who are Civil Servants are entirely personal and must not be taken to imply official policy of their Departments.

A.D.B.C.
A.M.C.

Acknowledgements

The success of the Study Group depended upon many people, and it is a pleasure to record our debt to them. First of all, the sponsorship of the Study Group by the Institute for Research into Mental Retardation and the hard work of its Secretary and Librarian, Miss Elizabeth Osborn must be acknowledged. The Department of Education and Science generously offered a grant towards secretarial and other expenses. Mrs. V. Barker and Miss J. Thorley undertook much of the local preparatory work and with Mrs. J. Steele contributed to the larger task of producing transcripts of the discussion thereafter; Mr. Clive Welbourn arranged tape recordings of the discussion. Lastly to the participants themselves we must record our gratitude.

Contents

Session I

Research Strategy and Methodology

What are the Problems? An Evaluation of Recent Research Relating to Theory and Practice

A. M. CLARKE and A. D. B. CLARKE

Department of Psychology, University of Hull

After some twenty or more years of post-war research into mental subnormality by behavioural scientists, this would seem to us to be an appropriate period to take stock of what has been achieved so far and to estimate what may lie ahead. This appears to be a matter of some urgency in the context of changing practices which are now in process.

The areas of research endeavour undertaken by behavioural scientists may be subsumed under the following headings:

1. *Description of the mentally subnormal,* whether clinical, observational or experimental.
2. *Fact-finding surveys.*
3. *Prevention* of subnormality by social or educational methods.
4. *Methods of amelioration,* whether by training, education or organisational change.

These areas to some extent overlap but we will proceed to outline several examples in each to indicate both the kinds of research undertaken, and the problems peculiar to the methods. Such an evaluation will, it is to be hoped, stimulate discussion and help to form a baseline in relation to which possible future trends may be considered. In so doing we shall be implicitly raising for discussion a fundamental question throughout: what are the aims and endeavours of research workers in mental subnormality? Obviously some research has an immediately and explicitly practical aim whereas other programmes are conducted in order to acquire knowledge for its own sake. In this latter case, does such 'pure' research lead ultimately to practical application, and if not, could it do so? If not, what are the barriers to it doing so?

The need for practical applications in solving or alleviating problems of subnormality is frequently stressed, and seldom more powerfully than by the American Association on Mental Deficiency, which, as Doyle (1971) points out, in 1959 published a list of what it considered the basic purposes of its research and grants. Of seven points, four involved expanding and improving facilities and services, e.g. improve facilities for professional in-service training programs; promote program planning and development in institutions; carry-on projects designed to produce materials for use by the profession, e.g. standards, handbooks and planning guides. The remaining three points dealt with dissemination of reasearch findings and provision of channels through which professional workers may be brought together to 'explore, define and appraise significant problems in mental retardation'. Only one point may be interpreted as perhaps involving basic research: 'To delineate promising areas of research, training and program development and encourage those individuals, institutions and agencies best equipped to further develop these areas.' This general attitude is also reflected in the stated purpose of the *American Journal of Mental Deficiency* (1959): 'To promote human progress and general welfare of mentally subnormal and deficient persons by furthering the creation and dissemination of knowledge of mental deficiency ... and encouraging highest standards of treatment of mental defect.' Nisonger (1963) echoes these sentiments when he writes that the aim and goal of research into subnormality is to 'minimise his disability at every point in his lifespan'. However, it seems to us, from an over-view of the experimental field, and from a literature survey which a colleague has recently conducted, that the emphasis on the need for practical applications of research, is far from being a primary goal in behavioural work.

As noted, one of our colleagues, Doyle (1971) has recently reviewed research trends in the field of subnormality during the last ten years by examining the contents of 12 Journals. This has yielded some interesting though crude data indicating what is occurring although not why it is occurring. Between 1959-1970 the most striking trend was shown by the considerable increase in experimental studies from 14.1% of *total* research in 1959 to 38.9% in 1970. This was balanced by a drop in training, rehabilitation and educational studies—17.2% in 1959 but only 5.1% in 1970. Earlier interest in the investigation and modification of attitudes of staff, parents, teachers and the general pulic has largely dissipated—12.0% in 1959 to 2.5% in 1970. Medical and psychometric studies appear to have remained roughly constant, both representing quite a large percentage of total research. There has also been a sharp rise in research of all types carried out by University-employed workers with a corresponding fall in that reported by institution-employed investigators. This reverses the 1959 position when over 50% of research was reported by institutions. While in 1959 most University research consisted of psychometric and theoretical studies, by 1970 experimental studies comprised two-thirds of behavioural reports and 27.9% of all research papers. There has also been a decline over the period in studies reported as co-operative ventures by institution-based and University-based researchers.

From all this Doyle concludes that there is something of a trend away from the complex world of practical problems. She notes that it is, of course, debatable whether a strict dichotomy between basic and applied research can or should be made. Medical research shows that the differentation should not be made in any other way than in terms of the researcher's objectives. Research is 'applied' to the extent that it is undertaken with the explicit intention of utilising results in practical situations. In the clinical field especially, though the research may deal with very simple unreal situations, the basic goal may be the same as in applied work. In addition to this, much apparently 'useless' work has had spectacular practical applications in the long term. Here one may consider the great practical contribution to medicine of basic discoveries in physiology and biochemistry. As Skinner (1961) says, 'The young psychologist who above all wants to help his fellow men should be made to see the tremendous potential consequence of even a small contribution to the scientific understanding of human behaviour'.

1. Description of the Mentally Subnormal

Although it is difficult to make a precise evaluation, it is our impression that the majority of published studies, whether psychometric, ethological or experimental, are basically concerned with desribing the subnormal rather than with the problem of amelioration or prevention of handicap. Ellis (1969) has made explicit what many investigators appear implicitly to believe: '. . . Given that there are behavioural differences between normals and retardates of equal C.A., the primary task for a behavioural science is to describe these differences.'

The basic rationale of descriptive work is the comparison of a defined population of subnormals with a control or contrast group of normal subjects. In psychometric studies, the controls are normally the C.A. match standardisation data of the test itself. Thus Alper (1967), analysing the WISC test results of 713 institutionalised children aged five to sixteen, found performance I.Q.s to be significantly higher than verbal I.Q.s; within the verbal scale the Comprehension and Similarities subtests were consistently higher than Arithmetic and Vocabulary, while within the performance scale Picture Completion and Object

Assembly tended to be high and Picture Arrangement and Coding lower. Belmont, Birch and Belmont (1967) compared WISC performance of a total population sample of home-based educable mental retardates aged eight to ten, in Aberdeen, with the performance of normal children. The subtest profile for the subnormal group differed from that of the normal, the outstanding feature being their lack of verbal facility, with Vocabulary the lowest subtest score. The factorial organisation of intellectual patterning also differentiated the groups and led to the suggestion that the limited level of functioning in the retarded children may be directly related to their less developed verbal skills and the non-availability of such skills in the service of perceptual-motor performance.

A large number of experimental psychologists have used as their basic paradigm a contrast group matched, not for C.A., but for M.A. In essence, the reason for this has been an important theoretical idea which has potential practical implications; is the subnormal person a *retarded* normal, in which case his behaviour at any stage of development should approximate to that of a younger M.A. matched normal, or is he qualitatively different, in which case such comparisons will yield significant differences? Among the many groups of researchers who have systematically pursued this approach over many years are Spitz and his colleagues, O'Connor and Hermelin and of course Ellis himself.

Zeaman (1965) was one of the first to question some of the methodological assumptions underlying this simple and apparently reasonable paradigm. He points out that the psychologist may attack the problems of subnormality in at least two ways, either by finding the laws, principles or regularities that govern the behaviour of retardates, or by finding the *unique* laws of their behaviour. If the latter is to be attempted, comparisons with normal children are essential but control in such comparisons is fraught with difficulty. 'If you match for C.A., then M.A. is out of control. If you match for M.A., then C.A. is necessarily out of control. If you assume C.A. is not a relevant variable and match for M.A., then other differences appear to be out of control. Length of institutionalization, home environments, previous schooling, tender-loving-care, and socio-economic status are factors likely to be different for retardates and normals.' To tackle such problems realistically would require heroic investigators matched by heroic budgets; hence Zeaman and some others confine their interest to laws about subnormal behaviour rather than unique laws.

Ellis (1969) makes a masterly contribution to this whole problem. The apparent rationale of an equal M.A. match is that this equalises 'development'. Rarely, however, is the meaning of 'development' scrutinised. There is the additional problem of whether equal M.A. scores are based on equal sub-test performance, and there is also the possibility that M.A. may reflect past and present motivational status as well as cognitive factors.

Ellis believes that the equal C.A. matching procedure is directed to the primary characteristic of subnormality. There are, however, serious problems with this design. Behavioural differences (except for the mildly retarded) are often so great that measurement on the same scale is impossible. 'Floor' and 'ceiling' effects are inevitable hazards (Ellis and Anders, 1968). Nevertheless, Ellis argues that for certain purposes C.A. matches appear to carry more theoretical significance than a comparison of adult mental retardates with normal children on the basis of an M.A. match

Baumeister (1967) discusses in detail the difficulties encountered in comparing normals and subnormals. He argues that such comparison is more appropriate where their behaviour is observed as a function of systematic variations in task or environmental variables; this calls for a multiple factor design in which subject characteristics are co-manipulated with experimental factors. The question then posed is not whether the subnormal is inferior but whether experimental manipulation will produce the same behavioural adjustment in both groups. One is thus no longer concerned with the showing that there are deficits in the subnormal (this is taken for granted) but with determining the conditions which produce variability in group differences. This procedure does not assume that the task is exactly the same for the two groups but that task and subject characteristics are constant for all values of the experimental variables. This latter is normally a far safer assumption.

Where after an M.A. match, performance differences emerge, the researcher has identified a difference not residing in the M.A. scores themselves. 'That this difference is any more fundamental and theoretically meaningful than one which happens to correlate with test performance is dubious. One might say that such a result shows that intelligence tests do not measure all adaptive behaviours . . . we may have done nothing more than to discover another way of diagnosing mental retardation' (Baumeister, op. cit.). Moreover, the M.A. is itself compounded of many factors, equal M.A.s may be reached by several routes, and are a reflection of an interaction between the content of the test, the experience of the subject and his 'true' ability. As such, the M.A. has little explanatory value. Baumeister notes that far more attention has been devoted to M.A. than to other variables such as reinforcement history, comprehension of instructions and so on. In effect, like Zeaman, he concludes that to understand the behaviour of subnormals one must study the behaviour of subnormals, and the study of normal behaviour 'is quite irrelevant to this purpose'. He does not entirely dismiss the usefulness of comparative studies but considers that observations of normals will not, of themselves, tell us about the behaviour of subnormals. At best it may raise hypotheses.

This debate goes to the root of the basic methodology of the majority of experimental studies and it must raise doubts in many cases about their usefulness both to theory and to practice.

A minority of descriptive experimental studies have avoided the problems outlined above by not attempting comparisons of this kind and instead, by addressing themselves to questions of differential response of the subnormal to different situations, training programmes or other experimental conditions. Among those who have confined themselves to the laws of subnormal behaviour, rather than attempting to elucidate any unique laws are Zeaman and House, Tizard and his colleagues, Zigler and Clarke and Clarke. Often the practical implications of such work appear more obvious than those based on M.A. comparisons.

For most practical purposes (i.e. education, training, and the provision of services) the C.A. match (either explicit or implicit) or the description and experimental manipulation of subnormal behaviour would seem to be the safest and most fruitful approach. Here the nature and degree of subnormal deficit can be outlined with respect to the average of the population, or the responsiveness to different procedures assessed. Some of these will be outlined under the section on Amelioration.

Despite the fact that most experimental studies have had a theoretical rather than an applied aim, and despite the methodological problems outlined above, a recent review of the literature (Clarke and Clarke, 1972) suggests certain consistencies in the findings which may have practical applications. *We enumerate some of our conclusions below:*

1. The question of whether the mentally subnormal is qualitatively deficient, due to general CNS impairment, or a retarded normal, remains to be resolved, if indeed it is susceptible of resolution. The fact that a large section of institutionalised populations are known to be the victims of chromosomal or metabolic defects, or conditions involving brain injury, makes the defect position tempting. There are, however, two problems: first, the fact that there is by no means clear evidence that the behaviour of diagnosed organically impaired retardates differs from matched groups in whom no impairment can be demonstrated (Haywood, 1966; Sternlicht, Pustel and Siegel, 1968; Zeaman, 1965); second, that the few comparisons made of normal with super-normal

children tend to show similar differences to those between normals and the mildly subnormal (Osler and Fivel, 1961; Blake and Williams, 1968). If the hundreds of studies comparing retarded with normal subjects were repeated, but comparing normal children (preferably from orphanages or other institutions) with superior children, it might be concluded that on the whole people with I.Q.s above 130 are qualitatively superior to those with I.Q.s of 100, and that the latter were inferior in CNS functioning to the former. Such a (hypothetical) conclusion might be entirely valid, but would invalidate suggestions that the majority of the mentally subnormal are to be regarded as a race apart.

Most of the evidence on perception, EEG studies, reaction time, hyperactivity, learning, memory, language and thinking shows clear differences between performance of retardates of whatever level and that of normal controls matched for chronological age. A number of research workers have also shown differences between mentally subnormal subjects and younger normal subjects, matched for mental age. The interpretation of these latter findings remains a matter of controversy. There is, however, no systematic evidence suggesting that the laws governing learning, including language acquisition, or retention, are essentially different from those underlying these processes in normal human beings, or, in some cases, other animals. Zeaman and House's analysis of discrimination learning in the subnormal bears a striking similarity to that of Sutherland (1964) and Mackintosh (1965) in the field of animal behaviour. The principles of operant learning, successfully applied in many cases to the subnormal, all originated in the animal laboratory.

Baumeister and others found that although reaction time is functionally related to intelligence, alteration of experimental conditions similarly affected the reaction times of normals and subnormals; Sen and Clarke (1968) showed within a defective population that susceptibility to external distractors was related to task difficulty, as previously demonstrated with normal subjects; factors affecting verbal mediation, such as meaningfulness, exposure time and free-association strength appear on balance to apply to retardate behaviour in a similar manner to the normal population. Blake and Williams (1968) showed that methods of concept attainment did not differentiate superior, normal and mildly retarded subjects, although there was a clear difference in levels of performance.

2. Zeaman and House's (1963; Zeaman, 1965) careful analysis of retardate discrimination learning have led them to conclude that this process is mediated, not by verbal behaviour, but by attention. Discrimination learning involves a chain of at least two responses, the

first being that of attending to the relevant dimension, the second being to approach the positive cue of that dimension; it is in the former aspect that retardates are deficient (this behaviour being M.A.-related) rather than in the latter. Learning and extinction, once the process starts, do not appear to be related to intelligence.
3. Although studies of short-term memory greatly outnumber those on long-term retention, and there is no consensus as to whether retardates generally are inferior to M.A.-matched controls, as they clearly are to C.A.-matched on short-term memory, there do seem to be reasonable grounds for tentatively concluding that the acquisition of new material is the chief area of deficit in the subnormal, while retention of well-learned material is good (Haywood and Heal, 1968).
4. The fact that subnormals often show variability of performance (Baumeister, 1968b), low degree of intercorrelation among tasks, and low correlation with intelligence test performance (Miller, Hale and Stevenson, 1968) suggests either a lack of a firmly based, well ordered repertoire of response tendencies enabling the subject to select an appropriate strategy when first confronted with a task, or fluctuating motivation to succeeed, or both in combination.
5. There is impressive evidence that retardates are particularly handicapped with respect to verbal and higher-order conceptual abilities (Alper, 1967; Belmont, Birch and Belmont, 1967; Miller, Hale and Stevenson, 1968). This is to be expected, almost by definition, and may reasonably be accepted as evidence of constitutional deficits. It should, however, be immediately apparent that differences between the subnormal and normal in these respects find a direct parallel in differences between the average and intellectually gifted. The extent to which social factors (whether in the home or the school) play a part in verbal and conceptual handicaps is not as yet precisely evaluated. It has been shown that even among the severely retarded, social factors significantly affect verbal performance (Lyle, 1959; 1960a b).

It is equally clear from the work of many investigators, and particularly Furth and Milgram that even fairly low-grade subnormals are not wholly devoid of conceptual categories, but that the greater the severity of defect, the greater the deficiency in *verbal formulation* of conceptual activity.

2.Surveys

These will receive only brief mention. Frequently they are conducted with an expressed practical aim, such as the assessment of probable need for residential provision in the next decade. Others may have a more theoretical orientation; in either event, while the techniques may be complicated, and time-consuming, and the interpretation of the data safe only in sophisticated hands, they are essentially non-controversial. The areas surveyed have, however, been rather limited. They include studies on the incidence of severe reading disabilities, the extent of oral vocabularies, or incidence and prevalence rates for severe handicap or the social structure in institutions. The work of E. O. Lewis, for example, in the nineteen-twenties is well-known, as is the comparison by Tizard (1964) of these results with his own on severe subnormality in Middlesex. More recently, Kushlick has carried out detailed prevalence surveys in the Wessex Region. Studies such as these are immensely valuable in indicating variations in incidence and in prevalence which may occur as a result of social change (e.g. earlier completion of families, family planning, decline in childhood disease, better medical care and improved social conditions) and also enable firm forecasts to be made of necessary social provision for the mentally handicapped. Where the mildly subnormal are concerned the situation is less clear in that the criteria for inclusion into or exclusion from this category are incapable of definition with any degree of scientific precision, involving as they do a number of social value judgments.

Another survey aim which has been exceedingly useful is the method of social follow-up. This may involve a clinically defined group (e.g. survival rates in mongols), or a group earlier classified as educationally subnormal, or as 'feeble minded' and certified. In general, so far as the mildly subnormal are concerned, originally homogeneous groups become increasingly heterogeneous as age increases (e.g. Baller, Charles and Miller, 1967). Such investigations tell us something of the natural history of the development of retarded individuals and help to indicate in what areas, and at what points in time, they may require expert assistance.

In general, the need for surveys is very considerable. Local variations in availability of expert staff, be they specially trained teachers or social workers, or in levels of employment, might be expected to influence the status of handicapped individuals in adolescent and adult life. Their relation to, for example, literacy or adult employment can in this way be revealed. Variations, too in local 'philosophy' may be linked with outcome. Society thus produces a number of natural laboratories which may be of use in suggesting better methods for the future.

3. Prevention

So far as prevention is concerned, a clear distinction must be made between mental subnormality arising from pathological and constitutional factors on the one hand, and, on the other, those in which there is a strong reason to suppose that social factors have played a major part. In the former, prevention will be primarily the concern of biological scientists, although behavioural scientists may well be in a position to ameliorate the defects, as noted in the section on Amelioration.

For thirty years, a number of studies have suggested an important casual role for adverse social influences in retarding early development. Many of these studies were, however, unsatisfactory in a number of ways. In particular, there was an inadequate analysis of the precise nature of these factors, and of their *modus operandi*. Despite inadequate preparation, a vast amount of money has been hastily and enthusiastically invested by the United States in Headstart Programmes aimed at the prevention of educational failure and mild retardation in children from slum homes. These programmes and their general failure (with certain outstanding exceptions) have been well reviewed by Jensen (1969) who, as you will know, attributes their lack of success to intractable genetic factors. Jensen, who is an intelligent and careful reporter of this literature, does, however, mention one or two schemes which have been relatively successfuly (e.g. Bereiter and Engelmann, 1966; Gray and Klaus, 1970) but does not analyse in detail the difference between the methods used and those employed in other Headstart Schemes. He does, however, point to the success of sharply focused programmes concentrating on essential verbal and conceptual skills, in contrast to those aiming to 'enrich' the child.

The important point to be made is that the relatively successful programmes of intervention have focused not so much on 'enriching' the child by putting him in a play situation with much apparatus, but rather by sharply defined and clearly directed instruction in verbal, numerical and problem solving situations, the sort of programme which would horrify modern infant school teachers and most teachers of the mentally handicapped child in this country. Other clearly relevant variables are duration of the programme and the degree to which parents are involved or the child removed from inadequate parents or institutions.

As you will know, studies by Skeels and Dye (1939), Skodak and Skeels (1949) and Skeels (1966) assessed the outcome of children of mentally subnormal mothers, fostered or adopted into average or above average homes. Although some of these studies can be criticised (because among other things the precise status of the father was usually unkown) most workers (including Jensen, 1969) accept that these consistent findings indicate in general a far better outcome than could have been predicted had these children been brought up in their native environments. Although genetic factors clearly play a part in the ultimate status achieved by children of this sort, it is absolutely clear that a large environmental shift is paralleled in most cases by a large shift in intellectual and educational attainments.

Total removal of children from their inadequate parents, although sometimes desirable, normally can only take place under unusual circumstances such as abandonment or illegitimacy. Heber (1968 and 1971), and Heber and Garber (1971) are in process of conducting a most important study in connection with the prevention of mild subnormality, without *total* removal of the children from their homes. This study, in a slum area of high prevalence for mental retardation, shows a statistical risk factor for 14 year-olds of 0.90 when the mother's I.Q. is less than 80, and only 0.13 when maternal I.Q. is 80 or above. Hence low intelligence mothers (and there was strong evidence of paternal/maternal I.Q. congruence) in this area have been randomly assigned either to experimental or control conditions. The newly born children of the former group were stimulated intensively from birth onwards to see whether or not it might be possible to reduce the occurrence of mental retardation. From four months of age the babies attended a special Infant Education Centre initially with a 1:1 teacher/infant ratio, and followed a daily programme of sensory and language stimulation from early morning until late afternoon. The major emphasis has been to facilitate achievement motivation, problem solving skills and language development. At the same time the retarded mothers were relieved of the day care of other pre-school children and offered training in home-making and child care techniques. Early results at age 3½ show striking differences between the experimental and control children on *all* behavioural variables, and in terms of I.Q. an average difference of 37 I.Q. points. While Heber is professionally cautious, he concludes that 'the performance of these children today is such that it is difficult to conceive of their ever being comparable to the 'lagging' control group. We have seen a capacity for learning on the part of extremely young children which exceeds anything which, previously, would have been believed possible. And the trend of our present data does engender the hope that it may prove to be possible to prevent the kind of mental retardation associated with both poverty and parent of limited ability. And should the means of prevention fall within our grasp, surely our society will have the responsibility to do so.'

This study provides an example of research in which the theoretical and practical problems which it illuminates are both of fundamental importance.

4. Amelioration

Twenty years of laboratory experiments and rehabilitation schemes have shown at least one matter with absolute clarity. The behaviour of a mentally subnormal person can be modified in a systematic way, granted both time and appropriately skilled teaching or training. The question is now not so much whether a handicapped individual can with tuition learn a basic skill which he would otherwise not spontaneously develop; the answer is usually affirmative. Rather the question has now become: 'What is the best way of teaching the particular skill, what circumstances of training and subsequent reinforcement favour its acquisition and retention, and what duration of tuition is necessary?' A further important problem relates to the limits of development, and on the whole these are usually less restricted than has earlier been anticipated. To this may have to be added the non-scientific but vital question 'what is the cost, what resources can be made available and for what ultimate purpose?'

We do not propose in this short section to review the many studies concerned with education and training of the mentally subnormal. Rather we will try to deal with what, after examining and reviewing a great deal of the literature, we see as some of the more important issues. The first is the distinction now usefully being made between 'capacity' and 'performance'. The former refers to behavioural potential and the latter to the use made of it in any given situation. For example, one of the tasks in an intelligence test at which the mentally retarded are likely to perform badly or fail is giving similarities between conceptually related objects (e.g. the question 'in what way are aeroplane and car alike?') The clinician may easily, on the basis of the subnormal's failure, conclude that the conceptual relationship between exemplars is totally lacking. He might well be wrong. Among the many investigations having a bearing on this is an important series of studies by Furth and Milgram (1965) who contrasted the performance of subnormal and normal subjects on a verbal similarities task and a parallel picture-sorting task. Milgram (1966) using the same procedure, compared severely retarded (trainable, institutionalised), mildly retarded (educable, non-institutionalised) and normal groups of similar M.A. (6) but with an I.Q. difference of 30 points between adjacent groups. No difference was found among the three groups on picture sorting but the severely retarded were significantly inferior to the other two groups with respect to verbalisation. Milgram concludes that the greater the severity of mental defect, the greater the deficiency in verbal formulation of adequate conceptual performance.

Similarly, O'Connor and Hermelin (1963) showed, in their

experimental work with the severely subnormal, superior performance when a sorting task could be learned with the aid of a spontaneously-used concept than merely by rote learning. Moreover, they postulate a disinclination to use speech as one of the language handicaps exhibited by such persons, as well as a relative inability.

We have conducted a series of experiments, some with mentally subnormal subjects and others with normal pre-school children, which show that, when faced with problems demanding categorisation for adequate performance, initial ability was very poor. However, granted certain conditions of training, a set to use categories could be induced, and an important cognitive process not normally the preferred one, and thus low in the behavioural repertoire, could be made available. We were able to show that memory for categorically related words, randomly presented, could be enhanced by a rather long period of training with different material in which the categorical relations among groups of words was made clear (Clarke, Clarke and Cooper, 1970). Other work on verbal mediation (Borkowski and Johnson, 1968; Penny, Peters and Willows, 1968; Gallagher, 1969) suggests that the subnormal can be shaped in the laboratory to use verbal mediators, but the strong possibility exists that without long-term overlearning they would quickly lapse back into their lower order response habits. Milgram (1967) found that subnormals, although benefiting significantly from verbal mediation instructions, were inferior to normal controls in their long-term retention of a mediational set.

Bortner and Birch (1970) in an important paper reviewing studies of young normal children, mental retardates and animals, state that these support the assumption that a meaningful distinction should be made between capacity and competence (performance). Moreover, the performance of the individual may not directly reflect his capacity but rather represents that fragment of his capacities which was in accord with the particular conditions of demand. This general proposition which, as the authors indicate, has more often been implicit than explicit, has led workers in many countries to concern themselves with delineating the appropriate conditions, both cognitive and motivational, for making demands which, in turn, would lead to performance that more truly reflect the capacities of the subnormal individual than he ordinarily exhibits. Bortner and Birch go on to underline the crucial nature of the interaction between the subnormal and the demands made upon him. The present writers consider that it is the variables of task or programme demand, and their duration and nature, which differentiate effective from ineffective programmes of amelioration.

It was a failure to make this distinction that led to the discrepancy between the long-accepted behavioural descriptions of Tredgold (e.g.

the imbecile cannot concentrate, has very poor motor co-ordination, cannot respond to incentives nor appreciate cause-effect relations) and, the experimental findings of Tizard, O'Connor, Gordon, Loos, Clarke and Hermelin, as well as the rehabilitation schemes of Gunzburg. A similar failure can be seen today in the work of Piaget, who, like Tredgold, carefully describes behaviour he observes at different ages, but has failed to delineate the independent variables which elicit or significantly affect the behaviour.

It is clear from the experimental work quoted that there is often a considerable gap between capacity and performance. This is one of the factors which makes precise predictions of individual responsiveness to particular training procedures very difficult. An obvious relation between initial performance and ultimate level is often non-existent, nor does the I.Q. score often predict competence at learning *specific skills* under *special conditions*. What an intelligence test may, however, usefully do is to give some indication of the overall incidental or spontaneous learning capacity of the subject, and may well predict the approximate number of behavioural skills which can be achieved, as well as the level.

The 'behaviour modifiers', following Skinnerian principles implicitly recognise the distinction between capacity and performance, and also the hierarchically-ordered repertoire of response availability. As Dent (1968) indicates in an admirably succinct review, man's interaction with his environment results in the development of both simple and complex forms of behaviour. According to behaviour theory, these behaviours are acquired, altered or maintained by the reinforcement received from the environment; the frequency of a response is subject to the consequences of that response. Broadly speaking, reinforcement may be positive (pleasant, rewarding) or negative (noxious, punishing). The former is assumed to increase, and the latter to decrease, the frequency of a particular response. There are four simple schedules of reinforcement: fixed ratio; variable ratio; fixed interval; and variable interval. Dent stresses that since society skilfully dispenses its reinforcement on a variable interval schedule, the ultimate goal in training the subnormal is to achieve control of the particular behaviour in such a way that it will eventually be maintained by society. This in turn suggests that the desired response should be established by means of a fixed ratio reinforcement schedule (i.e. rewards given in a fixed ratio to the subject's response rate) which is then gradually shifted to variable interval reinforcement; at the same time there should be a shift from primary reinforcers (e.g. edibles) to secondary (e.g. social approval).

Operant techniques are important, since they have often been applied to subnormals with I.Q.s below 35, and in particular to those of idiot grade who are normally regarded as unresponsive to the more usual modes of training. Positive reinforcement is used to create desirable forms of behaviour and negative (e.g. aversive) reinforcement to eliminate undesirable traits such as aggressive, destructive or self-destructive behaviour. Various studies have concerned the development, by means of operant conditioning, of personal self-care skills and social and verbal skills. Useful and comprehensive reviews have been produced by Watson and Lawson (1966); Spradlin and Girardeau (1966); Watson (1967) and Baumeister (1967a). An Orwellian twist has been provided by Henker, according to Dent (1968). She contends that the mentally subnormal can be trained to apply operant procedures in the training of other subnormals. This will create 'therapeutic pyramids' whereby a small number of professionals train a larger number of subnormals who in turn train a still larger number of their peers.

Nevertheless, despite the large number of studies reported, Watson (1967) concluded that although they indicate that severely and profoundly retarded children can develop skills when systematic training procedures are used, it is not clear what variables are responsible for the success of these programmes, and which are either irrelevant or possibly even interfering. Gardner (1969) examined the methodology and results of operant conditioning techniques, and concluded that, to some extent, all the studies have violated one or more of the following requirements of good experimental design: (1) exact specification of *all* relevant independent variables, (2) proper sampling techniques, (3) use of adequate controls, (4) proper assessment of the dependent variable, and (5) evaluation of long-term gains. Gardner recommends (1) direct and indirect measures of both specific and general changes in behaviour, (2) individual as well as group presentation of results, (3) pre- and post-treatment evaluations, including periodic assessment to measure long-term gain, and (4) multivariate manipulation of the independent variables, particularly specific techniques. Progress in elucidating these problems can nevertheless be expected.

In a challenging chapter on 'The role of social institutions in the causation, prevention and alleviation of mental retardation', Tizard (1970) argues that though the causes of socio-cultural (mild) retardation may be complex and ill-defined, it is nevertheless now open to all developed countries to deal with the needs of the retarded in a civilised and humane manner. His careful researches, and those of his colleagues, emphasise the importance of the mode of care and training, and the organisation within institutions, in the degree to which they may ameliorate handicap. He believes that it is through the re-organisation and improvement of services, and the study of factors which may affect their quality, that the most effective contributions will be made.

While Tizard is primarily concerned with residential services for those who need to live away from home, the problem of social interaction within the home is being explored by such workers as Susan Gray (1970).

Granted that the subnormal are impaired in their ability to learn, verbalise and abstract, the question remains open as to whether they can be made more competent in these respects. Such evidence as is available suggests that they can. On the other hand, the criticisms voiced by Watson (1967) and Gardner (1969) of studies of operant learning would with profit be borne in mind by any potential researchers in this area. Neither short-term periods of specific instruction nor blunderbuss educational programmes are likely to lead to the detailed understanding of how verbal and conceptual training of the retarded should most effectively proceed. Obvious, but frequently overlooked problems, are 'Hawthorne' effects and the personal qualities of the instructor. Both of these should be controlled in the experimental design, in addition to other variables. Research on higher cognitive processes, to be of any value, will probably need considerable financial support, and the services of a team of scientists; it seems to the present writers that it offers a most challenging and potentially interesting area for endeavour—whatever the outcome.

Summary

In conclusion, there are four major areas of practical endeavour in the field of mental handicap: description, (including diagnosis), social care, prevention and amelioration. In each of these, practical decisions are taken every day by doctors, teachers, social workers and parents, which profoundly affect the lives of the individuals concerned. There has developed in advanced societies a sense of compassion towards and desire to help the handicapped which must be accepted as the major motivating factor on the part of professional and non-professional alike. Yet there remains considerable bewilderment and frequent controversy as to the most effective course of action which can be taken in many cases. The efficacy of genetic counselling, for example, as an overall means of prevention has been the subject of controversy since the early days of the Eugenics Society; nor is there any unanimity on methods of teaching or even on a desirable curriculum for the mentally handicapped. We find passionate disciples of Glen Doman's methods, of the Rudolf Steiner philosophy, or of Skinnerian theories of operant learning. At present there is an on-going argument about whether Adult Training Centres should concern themselves in a major way with sub-contract industrial work, and whether different forms of handicap should be mixed. In the area of social care there are the passionate advocates of large institutions for the mentally handicapped, for the right of parents to be relieved of the burden of caring for a handicapped child, for the desirability and humanity of the less well endowed to live together, sheltered from the difficulties of a modern technological society. By contrast there are those who see the future in terms of a greater acceptance by society of their handicapped members and a better social integration.

In all areas it is to be hoped that fundamental research will help to make possible a rational evaluation, and suggest ways of resolving some of the conflicting philosophies. A distinction must be made, however, between value judgments and questions of fact. To take an extreme example, Sidman and Stoddard's (1966) demonstration of perceptual discrimination learning in subjects devoid of language, including idiots and low-grade imbeciles, by means of careful programming and specially devised apparatus makes it clear that any human-being of whatever level is capable of at least some learning. Whether the gain for the subject or investment in terms of skilled manpower would be justified on a large scale depends upon value judgments and the resources which society make available. Or again, in an under developed agricultural community with widespread unemployment, it might be absurd to suggest an industrial workshop for the adult mentally handicapped. The decision takers would, however, have to bear in mind the research and experience which has shown that this type of activity in a different context may be ideally suited to the needs of many severely subnormal people. Advocates of large hospitals for the mentally subnormal would do well to take account of the painstaking findings of behavioural scientists on the effect of such communities on both staff and patients and the evidence provided concerning alternative methods of care. Those who attribute the failure of most American Headstart programmes significantly to ameliorate the educational handicap of the pupils to intractable genetic causes should feel bound to examine closely both the evidence of teaching methods, which have made several programmes successful, and the recent experiment by Heber who adopted a policy of total daily removal of newly born infants from their families and carefully devised nurture over a period of years. It is open to any society to decide that the amelioration of sub-cultural retardation is too costly to undertake on any wide scale; it appears no longer justifiable to maintain that it cannot be done.

It is our, perhaps optimistic, conclusion that the guide lines for effective practice are to a large extent available. Either through resistance to change, or through lack of communication of research outside Britain (predominantly in the U.S.A.) we do not, however, see a sufficient impact of fundamental research on practices in mental retardation in Britain.

In this connection we are most concerned about the lack of development in this country of programmes geared to the needs of the child in the I.Q. range of 35-60. There seems little reason to suppose that operant learning techniques and programmed instruction with a clearly defined goal should not provide a better method of guiding the child towards adult status than the prevailing methods which emphasise spontaneous learning through relatively unstructured activity. The time is now ripe to discuss the issue of whether a teacher of the mentally subnormal should see her role as an active behaviour modifier regardless of which developmental level a pupil may have reached.

REFERENCES

Alper, A. E. (1967). An analysis of the Wechsler Intelligence Scale for Children with institutionalized mental retardates. *Amer. J. ment. Defic.* 71, 624-630.
Baller, W. R., Charles, D. C. and Miller, E. L. (1967). Mid-life attainment of the mentally retarded: a longitudinal study. *Genet. Psychol. Monogr.* 75, 235-329.
Baumeister, A. A. (1967a). Learning abilities of the mentally retarded. In 'Mental Retardation: Appraisal, Education and Rehabilitation' (ed. A. A. Baumeister). pp.181-211. London: University of London Press.
Baumeister, A. A. (1967b). Problems in comparative studies of mental retardates and normals. *Amer. J. ment. Defic.* 71, 869-875.
Belmont, I., Birch, H. G. and Belmont, L. (1967). The organization of intelligence test performance in educable mentally subnormal children. *Amer. J. ment. Defic.* 71, 969-976.
Bereiter, C. and Engelmann, S. (1966). 'Teaching Disadvantaged Children in the Preschool'. New Jersey: Prentice Hall.
Blake, K. A. and Williams, C. L. (1968). Induction and deduction and retarded, normal and superior subjects' concept attainment. *Amer. J. ment. Defic.* 73, 226-231.
Borkowski, J. G. and Johnson, L. O. (1968). Mediation and the paired-associate learning of normals and retardates. *Amer. J. ment. Defic.* 72, 610-613.
Bortner, M. and Birch, H. G. (1970). Cognitive capacity and cognitive competence. *Amer. J. ment. Defic.* 74, 735-744.
Clarke, A. M. and Clarke, A. D. B. (1972). Mental Subnormality. Chapter 6. In 'Handbook of Abnormal Psychology', 2nd Edition (ed. H. J. Eysenck). London: Pitman.
Clarke, A. M., Clarke, A. D. B. and Cooper, G. M. (1970). The development of a set to perceive categorical relations. In 'Social-Cultural Aspects of Mental Retardation' (ed. H. C. Haywood), pp.433-447. New York: Appleton-Century-Crofts.

Dent, H. E. (1968). Operant conditioning as a tool in the habilitation of the mentally retarded. *Proc. First Congr. Internat. Assoc. scientif. Stud. ment. Defic.* 873-876. Reigate: Michael Jackson.

Doyle, C. E. (1971). A general review of research in mental subnormality 1959-1970. University of Hull unpublished B.A. dissertation.

Ellis, N. R. (1969). A behavioural research strategy in mental retardation: defense and critique. *Amer. J. ment. Defic.* 73, 557-566.

Ellis, N. R. and Anders, T. R. (1968). Short-term memory in the mental retardate. *Amer. J. ment. Defic.* 72, 931-936.

Furth, H. G. and Milgram, N. A. (1965). The influence of language on classification: a theoretical model applied to normal, retarded and deaf children. *Genet. Psychol. Monogr.* 72, 317-351.

Gallagher, J. W. (1969). Mediation as a function of associative chains in normal and retarded children. *Amer. J. ment. Defic.* 73, 886-889.

Gardner, J. M. (1969). Behaviour modification research in mental retardation: search for an adequate paradigm. *Amer. J. ment. Defic.* 73, 844-851.

Gray, S. W. (1970). Intervention with mothers and young children: the focal endeavour of a research and training program. In 'Social-Cultural Aspects of Mental Retardation' (ed. H. C. Haywood), pp. 508-519. New York: Appleton-Century-Crofts.

Gray, S. W. and Klaus, R. A. (1970). The Early Training Project: a seventh-year report. *Child Developm.* 41, 909-924.

Haywood, H. C. (1966). Perceptual handicap: fact or artifact? *Ment. Retard.* (Canada). 16, 9-16.

Haywood, H. C. and Heal, L. W. (1968). Retention of learned visual associations as a function of I.Q. and learning levels. *Amer. J. ment. Defic.* 72, 828-838.

Heber, R. (1968). The role of the environmental variables in the etiology of cultural-familial mental retardation. *Proc. First. Congr. Internat. Assoc. scientif. Stud. ment. Defic.* 456-465. Reigate: Michael Jackson.

Heber, R. (1971). *Rehabilitation of Families at Risk for Mental Retardation: a Progress Report.* Rehabilitation Research and Training Centre, University of Wisconsin, Madison, Wisconsin.

Heber, R. and Garber, H. (1971). An experiment in prevention of 'cultural-familial' mental retardation. In *Proc. Second Cong. Internat. Assoc. scientif. Stud. ment. Defic.* (ed. D. Primrose), pp. 31-35. Amsterdam: Swets and Zeitlinger.

Jensen, A. R. (1969). How much can we boost I.Q. and scholastic achievement? *Harvard educ. Rev.* 39, 1-123.

Lyle, J. G. (1959). The effect of an institution environment upon the verbal development of imbecile children: I. Verbal intelligence. *J. ment. Defic. Res.* 3, 122-128.

Lyle, J. G. (1960a). The effect of an institution environment upon the verbal development of imbecile children: II. Speech and language. *J. ment. Defic. Res.* 4, 1-13.

Lyle, J. G. (1960b). The effect of an institution environment upon the verbal development of imbecile children: III. The Brooklands residential family unit. *J. ment. Defic. Res.* 4, 14-23.

Mackintosh, N. J. (1965). Selective attention in animal discrimination learning. *Psychol. Bull.* 64, 124-150.

Milgram, N. A. (1966). Verbalization and conceptual classification in trainable mentally retarded children. *Amer. J. ment. Defic.* 70, 763-765.

Milgram, N. A. (1967). Retention of mediation set in paired-associate learning of normal children and retardates. *J. Exp. Child Psychol.* 5, 341-349.

Miller, L. K., Hale, G. A. and Stevenson, H. W. (1968). Learning and problem solving by retarded and normal Ss. *Amer. J. ment. Defic.* 72, 681-690.

Nisonger, H. W. (1963). President's address: Changing concepts in mental retardation. *Amer. J. ment. Defic.* 67, 4-7.

O'Connor, N. and Hermelin, B. F. (1963). 'Speech and Thought in Severe Subnormality'. London: Pergamon Press.

Osler, S. F. and Fivel, M. W. (1961). Concept attainment: I. The role of age and intelligence in concept attainment by induction. *J. exp. Psychol.* 62, 1-8.

Penney, R. K., Peters, R.DeV. and Willows, D. M. (1968). The mediational deficiency of mentally retarded children: II. Learning set's effect on mediational deficiency. *Amer. J. ment. Defic.* 73, 262-266.

Sen, A. and Clarke, A. M. (1968). Some factors affecting distractibility in the mental retardate. *Amer. J. ment. Defic.* 73, 50-60.

Sidman, M. and Stoddard, L. T. (1966). Programming perception and learning for retarded children. In 'International Review of Research in Mental Retardation' Vol. 2 (ed. N. R. Ellis), pp. 151-208. New York: Academic Press.

Skeels, H. M. (1966). Adult status of children with contrasting early life experiences. *Monogr. Soc. Res. Child Developm.* 31.

Skeels, H. M. and Dye, H. B. (1939). A study of the effects of differential stimulation on mentally retarded children. *Proc. Amer. Assoc. ment. Defic.* 44, 114-136.

Skinner, B. F. (1961). Current Trends in Psychological Theory'. Pittsburg: Univ. Pittsburg Press.

Skodak, M. and Skeels, H. M. (1949). A final follow up of one hundred adopted children. *J. genet. Psychol.* 75, 85-125.

Spradlin, J. E. and Girardeau, F. L. (1966). The behavior of moderately and severely retarded persons. In 'International Review of Research in Mental Retardation', Vol. 1. (ed. N. R. Ellis), pp. 257-298. New York: Academic Press.

Sternlight, M., Pustel, G. and Siegel, L. (1968). Comparison of organic and cultural-familial retardates in two visual-motor tasks. *Amer. J. ment. Defic.* 72, 887-889.

Sutherland, N. S. (1964). The learning of discriminations by animals. *Endeavour.* 23, 148-152.

Tizard, J. (1964). 'Community Services for the Mentally Handicapped'. London: Oxford Univ. Press.

Tizard, J. (1970). The role of social institutions in the causation, prevention and alleviation of mental retardation. In 'Social-cultural Aspects of Mental Retardation.' (ed. H. C. Haywood), pp. 281-340. New York: Appleton-Century-Crofts.

Watson, L. S. (1967). Application of operant conditioning techniques to institutionalized severely and profoundly retarded children. *Ment. Retard. Abstrs.* 4, 1-18.

Watson, L. S. and Lawson, R. (1966). Instrumental learning in mental retardates. *Ment. Retard. Abstrs.* 3, 1-20.

Zeaman, D. (1965). Learning processes of the mentally retarded. In 'The Biosocial Basis of Mental Retardation' (eds S. F. Osler and R. E. Cooke), pp. 107-127. Baltimore: Johns Hopkins Press.

Zeaman, D. and House, B. J. (1963). The role of attention in retardate discrimination learning. In 'Handbook of Mental Deficiency' (ed. N. R. Ellis), pp 158-223. New York: McGraw-Hill.

Scientific Research and Individual Variation

JOANNA RYAN

Unit for Research on the Medical
Applications of Psychology, University of Cambridge

Much of the fundamental or pure research that is done on mental subnormality never reaches the classroom, hopital or home, in any form at all. This is particularly true of behavioural as opposed to medical research. This failure of application of research. to the actual needs of the subnormal is paradoxical, since for many individual research workers as well as for grant-giving bodies, the motivation for doing such research is its potentially applied and socially useful nature. I shall argue that the large gap that exists between most behavioural research and the requirements of those in charge of the subnormal is not simply one of 'communication', not simply due to an absence of suitable feedback from the research, as is often supposed. Instead, much of the research that is done is in principle inapplicable and irrelevant to any actual situation, and thus no amount of explaining it to teachers, parents, nurses or doctors, will make it less so. In fact, my experience of giving talks about research to any but an academic audience has often been that it makes its irrelevance increasingly obvious to everyone.

The reasons for this failure of application of pure research lie instead in some general features of the behavioural sciences, particularly in the adherence to models of explanation and procedures more suitable for inanimate matter than for humans. Detailed expositions of these features, as applied to psychology in general, can be found in Herbst (1970) and Ingleby (1970). Most of the research on the behaviour of the mentally subnormal has been directly influenced by the methods and theories of experimental psychology, and it is the purpose of this paper to show how this has prevented it from being of greater application. Two specific characteristics of such research will be discussed: its inability to deal with individual variation, and its definition of subjects in terms only of their I.Q. or mental age.

It is as well to raise the question of how applied it is desirable research should be. There is no simple way of answering this, since the conventional distinction between pure and applied science does not have the same meaning in psychology as it does in other sciences. Roughly, the model for the relationship between pure and applied science is one in which fundamental principles are discovered in the laboratory under controlled and artificial conditions that may bear little or no resemblance to natural conditions, or to any potential application. In psychology the hope has been that basic principles of human behaviour will be revealed in the simplified and standardised conditions of the laboratory, and that these principles will be used to predict, explain, or control behaviour in the more complex and less controlled conditions of everyday life. It can be argued that this is a mistaken enterprise for psychology, one that certainly has not succeeded in the way that it has in other sciences. There are several interrelated reasons why this is so, that can only be mentioned briefly here.

It is notoriously difficult to create standardised situations that are 'uncontaminated' by all the forces that normally influence people's behaviour: it is even more difficult to do so without excessive trivialisation, without excluding the most important phenomena from experimental investigation. Further, a standardised experimental situation that is, as far as the experimenter is concerned, the same for all subjects, is not perceived in a similar way by different subjects. Thus it cannot be said that the 'same' thing or event is being investigated, in apparently standardised conditions. The attempt to do pure research on human behaviour by the isolation of variables and the standardisation of conditions may thus defeat its own ends and this is why the usual distinction between pure and applied research is not such a useful one in psychology as in other sciences.

We have not yet developed a methodology to deal with the range and complexity of variables that influence human behaviour, nor with the relationships between such variables, nor with the fact that these relationships vary between individuals. The customary experimental procedures of isolation of variables and the treatment of individual variation as statistical noise are not likely to produce much that is of revelance to those faced with complex individual variation in situations where it cannot be dismissed but must be responded to appropriately—as in the classroom. Teachers and caretakers have to deal with individuals, and this is emphasised in the philosophy of 'special' education—education that is adapted to the special needs of individual children. There are several features of mental subnormality that accentuate the difficulties of psychology in dealing with individual variation, but that also increase the need that it shall do so. It is to these features that I now want to turn.

Variation in Groups of Subnormal Children

Teachers of subnormal children, despite the small size of classes, are faced with a degree of variation that is not usually found in any one class in an ordinary school. This variation is shown in measured mental age, in chronological age, in height, in medical diagnosis and physical condition, in the incidence of sensory and motor deficits, in patterns of activity, ranging from extremes of hyperactivity to extremes of slowness and apathy, in social background and class, in parental attitudes, in family stability and in experience of institutional and substitute care. The reasons for this great variation are related both to the causes and consequences of having a subnormal child, and also to the relatively small numbers involved.

The known causes of mental subnormality are both numerous and very diverse, as are the conditions often associated with it (e.g. epilepsy, cerebral palsy, etc.). Further, even in severe subnormality, there are still a large number of undiagnosed cases. No conclusions can at present be drawn from the limited evidence available about any specific or distinctive behavioural concomitants of these diverse causes and conditions, although some tentative suggestions can be made (Ryan, 1971). However, neither does the evidence allow Ellis' (1969) conclusion to be drawn, namely that etiological heterogeneity can safely be ignored as an important source of variation amongst subnormals. The possession of a common and low I.Q. is no guarantee of any other similarity, given the complex and varied patterns of causation that are involved,

Consequences of Subnormality

As regards the consequences of being subnormal, it is obvious that this must have profound effects on the behaviour of others towards the child, and thus the environment the child develops in. However, there has been very little direct study of this. There is some evidence of the kind of family crisis caused by the birth of a subnormal child (e.g. Menolascino, 1968), but there is very little knowledge of persisting attitudes and behaviour on the part of the family. We have no systematic information at all about mother–infant interaction where subnormal children are concerned, nor the likely effect of this on the child's cognitive development. However, there is much informal evidence to suggest that subnormal children, considered as a group, experience extreme forms of caretaking, ranging from over-protection and continual attention and encouragement, to rejection, neglect and institutionalisation. This is likely to be an important source of variation amongst any one group of subnormal children. There is also some indirect evidence of the range of social experiences subnormal children are exposed to, and how this differs from that of normal children. Jeffree and Cashdan's (1971) study suggests that their group of subnormal children were more heterogenous as a group than were a comparison group of normal children, as regards what they call 'experience' of common activities. An unpublished study (carried out from this laboratory) of social interaction during 'free play' sessions in a Junior Training Centre class showed a very wide range in the extent to which the children spent time either alone or with other children. Comparisons with similar studies of normal nursery school classes suggested that the variation between subnormal children in this respect was much greater than that between normal children. Follow-up interviews with the mothers of these children showed a similarly wide degree of variation in the extent to which their subnormal offspring played with other children, and were included in family activities. Further, the usual social class effects do not seem to obtain within groups of subnormal children. For example, Carr (1970) in a study of mongol infants, did not find the usual differences between social classes in rate of development. In a study of language development (to be described below), many fewer correlations were obtained between social class and various measures of verbal ability within the groups of subnormal children than within the comparison group of normal children. Thus, of 9 possible correlations with social class, 6 were statistically significant for the normal group, only 1 for the mongol group, and 2 for the non-mongol subnormal group. Such findings suggest, at least as one interpretation, an alteration in the usual patterns of parental behaviour, in the direction of less predictability and more variation with the subnormal children.

Such facts about the varied emotional and social experiences of subnormal children, as well as their etiology, may sound like truisms but they are worth spelling out and emphasising since they are commonly neglected when it comes to forming experimental groups. They, and the very different education subnormal children receive, are also neglected in the interpretation of apparent cognitive differences that are found between subnormal and normal groups. Most experimental groups are formed by matching solely on the basis of mental age, or sometimes chronological age, and all other co-varying factors are ignored. Estes (1970) has some trenchant criticism to make of the lack of control this implies by way of inequalities in opportunities to learn. However, the answer to these problems of adequate experimental control is not to increase the number of variables that are matched for, as is implied by Estes. To illustrate the reasons why this is not a solution to such problems I will draw on my own experience in trying to do just this.

Longitudinal Study of Language Development

The work in question was a longitudinal study of several aspects of language development in severely subnormal chldren. Two groups of subnormal children were used, one mongol, and one which can only be accurately described as 'non-mongol'. The main reason for subdividing the subnormal children in this way was to provide some insight into the effects of etiological and medical heterogeneity. A third group of normal children (i.e. of average I.Q.) was also used. My original intention was to form well-matched groups using selection criteria that are normally neglected. These criteria were not in any way extraordinary. They were chosen either because they involved factors known to be relevant to language development, or because they would reduce the variability within groups. The initial selection criteria were as follows: (1) living at home, not in an institution, (2) attending a Junior Training Centre in the case of subnormal children, and a creche or nursery school in the case of the normal children, (3) mental age between 2½ and 3½ as assessed by the Stanford–Binet test, (4) chronological age between 6 and 8 years for the subnormal children, and between 2 and 3½ years for the normal children, (5) absence of gross sensory and motor defects, including severe articulation defects, (6) social class of parents—Registrar General's classes IV and V, (7) sex—equal numbers of both in each group, (8) birth order— matching across groups, (9) both parents living at home and no history of family breakdown, (10) handedness—matching across groups.

It proved impossible to find enough subnormal children within a 50-mile radius of Cambridge to form sizeable groups, using these selection criteria. In order to obtain 30 children—15 for each of the two groups—10 different Junior Training Centres had to be visited, and several of the criteria had to be waived. The social class range was widened to include classes II and III, and the chronological age was widened to include children aged 5 and 9, and matching was not achieved on sex, birth order or handedness. A further confounding factor was introduced by the inclusion of three second twins in the non-mongol subnormal group, but not in the other groups. The variability within subnormal groups was also increased by having to use children from so many different Training Centres, all of which varied in the quality of teaching, and the attention given to language and speech. Other uncontrolled factors, of relevance to language development, were the age of parents, the size of family, and the kind of care received. Thus, despite considerable efforts, the resulting three groups were inadequate by most standards of experimental control, even though exact mental age matching was achieved. The attempt to be more rigorous and systematic than is usual in the formation of groups would, if strictly adhered to, have resulted in groups that were too small for statistical comparison. Such a *reductio ad absurdum* suggests that the procedures involved are fundamentally inappropriate for the investigation of the mentally subnormal. Essentially, exact matching of the kind that is desirable is impossible, because almost everything about the life of subnormal children is different from that of normal children.

The unsatisfactory nature of the groups in this study was reflected in some of the findings. Whilst details of the results cannot be discussed here, some general points are worth making. Several different aspects of verbal behaviour were investigated, as well as some relevant non-verbal abilities. The purpose of this was, in part, to obtain a large amount of information about each child—something that is rarely done in experiments with the subnormal. Differences were found on some tests but not on others. Some of these results broadly replicated other findings, and some did not—a common state of affairs in subnormal research, to judge from review articles of specific topics (e.g. Spivak, 1963; Goulet, 1968), and one which I have attempted to explain elsewhere (Ryan, 1971). Intercorrelations between the scores of different tests suggest that the groups differed in ways which make it very difficult to interpret the scores of any single test. Of 45 possible correlations, 18 were statistically significant for the normal group, but only two for the non-mongol subnormal group, and four for the mongol group. This means that there is much more consistency within the normal group as regards the relative performance of the children on the different tests than there is within either subnormal group. In this sense the normal group is more homogenous than either subnormal group. Similarity of clinical condition, as in the mongol group, does not seem to have much effect on the variability of scores within the group. Baumeister's (1968) work on the variability of reaction time scores also shows greater between and within subject variability for subnormal groups compared to normal ones. Such findings make the interpretation of any differences found between normal and subnormal groups on any single test very difficult. They also invalidate the attempt to generalise about subnormal behaviour on the basis of group studies and of comparisons within the normal groups.

In the light of this, it should now be clear why research with groups of subnormal children that aims to form generalisations about their behaviour will be of little use to those such as teachers who have to deal with individuals. With any group of subjects it is always logically possible that no one individual in the group will show the pattern of behaviour described for the group as a whole—this is one of the problems about inferring from the behaviour of groups to that of individuals. For the reasons cited above—the greater variation both in the composition of the groups, and in the scores on tests—this problem is particularly acute when the groups are composed of subnormal children. They appear to be especially diverse as a group, and particularly variable as individuals. Generalisations about groups that do not apply to any of the individuals within the group will be worse than useless, because misleading, to a teacher or nurse.

Summary

To conclude, it appears that if research is to be of greater application to the lives of the subnormal, new methods and approaches are needed. In particular we need to be able to make sense of the great individual variation that exists. There are at present large gaps in our knowledge of the development of subnormal children which if filled, would at least help in making research more relevant in principle. We need detailed information about the way in which parents, teachers, nurses, and other children behave towards subnormal children, and thus of the experience of a subnormal child in its interaction with the world. We need similar information about the expectations of others concerning the subnormal. There is also virtually no information about long-term developmental changes amongst subnormals. We should stop trying to find out about mentally subnormal by comparing them with those of higher I.Q. Instead we should investigate the effective world in which they develop, and try and relate their observed behaviour to this. In this way research will be of greater application to their needs, and to the needs of those in charge of them.

REFERENCES

Baumeister, A.A. (1968). Behavioural inadequacy and variability of performance. *Amer. J. ment. Defic.* 73, 477.

Carr, J. (1970). Mental and motor development in young mongol children. *J. ment. Defic. Res.* 14, 205.

Ellis, N. R. (1969). A behavioural research strategy in mental retardation: defense and critique. *Amer. J. ment. Defic.* 73, 557.

Estes, W. K. (1970). 'Learning Theory and Mental Development'. New York: Academic Press.

Goulet, L. R. (1968). Verbal learning and memory research with retardates. In 'International Review of Research in Mental Retardation', Vol. 3 (ed. N. R. Ellis). New York: Academic Press.

Herbst, P. G. (1970). 'Behavioural Worlds. The Study of Single Cases'. London: Tavistock.

Ingleby, D. (1970). Ideology and the Human Sciences: some comments on the role of reification in psychology and psychiatry. *The Human Context* **2**, 159.

Jeffree, D. M. and Cashdan, A. (1971). The home background of the severely subnormal child: a second study. *Br. J. Med. Psychol.*, **44**, 27.

Menolascino, F. J. (1968). Parents of the mentally retarded. *J. Amer. Acad. Child Psychiat.* **7**, 589.

Spivack, G. (1963). Perceptual processes. In 'Handbook of Mental Deficiency' (ed. N. R. Ellis). New York: McGraw-Hill.

Ryan, J. F. (1971). Classification and behaviour in mental subnormality: some implications for research. *Proc. 2nd. Congress of I.A.S.S.M.D.* Warsaw, pp. 155-160.

SESSION ONE
DISCUSSION

Chairman: Dr. C. C. Kiernan

Chairman: The function of Chairman's remarks will be to make additional comments or to point out particular issues which have been raised by the two speakers. I would like to do these two things in that order. I want to organise my remarks in terms of three broad categories; methodological issues, theoretical issues, and issues of value. As far as methodological issues are concerned, the main one from my point of view which comes out of these papers is that there is a confusion between pure and applied science which seems to lie at the root of a lot of difficulties which are described in the papers. There are basic differences in aim between the applied and the pure scientist. The applied scientist's main aim being to evaluate, to describe, to bring under control those variables which account for the bulk of the variance in behaviour of individuals. These are variables which if you like are the 'big' variables, so far as determining behaviour is concerned. On the other hand, the pure scientist is interested in how the system works, and quite rightly so. He is like the computer technologist who is interested in the operation of a particular relay circuit within the computer, whereas the applied scientist is concerned with how the computer works overall and would find it of very little interest to know about the operation of a particular small unit.

These considerations seem to me to be fundamental. Much of the difficulty with working in subnormality, as described by Professor and Dr. Clarke and as commented on by Dr. Ryan, seems to stem from the fact that people do not really know what questions they are trying to ask and I would suggest that, in the area of subnormality, an essentially applied area, the primary questions ought to concern the major sources of variance of everyday behaviour, the 'big' variables which affect behaviour.

The second methodological point relates in particular to statistical issues. Looking through the two papers, and also from what I know of the literature in subnormality, there appears a substantial lack of imagination in the research designs used. For example, there is little use of the more flexible designs recommended in educational research by Campbell and Stanley (1963). There is very little use outside the operant framework of the 'own control' designs which have been adequately developed since 1960 in fairly readily available forms (Baer, Wolf and Risley, 1968; Bijou, Peterson and Ault, 1968; Sidman, 1960). There is very little use in experimental psychology in general of time series analyses of individual data but this type of analysis is available and has been available in statistics for very many years (e.g. Gottman, McFall and Barnett, 1969).

In addition, many experiments seem to be designed around a single statistical test whereas quite clearly the need is for a much more flexible approach to the analysis of problems. It is a psychological problem rather than the statistical problem which is the central focus for much research in this area and, with great respect, I think that this is where Dr. Ryan experiences her main problems. The main point that comes out is that statistics ought, if they are going to be used at all, to be employed much more flexibly and since they do in essence determine the design of experiments then one ought to use them to their fullest extent.

On theoretical issues, the main one centres on the point which the Clarkes made concerning the need to broaden the basis of research in terms of examining behaviour against its context. They point out very clearly the dangers inherent in taking the behaviour of the subnormal child away from the context in which it occurs, in divorcing it from the independent variables which determine it. This to me seems again to have implications concerning research strategy which suggest that much more research should be done in the natural environment in which behaviour is occurring rather than in laboratory environments.

Finally, it seems to me that the issue of value is one which ought to be stressed. My background is in psychology and one of the characteristic features of psychologists is that they have always been very backward in coming forward to recommend that other people act on the basis of their research. Nowadays more than at any other time, I feel that the psychologist ought to be prepared to make recommendations about the conduct of practice based on his findings, in particular as they relate to the modification of behaviour in the natural environment. The main area where I would see this impact is in the provision of advice and training for parents and teachers, based on thorough research.

REFERENCES

Baer, D. M., Wolf, M. M. and Risley, T. R. (1968). Some current dimensions of applied behavior analysis. *Journal of Applied Behavior Analysis* 1, 91.
Bijou, S. W., Peterson, R. F. and Ault, M. H. (1968). A method to integrate descriptive and experimental field studies at the level of data and empirical concepts. *Journal of Applied Behavior Analysis* 1, 175.
Campbell, D. T. and Stanley, J. C. (1963). 'Experimental and Quasi-Experimental Designs for Research'. Chicago: Rand McNally and Company.
Gottman, J. M., McFall, R. M. and Barnett, J. T. (1969). Design and analysis of research using time series. *Psychol. Bull.* 72, 299-306.
Sidman, M. (1960). 'Tactics of Scientific Research'. New York: Basic Books.

Cookson: I'll start the ball rolling. I would like to take up this point which Professor Clarke made about the amount of structuring in teaching of severely subnormal children. Many people see this as being a very bad thing for the subnormal and normal child, and it remains a controversial point in both cases. I would like to start by saying that years ago, when so-called 'free activity' first became popular, it was a reaction against what occurred before that time. This tended to be groups of children sitting behind desks, perhaps reciting or chanting for half an hour, then silence, then various sorts of sense training for a period, possibly 20 minutes—short periods of detailed, intense practice in silence. There was no opportunity for the children to talk about what they were doing, no opportunity to select, no opportunity to go off something when they had become proficient at a particular skill. It was against this that one saw the move to the free activity approach, and what we see now is good nursery school practice being adopted. Dr. Woodward at the Fountain Hospital at this time did a piece of research in which she made some sort of a count and a measure of the amount of language, the amount of speech during varied sessions of so-called speech therapy in a classroom situation and against this, the kind, the amount of speech which took place in so-called free activity sessions in another group. It is fascinating to see, as one would expect, that there is a great deal more conversation in the group of children who were playing talking than in that group where specific words and groups of words were required from the children who were sitting otherwise behind desks. While I agree with Professor Clarke, who I know has always stuck to his guns about this point, that the children will learn in a structured way and may not learn so effectively in a free way, it seems clear that, if they are landed in groups of children in this old-fashioned way, then they also will not learn. The intense learning seems to be something which occurs on an individual basis, it seems to require individual reinforcement, individual programming and so on, and if they land in a large group then this kind of structuring isn't satisfactory.

Gunzburg: Wouldn't that problem really be that one wants to programme these activities? It isn't just a question of sitting them down and letting them do something in a structured situation, but the programme should structure the situation in such a way that in fact there is a stepping up from one level to the other, and I think what we have in mind is programming the teaching activities so that we will know exactly the aim we want to achieve, direct our attention and our effort towards it, rather than letting the child find its own way. I think we want to utilise the available time efficiently so that we reach our goal in a reasonable period.

Cookson: One thing that worries me is whether we know our aims, do we know precisely what we are structuring, do we know precisely what we are structuring to? Watching the practice in the special schools, I am very conscious of the fact that we have not got this hierarchy in any sense. I am never in a position to impose it, only tentatively to suggest it on occasion. I find the long-term aims are extremely confused, the short-term aims relate to specific skills but often do not clearly relate to long-term goals.

Chairman: I think we are slipping over to a discussion which may be relevant to a rather later paper and it is a terrible thing to do to have to stop discussion, but it's all there.

Cookson: Can I make this specific point that we don't know about the particular hierarchies or programmes. We haven't got these organised yet sufficiently well and we don't know precisely what we're working towards such that we can't go on into a school and say exactly what should be done and in what order.

Ryan: Actually I think, if I understand you correctly, part of what you are saying is that we just don't have our educational aims sufficiently defined. Is that right?

Cookson: Either our broad educational aims or our specific aims in any particular activity?

Ryan: And I think this is relevant to what we are meant to be discussing in that, if psychologists want to do something about the present state of research and its relevance to practice, clearly we can't get away without discussing what the aims are for any teaching programme or process through which subnormal children are put.

Chairman: I consider that we are overlapping into Mr. Cunningham's paper.

A. M. Clarke: Yes, I would agree. This is a very important point which is brought out very clearly in Mr. Cunningham's paper. I would like to suggest that it would be a good idea to have a whole session on this one.

A. D. B. Clarke: Could I perhaps sidetrack now in the hope of getting on to something which is certainly relevant, I think, to Dr. Ryan's paper. I've only got three queries which she may care to think about. She says there are no mother/infant interaction studies. I have a feeling that Dr. Carr has been up to something of this sort and if so I hope she'll say something. Secondly, Dr. Ryan believes one can't ignore causes of the condition because this is something linked with individual variation; one agrees, but leaving aside autism, one would add that so far attempts to find really significant behavioural differences between different clinical conditions have not proved very successful. Even differences between subnormals with organic injury and those with no demonstrable pathology have been disputed recently. I am putting this as an overstatement in the hope that someone will be provoked to discussion. And then the point about selective social processes which affect the way people are dealt with; this is old work and I would guess that Dr. Morris knows a good deal more than I about this, but didn't Saenger in New York do some very interesting studies on the reasons which cause some children to be institutionalised whereas other children were not?

Carr: I have in fact done a study of mother/infant interaction which is not yet published. I compared a group of mongol infants with a matched group of normal infants. First of all, they were matched for C.A., they weren't matched for mental age and they were matched for sex and social class, so that was all the matching I did. I think that there's a limit to how much matching one can do. I made two studies when the children were fifteen months old and when they were four years old to try to find out the sort of effects that these children were having on their families and to try to discover in what way the child-rearing practices being used with the normal children could be compared with those used by the mothers of the mongol children. There is, however, one small point I'd like to mention, that of the differences in social class effects between normal and retarded children. I made a study of the amount of stimulation which the mothers in the two groups (the two groups being working class and middle class mothers) were offering to their children. I measured this by making ratings of the amount the mothers talked to their children while I was there, the amount they said they talked to them, tried to teach them things to say, to do, the number of toys they had and so on. I made a constant rating of this and I correlated this with the mental age of the children when they were four years old. It is clearly shown that the brighter children were those who were more stimulated by their mothers and overall there was no correlation at all when I split the group into middle class and working class. I found, as I expected, a significant, positive correlation between the amount of stimulation the mothers gave to the children and the mental age of the children. With the working class, I found a significant negative correlation and this I found very difficult to explain; and I felt one couldn't really say that the working class mothers who were trying so hard with their children were having a deleterious affect on them. So I really had to look at it in a different way and conclude that this is a much more subtle thing than we have appreciated. I think it is very much more complex than hitherto realised and the best explanation of this phenomenon that I could come up with was that it depended on the different effect that the child had on his parent, *not* the effect of the parent on the child. That where the middle class mother found she had a fairly bright subnormal child, she was ready to make a lot of effort to teach him, to bring him up, to bring him out and to stimulate him. Where she could see that he was obviously hopeless she left him alone and let him be. The situation was quite different with the working class mothers. When they could see that the child was getting on quite well, not falling too far behind, the mothers left them just tagging on at the back of the family. When she could see that he was very severely retarded, then this brought out all her efforts and she really made great efforts to stimulate and to educate him, to bring along this very, very retarded child. There seems to be a completely different process in these two social classes.

Ryan: Yes, that's extremely interesting. It's just the sort of information I was saying there seems to be a lack of, and yet it is very relevant to the interpretation of the behaviour you mention. Could I ask you one question? Were your studies observational or were they mostly using interviews?

Carr: It was mostly interview. But if you're talking about this rating, this was partly observation. As I say, I watched how the mothers were talking to the children, how many toys there were around and partly it was interview; it was a combination of both.

Lambert: This is a very obvious point, but it's much more likely that research of the kind you mentioned, into parental expectation, is going to be done when a child is obviously easily diagnosable as subnormal from birth. As a practising psychologist, I find that many doctors and also many psychologists are particularly coy about making a diagnosis of subnormality until the children are about two or three years old. And so I suppose most research of the kind we would like to see on mother/infant interaction will be done on mongols and this is a very biased sample of subnormality, isn't it?

Ryan: Perhaps I should answer one of Professor Clarke's points. He raised the problem of the causes of subnormality and the fact that there is very little evidence of there being systematic differences between different aetiological groups and he referred to a particular study of attempts to find differences between organics and inorganics. The first point I would like to make is that I think that organic/non-organic a very bad classification and it doesn't surprise me at all that no differences have been found. All the work involved in classifications into organic and non-organic familial and pathological, seems to me to be based on really very tenuous theorising about sources of variation of intelligence. When it comes to attempting to differentiate characteristics of better defined groups such as mongols from other subnormals, there is the difficulty that though the mongol children are medically quite well defined, the comparison group never is and it is always 'all the rest' and these may well differ in different people's studies. Essentially, one is then comparing a mongol group against a varying set of other groups. But we cannot dismiss, as a lot of people would wish to do, the possibility that there are systematic differences. It seems to me it is an open question at the moment.

Mittler: I am not quite sure whether in this discussion we should be looking at specific points made by individual speakers, or whether it is the aim of the organisers in this discussion to stick to what seems primarily to be methodological issues which you have, Mr. Chairman, outlined with exemplary clarity. I am very sympathetic to the point of view put by Professor Clarke and to most of the points made by Dr. Ryan, perhaps for different reasons, but I am worried about the current tendency to erect a dichotomy between pure and applied research. It is a platitude to say that this is a continuum rather than a dichotomy but I feel that one of the dangers of this sort of Study Group is that we should be putting these two things on different sides of the fence. Now I don't think of it at all as a dichotomy; it seems to me one of the reasons why we are in difficulties at the moment is that here is a subject that we know relatively little about despite the enormous amount of research which has been done, despite the view which Miss Doyle produced, I still feel that the present climate of opinion is in favour of practical studies therefore I feel the conclusions reached as summarised by Professor Clarke (Miss Doyle's work) don't really represent the current climate of opinion here. But, we are at a very primitive stage at the moment and 'scientifically trained psychologists' react to a situation about which they know nothing by turning to techniques which they feel they know, although I think in the last analysis Professor Clarke and Dr. Ryan are probably right. Dr. Ryan in particular says that experimental psychology has nothing to offer, but I don't think that you can say this yet. When we know nothing we need to use laboratory type techniques and I see nothing wrong with this. We know what the limitations of these techniques are, we must get to the stage when we go beyond the techniques of the laboratory. The second related point to this is that what is defined as experimental in Miss Doyle's work? Where, for example, do operant studies fit in? Are these called experimental studies or not? It seems to me that operant studies very nicely illustrate the fact that research can fall on both sides. A third aspect of this is that experimental psychologists are usually castigated for pointing to the existence of developmental delays or deficits and not doing anything about it. Not in fact grasping the nettle firmly and saying well here are the implications of this deficit for remediation. I don't think it's entirely fair to blame experimental psychologists for this. Experimental psychologists ought not to interfere too much in education. I'm glad that Margaret Cookson began the discussion by bringing up the point that here we are working in an educational tradition with certain historical roots which she was quite right to point out to us. All we, as experimental psychologists, can do is first to help our fellow psychologists and this I think we can do quite well by looking at experimental techniques and saying here are implications for assessment. Let us take the work of O'Connor and Hermelin as a fine example of this. Here is a group of psychologists who have been working in this field for years, who have been blamed by many people, including myself, for not translating their findings into action but if you read their papers and, particularly, their two main books carefully, there are innumerable implicit suggestions in these for a whole hierarchy of assessment techniques which psychologists and others could adopt.

I only wanted to say that there are implications in work done by experimental psychologists which was originally not intended to have a practical application, which other psychologists can translate into action; in the first place for assessment and secondly, for remediation. As a corollary, the remedial aspects have to be set in the context of what teachers can be expected to accept, and our primary problem is to find the balance between what teachers think they ought to do (e.g. progressive methods of nursery and infant education) and such

techniques as I think we can now begin to offer. The dichotomy
between stimulation and structure which we are all talking about now is
again just as unfortunate as the dichotomy between pure and applied
research. When Alan Clarke or myself or other people talk to teachers
in these terms, they regard it as a threat and they say 'we have our
traditions of education, who are you to tell us what to do?' They are
probably right to criticise, but where they misunderstand us is in
suspecting that we want to change the whole daily timetable of the
school. I don't think anybody wishes to do this. Even Bereiter and
Engelmann who are the people often regarded as extremists, make it
perfectly clear that the techniques that they advocate are only part of a
wider spectrum of methods. So I would like to see experimental schools
where there is a normal curriculum but some part of each day set aside
for structured activity.

Currie: I wonder if I could pick up this point that Dr. Mittler has made
and link it with something else. This feeling that we have, sitting away
somewhere nice and safe, experimental psychologists doing the
traditional stuff, and teachers sitting away somewhere else paddling
their big canoe in a rather rough education water, seems to me to be
precisely the sort of thing that we've got to get over first. Teachers
want to know what you can suggest to them about the individual
difficulties of individual children. I think you, Mrs. Cookson, said that
you could only advise, you couldn't enforce and isn't perhaps the
answer, at least at this level of communication, to ignore whether it's
pure or applied research, because I don't think it matters? What really
matters is its impact, is it significant or is it not? Isn't the thing for us
to do then, to harness such bits of information as we have, be they
highly specific bits of information or so-called pure research, to the
particular needs that people feel at the time? Really and truly our
research is as useful as it helps to push out the frontiers a bit or as it
helps other people to do their job that much better.

Cookson: Can I take up this point you've mentioned of 'harnessing'?
Can we not see this harnessing as a piece of applied research? We are
trying to harness, or to use in some way, principles which have been
derived from research, or to suggest ways in which these principles
might be employed in the practical field. This can be done in the kind
of haphazard way in which I use it, or it could also be done much more
systematically, this would subsequently enable me to assess much more
effectively the principles I tried to use when in school, or when some
other agent has been instrumental in producing the results that have
occurred. I would like to see, in fact, as one of the outcomes of this
discussion group, some specific points which might be taken up as
hypotheses for subsequent research, that is to say certain principles that

we have to live with and see how these could be turned into hypotheses to be tested out in the practical sphere.

Currie: I think we'll make our impact most effectively if we do it through the needs which teachers feel. I think that we are most likely to be able to encourage teachers to say 'Well it worked all right with John, should we try this on a broad field?', or better still, 'Well now, it's worked all right with John, so that we ourselves suggest, do you think it's worth extending a little bit?' I think that if we do it the other way we are likely to raise the barriers and we shall be back here discussing this kind of problem once more and that'll be no good at all.

Chairman: The point which was made about the feedback from the practical situation into the laboratory is a very critical one. Too often what appears to happen is that research is funded on the basis that it is supposed to have application. The research is done, the application is attempted and the application is very partially successful. But what tends not to follow at this stage is that the investigator into the real-life situation nearly always has to find out why the variable he thought was important is not having an effect. It is all very well to know that there is a correlation which is significant between such and such a type of operation and such and such a type of performance but if this is not very powerful then no one should be interested in practical applications.

Gunzburg: During many years in the clinical world, it has been obvious to me that psychologists are always very ready to advise, always very ready to give a recommendation, and so on. They seldom seem ready to come forward and take the responsibility for action themselves. I give advice to the doctors, I give advice to the nurses, I give advice to the teachers, but they have to do what I advise, and I think we have got to come to the point where we say we make recommendations on the basis of our findings, and then we have to follow it up ourselves and not hand it over to other people to implement. The only way to test anything is to do it ourselves first of all and then, when it works we can hand over and go on to the next problem. But let's, for once, take responsibility and not always hand it over to other people.

A. D. B. Clarke: Dr. Gunzburg is being over-modest, he is at least one exception to the rule. He has, for the twenty years I've known him, always played a part in implementing his own recommendations. I think others, too, in institutions have done the same when allowed to do so. There are a number of people who are already practised in following the implications of their own research lines or their own assessment procedures.

Mittler: Dr. Gunzburg may have been getting at researchers in Universities and if that is so, it is partly correct but no longer as correct as it used to be. Again I have to refer to operant work. The operant movement, whatever its limitations, is a movement which makes a diagnosis, but does not rest content with a diagnosis. It then proceeds organically to try and do something about it, so that, I think, is a step in the right direction. But we are tending to talk now in terms of organisation and communication problems and to keep it relevant to the subject of the researcher. I think that the researcher in subnormality has two primary targets. The first is his fellow psychologists and the research psychologist should first and foremost learn to talk to educational and clinical psychologists in language that they will understand. When that happens, and it has not yet happened, then those psychologists will be encouraged to try to translate some of the findings of some of the research. Again I come back to O'Connor and Hermelin and reiterate my point that there is a wealth of information in their experimental studies which educational psychologists can try to use firstly in assessment without any apparatus and without calling it research. These are techniques and some of the things we are doing in Manchester, I hope will ultimately be of some use to psychologists. But, as I think Mr. Cunningham has pointed out in his paper, our main target, as far as children are concerned, is teachers and here I am profoundly depressed because I take as my model, not subnormality, but educational research over the whole spectrum. We have it on good authority on surveys done by the National Foundation for Educational Research that teachers do not read research at all. The majority of teachers read nothing but *'The Times Educational Supplement'* and the main journal devoted to research, namely *'Educational Research,'* is read by only a tiny proportion. So how do we get over to teachers what the results of our researches are? I think that educational and clinical psychologists have this function, working with individual children. The research psychologist should communicate with them; they will put the findings through the sieve of their own needs, and then translate to the teachers.

Ryan: I personally do not have much confidence in educational psychologists having any ability to translate academic research into practical education, and that clinical psychologists are obsessed with carrying out only assessment procedures and tests. Secondly, I am not so convinced as Dr. Mittler, about the relevance of much of the research done by O'Connor and Hermelin. He claims it has very broad implications for research into remediation. I am doubtful about this, because most of their research compares subnormal patients, who are inmates of institutions, with normal children, who live at home. The environments are so grossly different that we just don't know how to interpret the differences that they find. I have had a lot of difficulty in drawing any general conclusions from their research since it is rather piecemeal and does not add up to anything beyond the particular experiments. I would refer to the comment you made which was that we are in the situation of knowing next to nothing and in that situation you must use laboratory techniques. But for twenty years psychologists have used laboratory techniques and if we are still in the situation of knowing nothing, I do not honestly have the confidence that you do. What has been going wrong in various kinds of ways is that people feel that information which is obtained in standardised laboratory situations is somehow more reliable from the point of view of making generalisations than any information we find out from real-life situations. As I tried to show in my paper, the techniques and constraints of a laboratory situation are different from real life and it might be better to study everyday life as it comes.

Herriot: Might I ask how do you study everyday life?

Ryan: There are some quite well developed observation procedures. There are a lot of sociological theories which are probably relevant to deciding what goes on in the classrooms. We ought to study what teachers think they are doing, if we want to know what happens. It is important to try and learn what is actually going on between teachers and children. It would be difficult as it does not have the precision of laboratory studies, that's obvious.

Herriot: Presumably you have mentioned teachers, classrooms and children because you want to generalise about these? In which case, presumably, you will have to take groups of teachers, classrooms and children in order to be able to make any comments about everyday life at all, that are not in any way specific to one situation?

Ryan: I think for the time being, we should drop the attempt to generalise, it has become a bugbear of psychological research. What we are sadly missing is very first rate individual studies in subnormality. We do not have, for obvious reasons, first-hand accounts of what it is like to be subnormal. Some more imaginative and sociological descriptions of their experiences would help.

Gunzburg: What are all these laboratory studies over the last 20 years; how relevant are they for the development of the child? It seems that the questions researchers ask are the questions which interest them, little tidy problems, but which may have no immediate relevance to the children's problems. I think this is really why you feel so disappointed because you cannot give firm answers to the teachers. You cannot give an answer to the relevant question, and the relevant question is what matters to the child, not to us.

Herriot: In connection with translation of research findings, it might just be interesting to ask a question. How did the middle-class Swiss projections ever get into British schools? A study of how they did, might be very profitable. From a very cynical point of view can I suggest that they got there largely through preaching by people who liked the ideas because they appealed to them, and they trained teachers to like those ideas too.

Morris: Having said that, I wonder why Dr. Herriot asked what relevance sociological studies would have to this kind of work? It seems to me that that kind of question is relevant and I am surprised that one wants to make this dichotomy between sociological and psychological studies. Don't we need both, and might there not be a case for collaboration and co-operation in research? I am not sure that multi-disciplinary research is all that satisfactory, but at least subnormality could be an area where it might start and so far there is very little indication that psychologists might even consider that sociological research in that area is relevant.

Chairman: If I may just comment on that. Professor Tizard's group is translating a lot of what Goffman says into research terms and pursuing it. In that type of atmosphere there is a real attempt made to translate from one level to another, which I think is most profitable for the integration of sociological and psychological thinking. The two sides try to understand in their own terms what the other is saying.

Atkins: May I just put the point of view of a teacher who has found herself in the situation where she has a number of subnormals to teach and with very little knowledge of what is going on and just some of the difficulties that one meets? May I say that some sort of transformation process is required. If, as a teacher, one does seek out some psychological work, for a start, the jargon is incomprehensible and one is immediately met with the fact that the field seems full of controversy. The general rules about subnormal behaviour are not often applicable because of individual variation. There is controversy about methodology which is also incomprehensible to a simple teacher who does not understand what you are talking about. One is forced, first of all to learn something of psychology in order to understand the journals and then to learn enough to be able to criticise such things as the methodology. The thing that has annoyed me so far is that the literature, which is written incomprehensibly, is often outdated by the time it is published and it refers to journals which again are psychological and which one needs to comprehend. There is a booklet published by the University of Hull, called 'Aspects of Education' this goes a long way to mediate between psychology and education but it is really written for teachers of normal children. I suggest that a similar book, or journal, which is particularly written to mediate between psychology and teachers of the subnormal, is required. Educational research does not always apply to subnormals, but deals mainly with educational theory. Those researches that do apply to subnormals are often too obscure and deal with an individual psychologist's interests.

Lambert: Surely, to mediate between psychological theory and the teacher should be the function of the educational psychologist, providing he is not overloaded or understaffed? First of all, he has got to assess the individual child's problems and as Dr. Gunzburg has outlined earlier, he has then got to be up to date on the whole of research relevant to his problem. Then he goes into the classroom and talks to the individual teacher about the individual child. Is this not better than the contents of some research journal watered down?

Cooper: This again is the expert talking to the teacher. Educational psychologists have the role of expert, and teachers very much resent being told by them how to teach their children. They like advice and suggestions, but we have to get much closer than that and our research students have been trying to give teachers feedback about results of research in their teaching situation. We have some video-tapes and have been filming teachers in classrooms. It is a very small sample of teachers but we have looked at them individually and done everything with them. We have been on holiday with them, we have taken children away with them, we have tried to participate in being a teacher of subnormality. The effect on the teachers seeing themselves on video-tape has been that they begin to understand what the problems are, to ask sophisticated questions and to understand better their teaching methods and their relevance to particular children.

Mittler: May I come back to these two points because I think Mr. Lambert and Mrs. Cooper are really talking about two different aspects of the psychologist helping the teacher? The traditional role of the teacher is to come to the psychologist and ask for advice about a particular child. I think that psychologists are increasingly better equipped nowadays to give this kind of advice, despite what Dr. Ryan thinks about the poor abilities of educational or clinical psychologists. Some of this is partly up to the heads of psychology departments, like Professor Clarke, some of whom are interested in the applied field; partly up to the courses of professional training which are improving, both in teacher training courses and in courses for psychologists and they are really coming to grips with the problem of communicating information. I must record that I feel much more optimistic about this than Dr. Ryan. The particular difference between mental handicap and any other field of education is, that for reasons of role and structure and history, teachers in training in 'training centres' have never had this kind of experience before, therefore, while many in the previous existing education system would use a psychologist to help with the individual child, the teachers in the 'training centres' are really waiting for something much better. They are waiting for the psychologists to come to these new special schools, and offer a really good service based not only on the individual child, but in terms of asking the sorts of questions which Mr. Cunningham is asking in his paper. What are our long term objectives? Why do we do these things? This is why the influx of severely subnormal children into the educational system poses altogether novel problems. It is not that they are just children lower down the I.Q. scale. There are fundamental differences here which pose the very problems that the *Study Group* is here to discuss, namely, how *do* you translate research findings? I still maintain that this is a hierarchical process—you cannot communicate directly from our researches in Universities to teachers. You have to have some kind of intermediary. It is only the bad psychologist who tells the teacher how to teach—the good psychologist is the one who carries out a prior assessment and who then tries to work with the teacher in order to evolve a remedial programme.

Lambert: May I ask Mrs. Cooper, what kind of teachers were you video-taping and what were they teaching?

Cooper: Three were teachers in an autistic unit with children of age range six to eleven and three were teachers in a school for maladjusted children.

Chairman: I think we should allow Professor Clarke and Dr. Ryan a few further comments and then stop the discussion.

A. D. B. Clarke: I have five comments. These points arise from listening to what was a very interesting initial discussion, which tomorrow will blossom out and develop. First of all, the need for a greater study of the child's natural environment, and his interaction with it. I think we're agreed that this is very essential. Secondly, the guidelines are already available but this has been amplified by one or two discussants who pointed out that these were guidelines for groups not for individuals, and the need for a greater number of individual stud es. You, Mr. Chairman, talked about the particular statistical methods needed for individual case studies. The third point was our awareness of the rather knotty methodological problems that exist in this field. The fourth point is to hark back to value judgments and aims. You have to be aware that there are two quite contrasting groups in this field. One group which says 'let the child be happy, let the child develop,' versus the much more active group which says 'my task is to modify this child's behaviour in such a way that it functions to maximum capacity as dictated by constitutional factors and social demands.' 'Never the twain shall meet' and the value judgments put forward by these two groups have different consequences for research. I believe both pure laboratory-type research and applied research are important to mental subnormality. A matter which is often overlooked, in that there is frequently an unfortunate correlate of these types of research, and this is in terms of time taken to obtain results. The applied researcher, whether he be Kirk or Skeels or Skodak, knows he is unlikely to obtain useful data in a brief experiment; the 'pure' researcher too often seems to believe he can. I think we who teach in Universities are to blame for this. The student has his practical class on a Tuesday afternoon, he has time to put his subject through five trials, and then he analyses the results. If you do this with retarded children you will not get anything worth having.

Ryan: We have discussed at length what information we need and what we want to find out about subnormals. These are essential questions, for this whole *Study Group.* One of the answers which emerged somewhat tangentially during this discussion, is that we are seeking information that will enable us to help particular teachers in efforts of amelioration or remediation. Is this all that we want to know about? Are we narrowly concerned with the target of always improving the behaviour of subnormal children? What other sorts of information do we want to have?

Session II

Social Research and Problems of Institutional Management

Social Research and Social Policy

PAULINE MORRIS

*Legal Advice Research Unit,
The Nuffield Foundation, London*

Introduction

There has been a great deal of concern expressed over the past two or three years regarding the care of the mentally retarded, but a combing of both publishers' lists and the relevant journals indicates that whilst there is a considerable literature relating to medical or bio-chemical research, as well as to methods of teaching and training, extremely little specifically *social* research appears to have been carried out in this field. No doubt this is because, with a few exceptions, mental retardation has until recently been regarded predominantly as a matter for the medical profession and its ancillary services, or for psychologists, and few sociologists or social administrators have shown a wish to involve themselves in such work. It seems likely, however, that this may well change as the sociological implications of retardation and its treatment become more widely recognised. If this is the case, I think it of crucial importance to examine the likely direction of such research because there is a very real danger that, as has been the case in studies of other areas of deviant behaviour, notably crime, the findings and implications of social research will have little effect upon the underlying structure of services provided for the retarded, and there will be little questioning of current treatment ideologies.

The Aims of Social Research

These are essentially two, and they are in some measure contradictory:

1. Providing the necessary understanding of situations which will enable the researcher to make some contribution to the

resolution of contemporary social problems.* This immediately suggests that social research can never be value-free, since the very choice of a topic, as well as the implications for policy derived from any interpretation of the results, will be determined to some extent by the values of the researchers.

2. The discovery and verification of principles and limited general laws of social behaviour, and factors determining it, whether or not they are immediately useful in programmes to improve social life and social conditions. To this extent such research is scientific and should be as value-free as possible.

Priorities in Research

When deciding upon priorities it is unfortunately the case that the questions which social scientists are called upon to answer are, frequently, the wrong ones. There is a basic disjunction between, on the one hand the administrators (and this is a shorthand way of including both policy makers and practitioners), and on the other hand the specific skills of the sociologist.† Too often the administrators want to use these skills in order to give a semblance of intellectual respectability to their policies which it then becomes difficult for anyone to assail. The sociologist should, however, be asking questions *of* the policy makers and administrators, looking particularly at their processes of decision-making.

The role of the funding organisation is also crucial here; where the administrators and the grant givers are the same body, as for instance in the case of a government department, the pressures on the researcher to work within a consensus framework will be particularly strong. Even where research is paid for by some charitable Trust Fund, they are likely to have a 'social welfare' orientation and may be committed in a particular way to the specific project for which they are providing the money. Alternatively they may hope that the end product can be used for propaganda purposes in order to bring pressure to bear on governmental policy. At the same time it is worth noting that any

---

* This is not intended to imply that all sociologists doing research would see this as their aim—some would be more concerned with purely theoretical issues of a sociological nature rather than with specific social problems; in this paper I am referring only to such social research as is consciously directed towards social policy.

† Much of what is said in this paper may be relevant to other disciplines in the social sciences e.g. social psychologists, social administrators, etc., but rather than widen the discussion to areas about which I am in no way competent to speak, I shall refer specifically to the role of sociologists.

apparent 'politicisation' of work undertaken in their name is likely to lead to a loss of charitable status, or to the withdrawal of funds.

From the researchers point of view, the intentions of the sponsors are extremely important because the research design is likely to have to depend to a large extent upon the relative strengths of the interested parties, and this may induce biases in approach unless their nature is fully understood. Furthermore such *a priori* values and assumptions as are incorporated into the fabric of the research design will, in turn, affect the interpretation of the findings.

Questions for the Sociologist

Generally speaking sociologists when approached by policy-makers are asked to provide answers to three types of question. I want to refer briefly to each of these and then to suggest a fourth which I believe to be a crucial question, but one to which he is rarely invited to address himself.

1. What kind of services are needed in order to enable a particular type of deviant (whichever group is considered problematic at the time, the mentally retarded, mentally ill, homeless, criminal, unmarried mothers, blind, poor, etc.) to fit into our society in a non-deviant, politically inert way? How can we ensure that deviants will accept what is offered without questioning, queue patiently for their benefits, accept their institutional treatment without complaint, or conform to the norms of a society which periodically changes the rules?* Again much social behaviour is differentially defined as deviant depending upon the time and place at which it occurs, e.g. homosexuality, suicide, mental illness and more importantly violence which is not only sanctioned by society in certain instances, but demanded of people at times of national or civil wars.

Research couched in terms of answering questions like these is basically geared to providing quick answers to the immediate problems of administrators. This demand for a solution to specific problems must, I would argue, be resisted until some fundamental examination of all aspects of the problem we are trying to resolve has been carried out, in order to avoid the possibility of doing long-term harm following what appears to be short-term good. A failure to study all aspects of what are usually highly complex problems is likely to result in the provision of what Halsey (1969), in the field of education, calls "more of the same". Research which examines existing programmes and

---

* Even complaints are not too dangerous: most institutions have waiting lists and a complaint may simply lead either to the possibility of reprisals inside the institution, or to a request for removal

services without reference to the wider social structure will provide information which will allow us to 'tinker' with the service, in order to change its face, but not its underlying structure. Garabedian (1971), in the field of corrections, sums it up by suggesting that "most correctional research has had the latent function of perpetuating the existing system". Such research is used by policy makers as a back-up or justification for perpetuating the *status quo,* a situation which seems inevitable because it accepts the definition of the problem given by the existing structure.

2. How can we make the community more tolerant of people whose behaviour is a variance with what is conventionally acceptable? Like (1) above, the question is posed in such a way as to emphasise a concensus model; the previous questions required the researcher to provide answers which would enable the client to adjust or accommodate more readily to the norms of the existing system. The present question has certain additional 'advantages', some more questionable than others. It may, for example, be cheaper for the Government, fostering is one example of this; the wish to imbue the community with a sense of 'involvement' reflects a return to Tonnies' (1955) *Gemeinschaft* or Redfield's (1955) 'ideal type' of the 'little community'. Clearly other factors than cost enter into policy decisions; there is considerable evidence that for many offenders probation would be just as effective as prison in terms of recidivism over a given period. The Government seems, however, more prepared to build expensive new prisons than to pay probation officers a salary comparable to other types of social worker. The use of voluntary workers has long been extolled as a virtue in this country; there is thought to be something intrinsically 'good' or 'better' about work which is unpaid although in Denmark it is a matter of policy *not* to use voluntary workers since this is said to emphasise the charitable, hence degrading role of the recipient—though whether it does more than provide an opportunity for the middle-classes to resolve feelings of guilt (not usually their own but a kind of collective guilt resulting from the reluctance of the community to accept deviants amongst them), is difficult to say. (*Note* the reluctance of residents to allow hostels, prisons, schools for maladjusted children, etc. in their neighbourhood.)

3. What is the incidence and aetiology of a particular form of deviance? Is the problem getting worse, and how does it compare with similar situations in other countries? Certainly in terms of the provision of existing services such 'headcounting' is important—we need to know how many hospital beds will be required, how many social workers, how much social security or unemployment benefit is likely to cost, etc. It is my contention, however, that this is primarily an

administrative task which can best be carried out with the aid of economists, and it does *not* require the specialist skills of the sociologist. Furthermore, by contributing to it, the latter is again working within a consensus model.

Finally we come to the fourth question, the one so rarely asked, but which I have earlier suggested seems to be of crucial importance in terms of the sociologists' contribution to social policy. It is the question that he must ask of the politician and of the administrator, namely how do *they* define this specific form of deviance that we are studying; by what criteria do they decide that a person should be so labelled. (For an interesting discussion of the problems of bureaucratic decision-making in relation to marginal cases, see Gusfield, 1970.) Answers to such questions would enable the sociologist to show how definitions of deviance reflect the values and norms of a given group of people within the society; how they fluctuate and are essentially subjective terms to identify what is, and what is not, morally tolerable. Then by examining the ways in which the deviant himself defines the situation, the sociologist is able to discuss the implications of the interaction between definers and defined in terms of the control, or treatment, processes.

By asking these kinds of questions, and by adopting a conflict model, it will become apparent, for example, that white collar crime is *not* a crime; that a skid-row alcoholic is treated as a deviant not because of his *alcoholism,* but because he disturbs the 'good order' of our society. If this were not so, the middle-class alcoholic would also be defined as a deviant, whereas he is likely to be defined, if at all, as 'sick' (more likely the whole matter will be ignored by outsiders except for a certain sympathy expressed towards his wife.) For the sociologist the important point here is that if society were to apply its definitions in a consistent manner, or in accordance with the behaviour exhibited by individuals rather than in accordance with their status in that particular society, the social order would be upset. Hence the process of defining deviants performs an important function in maintaining the *status quo.*

Cross-cultural comparisons show how the treatment afforded by different societies to the same category of deviant reflects differing ideologies, even where definitions are held constant. [For an interesting comparison between Britain, U.S.A., Russia and Sweden in terms of attitudes to blindness and its treatment see Scott (1970).] In relation to the treatment of the mentally retarded much has been made recently of the concept of 'normalisation', but I believe that the term is being used differently as between this country and Sweden, and that this reflects basic differences in treatment ideology. The Swedes would appear to understand by this term the abandonment of the hospital as a means of caring for the retarded at any stage (Grunewald, 1971), except where some physical treatment is necessary, and then on an out-patient or short-term basis. In England, on the other hand, normalisation seems to mean that attempts should be made to humanise hospitals so that they become "a preparatory stage before placement in *normal* conditions" (Gunzburg, 1970) (my ital.) thus recognising that hospitals do not provide a normal environment. In other words we are adapting the term to meet the demands of existing practice, rather than questioning the values implicit in our definition in so far as they affect treatment.

Sociologists of deviance have paid scant attention to the position of the mentally retarded *qua* deviants in our society,* there is surely a need to examine mental handicap as a form of deviance (as has been done extensively in the case of mental illness: the literature is too extensive to be listed here but see, for example, Scheff (1966), or Szasz (1961) and to study our reasons for treating such deviants in one particular way rather than another. This will require that we look at the mentally retarded outside the medical context (whilst acknowledging the medical component in its aetiology and possible development), since the *behaviour* of the retarded person, and of those so labelling them, is a social phenomenon.

The Dissemination of Research Findings and Their Use

It is probably unrealistic, or at least over-optimistic, to believe that sociologists who wish to work in this field will not be asked to answer the kinds of questions subsumed under 1, 2 and 3 above, namely problem-solving within the existing structure, with a view to providing suggestions for ways of modifying existing services.† Yet at the same time, some people working in allied fields are now asking why it is that social research has played such a relatively minor part in policy decisions. This, as I have suggested earlier, is perhaps at its most obvious in the penal field where one of the saddest aspects of much social research is that often it offers evidence of *resistance to change*. This, I believe, is largely because so much research is confined to answering the questions posed in (1) above. By asking what kind of services are needed, there is a clear implication that the existing ones are in some way unsatisfactory, and this, combined with the fact that such services tend to be studied in isolation, presents very considerable problems in terms of the acceptance and implementation of research findings.

---

* For a notable exception see Edgerton (1967).

† A recent advertisement for a research assistant, financed by a grant from the South Western Regional Hospital Board in furtherance of a recommendation of the Farleigh Hospital Committee of Enquiry, calls for research into 'ways of preventing violence and managing very difficult patients at ward level'.

There are a number of reasons for this: the hospital system, the penal system, or any major bureaucratic system is beset with inertia, the formal limitations on government departments, the structural constraints implicit in long chains of command, make change a monolithic task. At a lower level in the hierarchy, that of the institutions themselves such as hospitals, schools, prisons, etc. change is seen as threatening the very existence of the service they offer. Staff feel threatened not merely in terms of possible unemployment, but more significantly in terms of the implication that what they have been doing for so long is not good, or at any rate not good enough. Where research is concerned to evaluate some innovatory service, those involved in its provision have usually a heavy investment in proving that their approach is 'right', and they will have little tolerance for the sometimes discordant findings which may attend objective enquiry.

The non-implementation of research findings may also be the result of one hand not knowing (or not wanting to know) what the other is doing; in other words money is given for research in order to find answers to particular questions, but when provided with some of the answers, the potential beneficiaries (those concerned with the day-to-day problems the research set out to study) are not structurally in a position to implement them. Even the administrators may be unable to do so, because the findings may imply the necessity of a redistribution of decision-making authority, and this may not be viable within the wider system in which a particular organisation is functioning. There is an interesting example of how different structures may affect the situation if one compares the penal service with the health service: policy in prisons is *centralised,* the law requires that imprisonment in one place should be the same as in all other places, and despite some attempt at regionalisation, and despite minor differences in regime, in overall policy terms these make very little difference indeed. Thus policy change can, in theory, be implemented through central government, but since any such change has to include *all* those in the system, considerable caution is exercised before implementation. In the hospital service there is considerably more local autonomy, and regional hospital boards and even hospital management committees have opportunities for greater flexibility than exist in the prison service. In theory such a structure more readily permits innovation and change and it should be more responsive to the findings of research. On the other hand such autonomy may limit innovation and change where, for example, local democracy obstructs central government policies. (It is interesting to note that this was both the strength and the weakness of prisons under local government before 1877.)

Again one must bear in mind the political and economic factors which may negative the results of social research. The extent to which research findings are implemented is likely to reflect the relative power and status of those involved—the government department, the administrators, the grant givers and the researchers. Sociologists engaged in social policy research should, as I suggested earlier, be concerned with questions of values and definitions of need and about priorities. New services, when they are set up, may reflect the views of a *different* group of people having access to power, but they are nevertheless conceived of within the definitions and values of those setting them up, based upon their experiences and their understandings of the situation. As sociologists we should be looking at the implications of such change not only in terms of social and economic costs, but in the light of the relationship they bear to other aspects of the social structure.

I am conscious of the fact that in this paper I have not discussed the practical problems of social research, in particular the relationship between the researcher and the researched, and these may be of considerable importance at a symposium of this nature. Such issues may well affect the implementation of research findings and will almost certainly affect the willingness or otherwise of those working in the field to co-operate with researchers. I hope that those attending the symposium will feel free to discuss not only the issues raised in the paper, but these other, more practical and day-to-day issues.

REFERENCES

Edgerton, R. (1967). 'The Cloak of Competence'. University of California Press.
Garabedian, P. G. (1971). Research and practice in planning correctional change. *Crime and Delinquency*, **17**, 1.
Grunewald. K. (1971). The guiding environment: the dynamics of residential living. International Conference on Action for the Retarded. Dublin.
Gunzburg, H. C. (1970). The hospital as a normalising training environment. *Journal of Mental Subnormality, December.*
Gusfield, J. R. (1970). Moral passage: the symbolic process in public designations of deviance. In 'Crime and Delinquency' (ed. C. Bersani) London: Collier-Macmillan.
Halsey, A. H. (1969). The dilemma of priority areas. *Encounter,* May, 1969.
Redfield, R. (1955). 'The Little Community'. University of Chicago Press.
Scheff, T. J. (1966). 'Being Mentally Ill: A Sociological Theory'. Chicago: Aldine Press.
Scott, R. E. (1970). Construction of conceptions of stigma by professional experts. In 'Deviance and Respectability' (ed. J. Douglas), New York and London: Basic Books.
Szasz, T. S. (1961). 'The Myth of Mental Illness'. New York: Hoeber.
Tonnies, F. (1955). 'Community and Association'. London: Routledge.

The Rôle of the Psychologist in 'Manipulating' the Institutional Environment

H. C. GUNZBURG

*Psychological Services, Subnormality Hospitals,
Birmingham Area*

This paper is not concerned with arguing the pros and cons of institution versus community facilities (Tizard 1964; Kushlick 1966; Morris 1969) but will proceed on the assumption that a type of community settlement will have to continue for some time to come and might even experience a revival in a vastly changed form in the near future (Gunzburg 1970; Browne *et al.* 1971). I also make the assumption that the right type of psychologist—and I stress the qualification 'right type'—would be potentially capable of contributing to a large extent to desirable developments by introducing the behavioural approach to the management problems (and I take this term in its widest meaning relating to education and training) and by acting as a link profession not only between the various disciplines involved but also between the various govenmental departments which are concerned with the mentally handicapped—such as Department of Education—Department of Health and Social Security—Directors of Social Services etc.

I have to say this because some people are of the opinion that it is nowadays rather flogging a dead horse if one spends time to consider the rôle of the psychologist in a residential community. If in the past his presence has been ignored and his potential contributions been disregarded, it may well be due to the fact that he has failed to apply his expertise to the practical problems and was not seen often enough coming forward with realistic solutions to the problems.

Any survey of the literature on mental deficiency will indicate that by and large the medical, nursing and psychological contributions have tended to fragmentise the handicapped person by dealing with him as a medical abnormality who has to be supported by a medically oriented nursing environment and who shows a large number of deficits which can be measured, analysed and compared. Most of the actual training and rehabilitative work has aimed at dealing with specific weaknesses and finding the most appropriate methods for improving the level of functioning in various areas or discovering ways how to avoid the consequences of dysfunctioning without really doing something about the actual condition (e.g. feeding the patient in efficient ways rather than teaching him to feed himself, locking him up or stepping up medication rather than re-educating him). To some extent, such atomistic approaches were not only determined by historical development and inadequate knowledge but also by material conditions, such as inadequate staffing, inadequate financial resources, inadequate organisation. It will probably be accepted by most workers in the field that the piecemeal approach whereby a 'patient' is being 'processed' through the various departments of the hospital whilst being stored in the wards in indifferent or downright slum conditions—the absence of a systematic planned approach to improve the all round level of functioning of the individual person—the failure to recognise that the development of the meagre abilities of the mentally handicapped needs the *involvement* of all disciplines concerned—have contributed substantially to the rejection of the present residential (hospital) provisions for the mentally handicapped. And it is probably not an exaggeration to say that the whole organisational structure came into disrepute because of basic misconceptions in human management terms. To some extent this inadequate approach is highlighted already in the planning stage of such residential accommodation, when the architect's main concern is to design a place which is easy to run (for the staff!). No one in the briefing team considers seriously whether streamlined management of human problems is necessarily to their benefit (e.g. designing a residential facility around the toilet block—Dybwad, 1967), whether the argument of relieving staff of certain chores, necessarily leads to improvements in other directions and whether sophisticated approaches in one area (e.g. conditioning) do not cut across the efforts in another area and whether the departmental approach encourages sufficiently support for experimental efforts.

In short, there is an astounding and disheartening absence of an overall philosophy of work which would determine the direction of individual and departmental efforts, of integration of planning of programming rehabilitative approaches, of assessment and evaluation. It is the absence of active guiding principles which fails to prevent the emergence of such labour saving management practices, which leads to the much criticised block treatment of depersonalisation aspects of institutional regimes (King and Raynes, 1967).

I am here not talking of the well-known difficulties in communication, of departmental aspirations at independence and departmental jealousies. Rather of a lack of realisation that the task of dealing with the whole person requires the total impact of the environment and that this must be shaped and directed to serve this purpose. After all, the main purpose of our efforts is to help the mentally defective *to live* and not to work better, to read better and to conform better. The sequence of more or less inadequate activities, many of which are considered to be 'good and beneficial' without a clear realisation of their potential value, and which are seldom mutually supportive, has seldom been programmed from the point of view whether these activities are relevant to a particular person's future role in whatever community he will finally settle.

Even though there are many factors which prevent ideal conditions—shortage of staff, money, building facilities, vested interests, professional jealousies and apprehensions, traditions and prejudices—it seems that—at least for some time to come—some form of institutional framework will have to be used and it is essential to consider how the present scene can be manipulated to the advantage of the mentally handicapped person to enable us to apply research findings widely and not only in some isolated laboratory corner.

Three Essential Conditions

There are three essential conditions to be met and the experienced psychologist ought to contribute substantially to their practical execution.

1. Formulation of Basic Principles

The first is formulation of basic principles, which must govern the institutional policy from large to small issues. I suggest that such a guiding principle is represented by a suitable modified form of the approach known as 'Normalisation' (Nirje, 1970). This means that an attempt is made to create conditions and practices in the institution which are as near the 'normal' conditions and practices 'outside' as possible, in order (a) to prepare better for normal life demands, (b) to avoid the typical reaction to dehumanising conditions and (c) to give opportunities for making better use of limited potentials. (Such an 'operational policy' does *not* suggest that most, if not all, mental defectives should be prepared to live in the open community as has been often assumed, but gives a better chance for 'survival' to those whom the community is prepared to accept fully by giving adequate support and it gives near normal conditions of living to those who require the 'protective corner' of the community, into which our institutions will have to develop).

In this context it is irrelevant whether the prognosis for the people in this setting is favourable or not—the principle applies to all levels—but, and this is the vital point in the application of the principle: *'Normalisation' must not be a slavish aping of what is considered 'normal' because it will be necessary to utilise it as a teaching medium, an educational tool adjustable to the needs of the mentally handicapped and his particular difficulties in learning.* Considering that psychologists stress always the need for overlearning, for constant practise, for programming in small steps and point to the subnormal's difficulties in transfer of learning, of overcoming of obstacles etc.,—this new normalising environment will have to avoid the pitfall of institutional uniformity which fails just as much in providing adequate learning opportunities as does the provision of 'normal' ordinary settings, which have comparatively few opportunities for inculcating relevant skills because they have not been planned for this purpose.

As an example, one might consider the attempt to 'normalise' the building environment of institutions. Apart from the pitiful attempts to 'upgrade' the environment by slapping on some paint and putting up room dividers, whilst still thinking in 'ward terminology', one possible way of creating a new, normal climate appears to be the building of ordinary houses as one would for staff. By designing in terms of 'normal' people rather than 'patients', certain standards are automatically accepted, which in themselves will help in the creation of an environment which does not interfere with the rehabilitative work. Yet, it is by no means certain that this 'normal' environment with a limited number of learning opportunities will be adequate to provide that variety of practical experience, which will be required by the mentally subnormal to become relatively familiar with the many variations of normal life, nor that it will give the staff enough opportunities to manipulate therapeutically complete life situations. Thus, the provision of a row of 'normal council houses' on institutional grounds, whilst giving the appearance of normality, would introduce 'normal uniformity' by the back door and fail to exploit fully the opportunities offered by the variety of normal life, unless we design specifically a variety of life sized learning opportunities within this 'normal' environment. Thus it might well be not only that different types of normal buildings should be requested, but also that the designs should be modified to provide more than normal learning opportunities for the mentally handicapped.

I cannot see how the psychologist, a student of human nature, interested in learning processes, can fail to see the oportunities of consolidating and widening the learning in the classroom by ensuring that further learning takes place in other situations and that environment provides additional stimulation which can be utilised by the staff (A. L. Gunzburg, 1967). He must thus interest himself in the designing of the environment with a view of incorporating extra learning opportunities. For example, he may well suggest that a corridor should have a corner which will give opportunity for learning the hard way about different sizes of tables and chairs when they have to be negotiated round corners. Perhaps, having to learn to pass each other in a narrow corridor will help towards better social relationships and help to overcome much of the physical clumsiness of the mentally handicapped. The suggestion of having individual bedrooms for each patient should be investigated not merely from the point of view of 'normality' but whether it is beneficial for him and whether perhaps another arrangement might not be better.

I have taken these examples of architectural institutional manipulation because the physical environment is so often taken for granted and it is little appreciated that it has a powerful subtle influence on 'patient' and 'nursing staff' alike. I also attempted to show that a psychologist, who cares for the person—not necessarily the one who is primarily interested in his deficits—would be in an ideal situation to influence the physical conditions by recognising that this aspect could be manipulated to the mentally handicapped person's benefit in the same way as other variables in a controlled situation.

This guidance by an operational philosophy, based on psychological principles, extends to many other aspects of institutional organisation which have not to be merely 'normalised' but have to be adjusted to serve the purpose of learning something useful. For example: workshop efficiency could very easily result in well managed remunerative concerns, which dominate to such an extent that there is no time for programming essential other aspects—such as leisure time activities, social relationships, education; or traditional ward practices and management continue because 'it was always so'. It would be the psychologist's job to devise new normal and practical ways of organising and introducing normal life patterns as part of an educational process, which involves the nurse as a social educator rather than as the keeper of an indifferent lodging house (Gunzburg and Gunzburg, 1970). Nowadays on account of a different government department being responsible for the education at the hospital school, that school, considered as a character training factor, may not exercise enough influence on the ward environment to get the necessary support unless an agreement on operational philosophy is hammered out by the educationist and the hospital staff to ensure an integrated approach. The 'nurse', the present key figure has to be encouraged and guided to become a 'normal' human being combining the functions of assistant educator and guide and friend, instead of leaving the task of training and education to the respective professions and wasting the educational opportunities of after school hours and week-ends.

In short, *the guiding philosophy of 'normalisation' is not simply making everthing as 'normal' as possible, but to create additional, designed normal learning opportunities, using our knowledge of the psychological impact of various teaching situations, in order to promote in the mentally handicapped person a better all-round functioning.*

2. Multidisciplinary Approach

This brings me to the second point—it has been widely accepted that mental handicap requires a multidisciplinary approach. Generally this is being interpreted as providing a number of specialists who give their opinions, but, at present, they either do not take or are not asked to take any responsibility for their decisions. If a normalising institution environment is to be created, which is to provide an adequate setting for an intensive psychological contribution, the senior psychologist must not only be consulted but must actually become *involved* in the management problems. There is a ghastly American term that refers to 'human engineering', but one has to accept that a psychologist cannot make an effective contribution to the work if he is content with controlling the laboratory variables only, but opts out of tackling the life sized issues which affect the results of his work.

Having 'grown up' as a 'clinical' psychologist in the medical/nursing setting of the 'hospital', he is generally only too willing to accept his role as a 'backroom boy'. He explains and predicts behaviour, he designs experiments and researches to answer questions in which he is interested, but he keeps usually carefully away from the everyday problems of human management, of learning and training in ordinary conditions. Whatever the reasons, many of which are due to frustration, staff resistance to change, inadequate preparations before starting work, 'academic' preoccupation etc., there is no doubt in my mind that a multidisciplinary approach to the problem requires a multidisciplinary management of it, an involvement of relevant disciplines on equal terms with the psychologist taking part in it. In other words, *the senior psychologist must become a responsible partner in the management of the institutional environment in order to widen the general outlook, to ensure that the principle of 'normalisation' is safeguarded, to advise constructively on all matters which may influence the behaviour of the mentally handicapped.* It is his expertise which is required in altering arrangements, such as incentives—money, social club activities, supervision, dining arrangements etc., areas in which decisions are made at present nearly always in order to ease administrative difficulties, but where no consideration is given to lost learning—education and training—opportunities.

There have been valuable papers by psychologists reporting the effects of different types of supervision (Tizard, 1953), of incentives (Claridge and O'Connor, 1957), of the presentation of incentives (Clark, 1960), of programming the learning in workshops (Clarke, 1962), but, on the whole, these investigations were few in number and shortlived. There have been no opportunities for psychologists to apply their knowledge consistently to the overall management of the institutional situation and I know only of two examples in this country—Tizard's Brooklands investigation (Tizard, 1964) and my own participation in the Slough experiment (Gunzburg, 1968; Baranyay, 1971).

There is obviously some considerable reluctance on the side of the present 'establishment', the tripartite administration, to accept fully a new discipline on management level. There is probably an equal reluctance by the pure 'scientist' in psychology to venture forth into a situation for which his academic training has not prepared him. All three present management disciplines have grown up in a tradition of shouldering responsibilities—psychologists have never yet really looked at their problems from that point of view.

A management team of professional people (Elliot, 1970, 1971), which includes the senior psychologist and which has executive powers, need not necessarily be chaired by a particular discipline, and the *primus inter pares* concept need, or should not apply automatically. It is much more preferable that a temporary leadership role is taken by one or the other discipline, depending on the type of problem to be solved, without claiming that it is his responsibility alone and thus the psychologist will be able to initiate developments, which he regards essential from his point of view.

A professional management team must not be considered simply as an administrative body of departmental heads who consult together. It is a partnership in management and its members must not be concerned with scoring points and defending their respective departments. Irrespective of their particular disciplines, they are concerned with creating together, within the institutional framework, those opportunities for staff and 'patients' alike, which would enable everyone to function better. Rightly or wrongly, they are given the task of deciding and executing on behalf of everyone else in the place. Without the existence of an operational philosophy of a comprehensive education and training concept, present management practices are only too often limited to pitiful patching up of deficiencies according to personal idiosyncracies, developing isolated 'bright' ideas etc. out of context, and living from day to day. On the other hand, adherence to a concept and application of it to day-to-day issues, will assist considerably in pursuing systematically and consistently a therapeutic approach (Gunzburg, 1970). Very often it could be the senior psychologist who will have to act as a guide to his colleagues in this particular area and who must ensure that the principles of the operational philosophy are recalled and applied whenever the occasion requires it.

The demand that the senior psychologist should join the local management team alongside other professions is not an attempt to enhance his status by making him one of the establishment. It appears, however, the only constructive way for giving him that weight which would entitle him to participate on top level in decisions which influence the lives of the mentally handicapped and to which he is able to contribute a particular outlook, so far entirely missing in management considerations.

A team of profesional workers cannot, as legislation stands at present, accept responsibility where it is clearly stated that it is the doctor's, the nurse's, the administrator's responsibility. Yet, there are thousands of opportunities where the team, adhering to a particular policy can exercise some pressure and influence on decision and modify practices which are often the results of traditional, unchallenged personal viewpoints. A psychologist, using this medium of a professional management team, may well tackle such touchy problems as nurses' uniforms, locked wards, punishment, and changes or replacement of staff. Each of these areas has, like so many others, direct bearing on the level of functioning in the mentally handicapped and many of the research results have no chance whatsoever to be more than interesting findings, unless the psychologist himself is instrumental for their introduction in practical settings.

3. Rôle of Psychologist in Communication

A third point derives from these considerations. Psychologists are notorious for commenting on the origin of all institutional evils—namely lack of communication. The psychologist, being now, according to the model outlined—at the source of decision making, having participated in designing a philosophy and policy, is now in an ideal

position to make positive contributions towards communications—
'vertically and horizontally'. In this area the psychologist would be able
to establish a key function of therapeutic impact by turning, for
example, the traditional 'case conference' into a means of reshaping the
institution environment and practices. Instead of limiting himself to
presenting his test findings alongside the observations by others
contributing to a diagnosis and a doubtful prognosis (Wolfensberger,
1965), he should ensure that this occasion is used to ask some
pertinent questions which lead to actions which he will be in a position
to initiate and follow through as a member of the professional
management team. This would mean, for example, that the discussion
of a patient's particular problems would not only lead to stating clearly
his needs as far as training, education, therapy or treatment are
concerned, but would also arrive at a conclusion how these needs could
best be met. At the present time action is generally confined to
selecting among a very limited range of placement possibilities that one
which is *least unsuitable* and even that choice will depend whether
there is a vacancy in the particular department. It will be the task of
this type of multidisciplinary conference on individual patient's needs
to make constructive suggestions how to redeploy the hospital's present
resources and how to arrange best any additional resources 'in the
pipeline' to make full use of research findings, assessments, treatment
suggestions, programmes etc., which apply not only to the particular
patient who was the subject of the meeting, but to many others who
would benefit by a more active individualised policy.

This type of meeting, which is a cross between a clinical case
conference and a consultative body dealing with patient management
problems, provides an ideal opportunity for getting staff actively
involved in problems relating to making best use of available resources
and for establishing communications between the policy making level
and the 'firstline' staff who are in immediate touch with hard reality.
Instead of turning into a somewhat abstract clinical labelling exercise,
these meetings could provide the venue for explaining and demonstrating why particular 'clinical' findings require urgent action now, which
very often demand extra time and attention and cause perhaps
inconvenience and disturbance, and lead to the postponement of other
cherished ideas.

As far as the psychologist is concerned, this additional demand on
his professional contribution is quite considerable. We will still have to
carry on fully with the tasks of assessment, initiation of therapeutic
programmes, guidance and supervision of rehabilitative measures, group
therapy, education, research, as has been described fully on previous
occasions (Gunzburg, 1956; Clark, 1968). Now he has to accept that he

himself, for the benefit of the person he tries to understand and help, and for the benefit of his own discipline, must involve himself fully in the creation of the setting in which the particular findings and theories of behavioural sciences can be applied and tried out. The atomistic, departmentalised approach, essential as it is for grasping the problem and suggesting a possible solution, will have real significant impact on behavioural practices only if it recognises that its 'message' will have to be 'sold', brought home and incorporated into daily hospital life by the hard and frustrating work outside the shelter of laboratory and testroom and the only one who can do this at present must be the psychologist himself.

Future Rôle of Psychological Services

The foregoing has important repercussions on the size and quality of psychological services in the subnormality institution. The establishment does not depend on the number of admissions, the frequency of I.Q. assessment nor even the amount of 'fundamental' research undertaken by ambitious staff, but on the involvement with the general policy of such a place. The consistent application of psychological findings and suggestions, the modification of the programmes, the evaluation and permanent incorporation in life practices of what has been found valuable, requires full time attention to the actual frontline, the 'ward' or, as it is rechristened now, 'the Living Unit'. It can easily be visualised that there is no limit to the number of psychologists who could be usefully employed in introducing their knowledge on a practical plane. They must also be psychologists who can see and accept that we are dealing with human problems and not merely with research material. In such a service the head of the psychological services should not see himself as the chief of a numerically powerful department competing with the other established services, but as a co-ordinating influence, concerned partly with the very essential task of lubricating the machinery of departmental co-ordination (Clark, 1970), and partly with safeguarding the principles of a therapeutic environment, which are too often and too readily and sometimes unnecessarily sacrificed to expediency. One would like to see this type of psychological service as a kind of task force, which will be redeployed in other developments such as residential work in the community, once the task of creating a normalising residential environment has been completed, where behavioural sciences are applied. This further development is a long way away yet, but it has to be said now so as not to give the impression that the psychologist should 'take over', where in fact he should merely take an 'active part' in creating his own working conditions and applying his own findings.

REFERENCES

Baranyay, E. P. (1971). 'The Mentally Handicapped Adolescent'. London: Pergamon Press.
Browne, R. A., Gunzburg, H. C., Johnston Hannah, L. G. W., MacColl, K., Oliver, B., Thomas A. (1971). The needs of patients in subnormality hospitals if discharged to community care. *Brit. J. ment. Subn.* XVII, **32**, 7-24.
Claridge, G. S. and O'Connor N. (1957). The relationship between incentive, personality type and improvement in performance of imbeciles. *J. ment. Def. Res.* **1**, 16-25.
Clark, D. F. (1960). Visual feedback in the social learning of the subnormal. *J. ment. Subn.* **6**, 30-39.
Clark, D. F. (1968). A reassessment of the role of the clinical psychologist in the mental deficiency hospital. *J. ment. Subn.* **14**, 3-17.
Clark, D. F. (1970). The psychologist and interpersonal relationships in a mental subnormality hospital. *J. ment. Subn.* **16**, 30, 33-44.
Clarke, A. D. B. (1962). Laboratory and workshop studies of imbecile learning processes. *Proceed. Lond. Conf. Scient. Stud. ment. Defic.* 1960, I. 89-96.
Dybwad, G. (1967). Changing patterns of residential care for the mentally retarded. *Proceed. 1st Congr. Int. Assoc. Scient. ment. Defic. Montpellier,* pp. 575-580.
Elliot, J. (1970). Point of view. *Brit. J. ment. Subn.* **17**, **32**, 3-6.
East Birmingham Group. *The Hospital* **66**, 84-88, 225-228, 336-340.
Elliot, J. (1970). Point of view. *Brit. J. ment. Subn.* **17**, **32**, 3-6.
Gunzburg, A. L. (1967). Architecture for social rehabilitation *J. ment. Subn.* **13**, 25, 84-87.
Gunzburg, H. C. (1956). The role of the psychologist in the mental deficiency hospital. *Int. J. Soc. Psychiat.* **1**, 31-36.
Gunzburg, H. C. (1968). 'Social Competence and Mental Handicap'. Baillière, Tindall and Cassell.
Gunzburg, H. C. (1970). The hospital as a normalising training environment. *J. ment. Subn.* **16**, 31.
Gunzburg, H. C. and Gunzburg, A. L. (1970). The nurse and institutional design in mental subnormality hospitals. *Nursing Times*–Occasional Paper, August 20th, 121-124.
King, R. D. and Rayner, N. V. (1967). Some determinants of patterns of residential care. *Proceed. 1st Congr. Int. Ass. Scient. Stud. ment. Defic., Montpellier,* pp. 642-649.
Kushlick, A. (1966). A community service for the mentally subnormal. *Social Psychiatry* **1**, 73-82.
Morris, P. (1969). 'Put Away'. London: Routledge and Kegan Paul.
Nirje, B. (1970). The normalisation principle–implication and comments. *J. ment. Subn.* **16**, 31, 62-70.
Tizard, J. (1953). The effects of different types of supervision on the behaviour of mental defectives in a sheltered workshop. *Amer. J. ment. Defic.* **58**, 143-161.
Tizard, J. (1964). 'Community Services for the Mentally Handicapped'. London: O.U.P.
Wolfensberger, W. (1965). Diagnosis diagnosed. *J. ment. Subn.* **11**, 62-70.

SESSION TWO
DISCUSSION

Chairman: Mrs. Sonja G. Harbinson

Chairman: Dr. Morris has posed questions concerning value judgments within our social structures; to what extent do they, and should they, govern social research? She sees the danger that, by their nature, our institutional structures foster:

(1) incorporation of *a priori* values and assumptions into the fabric of research design,
(2) maintenance of the *status quo,* with superficial modifications to meet short-term pressures, and
(3) consensus models, when problems may call for fundamental change.

Hence, what areas of research should the researcher tackle, and how should the researcher cope with assumptions and value judgments of society which may in themselves determine sponsorship upon which research is dependent?

If my understanding is correct, perhaps it would be useful to look at the separate areas of activity of, on the one hand, the administrator, and on the other hand, of the researcher, by considering the time scale within which each must work, to see whether this allows for reconciliation, since it would be unrealistic to assume any revolutionary changes in the social and institutional structures of this country (the U.K.).

I should like to query whether administrative decisions taken for the good of the short-term, need necessarily be at the expense of long-term good? Surely a dynamic society requires a dynamic administration: that is to say, response to, and resolution of, a succession of problems as they arise in the relatively short-term, not once-for-all irrevocable decisions relating to some static long-term problem. This is a question faced by administrators and researchers, if their work is to be relevant, contemporary and useful. They must take account of this just as administrators must take account of the democratic political processes which give expression to the value of our society. How then is research to influence the values of society?

I would like to ask whether Dr. Morris considers that such issues, as were touched on in Session 1, for example, a service directed towards the mixing of handicaps, the experiences of the mentally handicapped child in his interaction with his environment, or the prediction of need for new or changing services to meet social, economic and technological change, for instance, the advance of automation, can be usefully examined by sociologists, in view of the problem she has raised. Or does she consider it more meaningful that the researcher should address himself to her second aim, that is, to discover and propound general principles, hoping that these will provide a frame of reference for administrators in resolving immediate problems?

Dr. Gunzburg's paper deals with a sensitive problem, not only with the rôles and responsibilities of clinical psychologists in subnormality hospitals, but indirectly, with the whole staffing structure and organisation of the hospital service. It also raises the question of the degree of involvement which is necessary or desirable for a psychologist to have in day-to-day management of individuals, not only in hospitals but in a much wider context.

Although it seems that the last word has by no means been said on whether or not a relatively large group of mentally handicapped people can live together without adverse effects, the *status quo* involving as it does, about 52,000 people of all ages in England and Wales, cannot be swept aside.

In recent years, the intention to provide a reasonable standard of living for patients has become explicit. Nevertheless, whilst the adverse effects of institution living on both staff and patients and the consequent need for provision of adequate training, educational and recreational facilities, are acknowledged, these are too often not clearly defined.

Examination of individual patient needs and their diversity, re-deployment of resources, for example in the creation of a more normal than usual environment, and perhaps most important of all, reorientation of staff rôles, is a mammoth task. Yet without such major reorganisation it would seem unlikely that minor and isolated adjustments would have sufficient impact quickly enough on the lives of patients, to be effective.

I hope that lessons are being learned in the development of a community service, from the traditional organisation of hospitals. The 'atomistic', as opposed to the 'systematic, planned approach', absence of guiding principles, staff-orientation and professional jealousies described by Dr. Gunzburg could result in small, isolated 'institutions', ostensibly in the community, which would do no more than larger establishments to enhance the social adjustment or quality of life of mentally handicapped persons living or working in them.

The development of day and residential services in the community will only succeed in inducing positive change in mentally handicapped people if a multidisciplinary approach with clearly defined principles and strategies of teaching, training and care, which are communicated to those with whom the mentally handicapped spend most of their time, for example, parents, teachers and residential and training centre staffs, is achieved.

Hodgson: I am very confused because I don't really know what is meant by the term 'behavioural science'. I don't know what it includes or what it's about and I wonder if somebody, or the *Study Group* as a whole, would define this for me and enumerate for me the professions involved. I had to get this clear before I could even begin to understand the first study talk. Would you, for example, include architects, are they ever behavioural scientists?

Dybwad: I think this is a very interesting question. Within the past ten years, a considerable number of architects around the world have become interested in moving out from the formal construction and mechanically oriented profession due to an increasing scientific inquiry as to the effect of space and form on human behaviour and I could name at least ten people who would feel that, as architects, they are very much concerned, in a scientific way, with carrying on research on behavioural factors.

Hodgson: Yes, this is one of the things that prompted my question. May I ask you another one? What about the developmental paediatrician? Is he in any way a behavioural scientist or not?

A. D. B. Clarke: Can I perhaps say what was in the mind of those who organised this *Study Group?* Of course, what was in their minds has not been fully represented here because a number of people we invited were unable to come, among them Dr. Kushlick and Dr. Kirman who are experts in several fields. I would, however, take the simple view that a behavioural scientist is someone who is not only interested in behaviour but has the training to undertake scientific research in the behavioural field. This is not true of architects. The architect may well be interested in behaviour and this is splendid. He may want to collaborate with behavioural scientists, and this is excellent, but I do not think any architect I know actually has training in the application of scientific method to behaviour. Many doctors are increasingly interested in behaviour too, but only a minority have any training in the very complex methodology of behavioural research. The professions we thought of mainly as being behavioural scientists were sociologists, psychologists, anthropologists, (of whom we have none here), and educators in so far as they use research methods in education, and they are rather few and far between. The other half of the mix—and equally important, possibly more important—is represented here (very well if I may say so), by people who are in teaching or administrative positions or in advisory positions who are interested in subnormality, interested in behaviour, therefore hopefully interested in both the strengths and the weaknesses which behavioural research shows. This is my short answer to Dr. Hodgson's very important question.

Mittler: Can I move on to another issue raised by Dr. Morris' paper? I was interested indeed in her comments about the rôle of funding organisations in research, but in addition, to the purposes which she lists that funding organisations have (and this includes the Government), that there is also the question of researchers being asked from time to time to evaluate an experimental service. I do not want to go into detail, but I want to use it as a demonstration, of what is something of a dilemma at the moment in relationships between funding organisations and research departments. If you are invited to evaluate a new service, this is a perfectly legitimate question for a funding organization to ask of you. If a Government is introducing a new way of caring for the mentally handicapped it is absolutely right that they should invite somebody independently to evaluate this. The difficulty is that research workers are now more and more anxious about the limitations of the techniques which are currently available to answer that kind of question and I would like to take as examples educational research rather than service research. In education, we have a large number of examples, or new schemes, being introduced, or new methods of organisation in schools, but the most obvious example that comes to mind is that of streaming in the primary schools. The Department of Education and Science wants to know whether the children who are educated in streamed classes do better or worse than those who are brought up in non-streamed situations, and they quite rightly commission a very large expensive piece of research. However, the research techniques which are currently available to answer these questions are not altogether satisfactory and most of these researchers (and I can mention several other examples) have come up with completely negative findings, that is to say, that there is no real difference arising from the varying size of group A and group B. There are other examples, such as the use of French in primary schools, progressive versus formal methods of infant school organisation. All of these questions are being well and thoroughly researched.

One of the reasons why we are dubious about the research techniques which are available to answer such questions bears on the sort of problem we were discussing in Session I on group research, although clearly when you have a population of 100,000 to look at, it is better than the small numbers we usually have available in subnormality. I am raising this general question because this is one example of the communication problem between governments who are asking important questions and research workers who are not sure that they have techniques adequate to answer them. To sum it up, governments say 'is there any difference between method A and method B of caring for the mentally handicapped?' We can try to launch a very good piece of research to answer these questions but I think we should come up with inconclusive findings, therefore, extinguishing further sources of Government support for the next project. But I am not suggesting it is always as black as it seems, for there is an alternative, but it is one that has not been tried very much, and it is to describe in great detail and with great precision, exactly what is actually going-on in a new service, without necessarily comparing the new service with the old. If you are introducing a scheme, the task of the researcher can be to monitor it—to describe the patterns of changes. This is an area where I think sociologists are of enormous value in helping us to structure our thinking. The people concerned with the research can evaluate but in a new sense. I am asking for a new definition of the word *evaluation*.

This seems to be low level research but I wonder if it can be made more high-powered than it is at the moment! I would like Dr. Morris' comment, as a sociologist, on whether it is possible to do good descriptive research, say in the field of mental handicap, as opposed to telling governments that this new method of looking after mentally handicapped people produces better adjustment, or raises the I.Q., or reduces admission rates to hospitals, or whatever are the criteria for improvement.

Morris: I think that it is possible to do this kind of monitoring of services and to make it perhaps slightly more high-level—certainly more sociological. I would want it linked to the effect that it has, outside the immediate service that you are monitoring, so that if you are specifically looking at a service in the field of education of handicapped children—then let us also see what effect this has on the wider social attitudes to subnormality, to the parental attitudes, and so forth. I would agree that this is probably an effective way of looking at new services.

Cave: I was very interested in Dr. Mittler's remarks here. It seems to me that he was attempting to define what we can legitimately expect of research and what we ought not to try and expect. He instanced the investigation into 'streaming', while the one that came to my mind first of all, was the investigation into comprehensive education. I think our research venture is to look at two forces or organisation and to say that *this* one produces this, that, or the other result. The investigator does not necessarily say it is better. I do not think a researcher can make a judgment of whether it is necessarily a more desirable educational organisation because all sorts of other values, their value judgments, come in. Therefore, I think there are restrictions which we must accept,

but this does lead me back to the second paragraph of Dr. Morris'
paper. Here she has made some provocative remarks which one has
come to expect from her. It seems to me that the nub of this is in the
end of the paragraph in which the administrators are alleged to want 'to
use these skills in order to give a semblance of intellectual respectability
to their policies which it then becomes difficult for anyone to assail.' I
think this is perhaps a little unkind, but it does raise a major question,
and maybe we ought to be looking, in this study group and elsewhere,
at the other side of the coin. After looking at certain services, the
researcher seems to the practitioner to be able to come up with certain
advice on the provision of services which will produce certain desirable
results. For example, we ought to be getting from the researchers some
indication of the way in which the mentally handicapped learn, how
they function, are these materially different ways from those in which
other normal children function? This is the question Alan Clarke
referred to when he was talking about our policy differences. So far, we
have not really had any clear indication and I am responding to the
challenge provided by Dr. Morris. Is this view of research an adequate
one and is it not too destructive? Ought it not, in the long term, to
come up with the constructive side which enables the administrator, the
educationist, the teacher, to provide a better service?
Morris: I am not sure whether you have really thought about this,
because the kind of examples you give of research that you want done
are not in the field of sociology, but in the field of psychology.
Certainly, I do not think, if we are talking sociology, that one can
divorce this from value judgments and one cannot say that this is the
right service, or a better service. One can only say these appear to be
the results of providing a certain service or an alternative service. There
is no right or wrong. The decision about what to do is a value decision
which is taken by the administrators.
Cave: I agree that I was mentioning psychological rather than
sociological research, but I do not think it always comes out to a
decision based on value judgments. I think there could be more
information provided from investigations of services which would
enable administrators and others to make right decisions. At the
moment, we desperately lack the kind of factual information which
research can give on which to base judgments, including our own sense
of values.
Hodgson: I agree because what is happening is that the researcher says
'well, I have looked at this and this is what happens. I have looked at
that and that's what happens—now you decide what sort of service you
are going to build'. This is very difficult to do, since usually the
criticism of the service then comes from the research worker, and really

they give you very little assistance in which way to design your services. Take for instance medicine; we read of many differences of opinion on the subject. One says this, someone else says that, but we are left to decide what sort of service to build. I think we should expect a little more from research, and there should be some indication as to what is *better,* and what is *worse,* not just an observation of what happens, because in many instances one could do that oneself, in fact, one need not have asked for the research to be done in the first place.

Morris: I find it very difficult to know what you mean by 'better' or 'worse' because this is basically not a question which a sociologist can answer in a field with which he is not specifically connected. I mean, he is not an expert in the field of, say, retardation or medicine, or anything else if it comes to that, he is a sociologist and the decision of what is *better* or *worse* is more appropriate for those in power at a particular moment in time.

Hodgson: I am sorry—*better* for the person receiving the service—that is what concerns me. People keep saying that it is *better* for the person in power, but the person in power is trying to find out what is *better* for the person who is receiving the service. The decision makers get very little help from research.

Morris: We know, for example, from areas of research in institutional care, that locking people up either in prisons or putting them in institutions is not a particularly good way of dealing with their particular problems but it does not prevent us from going on doing it. This is a decision, that for various reasons, (one could be financial and another that there was no alternative available, or nobody's going to make the money available), is often taken.

Hodgson: I do not agree. What I am saying is, could not somebody come up with a reasonable alternative? So often there is just the criticism and no offer of a valid alternative based on fundamental research.

Currie: I wonder perhaps if this underlines one of the things which I think the community, as a whole, unreasonably demands of the researcher. It is so easy to say 'right, now we want to do something for a particular group (unspecified at the moment), let us ask such-and-such a team who are good researchers in the field to come up with an idea'. I wonder whether we can expect researchers to be our all-purpose magicians, who can systematically study, evaluate and come up with some observations of what actually happens. At the same time to inform us of the limits within which they make these observations, and what our expectation might reasonably be in this field.

I wonder if it is reasonable to expect them to be our all-purpose magician when your job is to 'think up' the good services. What we have to accept is that we each have only twenty-four hours in the day and we each have our own particular areas of experience which give us a little extra opportunity to observe. Those of us who have anything to do with the services or caring organisations perhaps should approach the problem in these terms, and maybe not to say to the researcher 'well, you just give me that information and then I will make of it what I will' but rather 'could you join us in this planning organisation and can we together then thrash out in a face-to-face collaboration, what seems to us in the light of the best information at the time, to be a solution?'

Serpell: May I question an implication in Dr. Morris' statement. She is appropriately cautious of treating the problems raised by sociological research as the same as those raised by psychological research. We have heard some discussion earlier about whether behavioural sciences are a unitary group. It seems to me that what Dr. Morris is saying is not what Mrs. Currie said at all, that administrators are asking too much, but rather that they are asking too little of research work. She is saying that we should be looking on a much broader scale at the radical changes necessary in the services rather than looking at particular problems, because she feels constrained to a particular moral viewpoint by the definition of problems presented to research workers by administrators. This may well be a problem in the field of sociological enquiry, which is very largely concerned with normative issues all the time. It seems to me that in the field of mental retardation very often the questions which are asked of psychologists by administrators, some of which were outlined by Mr. Cave, are in fact not all normative questions, they are very technical questions and we can approach these without too much feeling of embarrassment. We can quite reasonably approach the question of, given that a particular form of learning is required, how technically can we bring this about without wondering all the time should we be promoting this kind of learning? Some people seem to be a little embarrassed talking about amelioration and improvement in this *Study Group*, as if there was something very controversial. It seems to me that this is almost pedantry; everybody in this room could arrive at a common scale of value judgments which are very general with regard to the fact that this particular kind of deviance, as Dr. Morris calls it, is not in fact a very difficult one to accept as being deviant.

Dybwad: Will there be any time for a general question period later on, because maybe we need to address ourselves to the problem of deviance.

A. D. B. Clarke: We have two and a half hours available virtually unstructured on the last afternoon and I have briefed a number of people to keep their eyes and ears open for these sorts of points which I hope will be raised one-by-one on the final afternoon, and use this opportunity to draw the threads of discussion together.

Chairman: Can we go straight on now to Dr. Gunzburg's optimism about staff co-operation and the multi-disciplinary approach in hospitals? I think perhaps one of the chief difficulties is the effect on the staff working in a large institution with a hierarchical structure and many traditions which are very difficult to break down. I wonder whether there are sufficient psychologists of the appropriate calibre and also interest, for any significant contribution to be made to this normalising environment. I wonder whether the training of other staff in the hospitals, if it were less diversified, would bring them together and make it possible for a multi-disciplinary approach to occur because it seems a very difficult step to get over. We already have a very false environment, exaggerated by staff difficulties. How can we bring it towards normal community living? Can I therefore throw open this discussion?

A. M. Clarke: I would like to bring the two speakers and the problems presented by them, together. I share with my husband the great regret that it was not possible to attract more sociologists to this meeting than we have in fact been able to do, but I count this *Study Group* very fortunate indeed to have Dr. Morris here. It seems to me that before Dr. Gunzburg or any psychologist, or other professional worker can get cracking, it is necessary to ask the sociologist as a scientist, working within a particular social structure, to answer a number of questions. I think Dr. Hodgson asked Dr. Morris a question, which was implicit in Mr. Cave's remarks. Dr. Morris has undertaken a detailed analysis of some of the activities and the interactions among staff and patients within a number of large institutions. I have little doubt that she must have a private view based on her findings, but perhaps not publicly expressed, as to the desirability of having residential institutions, what might be their optimum size, the nature and members of staff, and their purpose in the context of the wider community. This is a matter of urgent need for sociologists with their very special techniques of observations and data analysis that we must be allowed to ask them whether a particular society is ready to accept large numbers of handicapped people in their midst. I am not saying that ours is, but maybe, it is potentially ready to accept the majority of the mentally handicapped in the community, instead of in institutions. The psychologist, the doctor, the social worker, the teacher, will then have a prescription for the kind of direction which they will take in their day-to-day interaction with this person, because they will have a purpose. If it is suggested by the sociologist that either this society is not ready to accept a majority of the mentally handicapped in their midst, or that it is desirable for a number of other reasons that the mentally handicapped should be segregated into communities, then the kind of activity which will be prescribed by those directly concerned with behaviour modification will be different. In other words, one wants to know what is the purpose of the particular social structure in which the mentally handicapped finds himself segregated outside society. Will he need to acquire skills, behavioural skills, suitable for an adjustment within that segregated society, or is the prescription to be that the function of an institution is short-term care in order to help him to adjust better to the community, in which case it will be a slightly different set of skills which will be required of him? Or, will the sociologist suggest to him that large institutions should be avoided, small institutions are better or no institutions at all, in which case the direction which will be adopted and indeed the professional workers involved might be different? But I think that we must ask the sociologists whether they can answer this as scientists, or whether they feel that, at the moment, this really depends upon individual value judgments?

Morris: I think inevitably at this stage it must be admitted that this can only be based on value judgments. I don't think we can answer it scientifically. I think one would need to go around and ask people's views about whether we think they could be more tolerant, but all we would get, I suspect, is—it would be very interesting—a reflection on existing services. In other words, that you would tend to get people saying 'No, we won't accept people back into the community' because there aren't going to be any services for them, there aren't going to be workshops where they can go, there aren't going to be facilities for nursing them when they need it, or for going into institutions for a short period if they should need that. In other words, you are only asking people about their attitudes under existing conditions, and in fact, if one is thinking in terms of new services and new opportunities, then what one might want to do is something quite different and then you come back again to this whole question of priorities in terms of political attitudes, how much money one wants to spend on one service, compared with any other.

Although you have been asked to ask a lot of these questions, you might get some interesting ideas out of it, I don't think the result would be scientific in the sense that I think you mean it, and we are really only repeating certain values that we feel to be desirable. But I think it also comes back to this question that we do want to know on what criteria people defined the mentally retarded as deviant, within the existing system. Why do they define them in this way? What is it that makes us want to treat them differently?

Gunzburg: Two points, first of all, quite frankly I wouldn't like to wait for the sociologists' or psychologists' answers; we have got to do something now. Secondly, I don't think there is any difference whether they go into the community, whether they go into large institutions or small institutions. I would have hoped that we aim, generally, at making life normal and teach them normal life skills and so on. In fact, if they make it, then very good, let them go on. If they do not, we should not be preparing them for a different life, but a normal life within that protected corner of the community. We are not teaching them differently because they have got a different prognosis, we teach them the same thing but they do not achieve the full sort of expectations, but they will live somewhere else, still in normal conditions. Indeed, I really see the whole thing as one road, and the various levels of handicap sort of drop off at various stages, but it's always on the same main road, not different roads.

A. M. Clarke: It is presumably an ideal situation you are talking about?

Gunzburg: Why should it not be a very practical thing? Madame Chairman talked about the difficulties, that she wished she could share my optimism. I have just worked out how many years I have been an optimist—for thirty years! I still believe it is possible, and I still think the problems can be got over. I get valuable assistance from my colleagues. When they are very young, they come from the University and they are full of ideas that they want to do something, but when they get older they sort of drop-out and devote themselves to research!

Kiernan: I would like to take up what might be a different aspect of Dr. Clarke's point. I am somewhat involved in having to introduce an operant programme for the Ward Nurse at a subnormality hospital. One of the things which has become clear from this project is that if you do manage to modify the behaviour of the nurses on the ward, which is a difficult enough job in itself, then you've still got the great difficulty of dealing with the hierarchy. Now this is obvious, but it's one where I think Dr. Clarke's point becomes particularly important. In the operant area at least (and I wouldn't like to speak for people outside the operant area), there is I think a general lack of knowledge about sociological and other studies which are relevant to the organisation and to the impact the organisation has on the individual. If, as in the case of our project, the need becomes apparent to emphasise to the nurse in the ward situation that she is the primary change-agent, that it's her behaviour which modifies the behaviour of the child, then you immediately run into immense difficulties, creating conflicts within her view of her own roles, and also conflicts between that ward and the institution which sees the nurse as the end of the line of orders, sees her as a person at the bottom of the heap and sees her as the person who has no right and no comment to make on decisions which are taken at a high level. So, although I would feel that the notion of 'sociological research in advance' is something which could run into difficulties, none the less the existence of sociological research and, more important, the co-ordination of the research sociologists with changes which psychologists may make, seems necessary. There is a very small point here, and I'm going right outside anything I know much about, but as I've found it, many sociologists can claim that their research cannot be experimental. This may represent an opportunity where experimental research can be done in conjunction with psychologists, where the sociologist can co-ordinate his efforts with those of someone who is modifying behaviours, which the sociologist often speaks about but has little opportunity to actually change.

Dybwad: I was so very glad that Dr. Gunzburg introduced, besides the psychological considerations, also aspects of administration, and I think we can now deal with the science of administration which can claim equal rights. I was particularly interested in his idea of a team concept. I would like to call your attention to the fact that we have in Denmark over ten years now, an example of a team consisting of a physician, a sociologist (more than a social worker) and an educational psychologist. They have been operating as a decisive team, governing the eleven regions in mental deficiency work. Obviously the team does not sit to decide which child should have a tonsillectomy or not, you always can ridicule such a team effort in this kind of thing. But within even their discretion they acted, but they have managed over ten years now, with difficulties which would be worth studying, to operate as a team. We are now trying in the existing larger institutions to reduce the power of the superintendent which has been at the core of the disaster that we have had in all these institutions, to dissipate the power of the superintendent, by sub-dividing the institutions into treatment areas. He can still decide what amount of toilet paper is to be ordered from whom, but the treatment aspects will be handled from the team aspect and there is some good work going on now worth studying. I was glad that you spoke of the changing role of the psychologist and you mentioned in the last book which you published, in your concluding chapter you have the psychologist in society and I was very much interested in your formulation because Stanley P. Davies who, about 30 or 40 years ago, wrote a book *Social Control of the Mentally Defective* republished this 30 years later as *The Mentally Retarded in Society*. I found it very nice that a psychologist joins now the mentally retarded in society in terms of the kind of considerations which are important, and just as a concluding comment, I hope very much that the question of deviants and who makes and persists in making people deviants and the rôle of professional individuals, or individuals in the professions, in maintaining the deviance of individuals might perhaps be one of the topics to which we can address ourselves in the concluding session.

Borkwood: May I go back to an entirely different point which Dr. Gunzburg brought up in his paper when he spoke of the operational policy. He defined the policy in concrete terms and gave us an example of the potential of the subnormal. I've never considered myself a research worker. What I've done is listen whenever possible and read as much as I possibly can, of the work done by psychologists, psychiatrists, doctors and sociologists, in the field of mental subnormality. What I do is to pick out what is of immediate use to the work I'm doing at that time with a specific subnormal person. I have previously studied the needs of this person and looked at his potential and I've based my practical teaching from that point. Rightly or wrongly, I put the I.Q. in the background. Quite a lot was said last night, and has also been mentioned this morning, about how the research workers might help in the teaching field. I would be quite happy at any time to have any research worker actually in the classroom while I might be implementing a suggestion which they may have offered, and I, the teacher, would like their reactions to see somebody put this idea into practice, and to see how it works.

Kiernan: As someone who advocated this type of research last night, may I comment on this? I think this is the type of research which is critically important in the development of work in subnormality, and I would emphasise that I think this is the case mainly because the teacher is the person who is concerned about the variance—Dr. Gunzburg refers to urgent variables, problems which account for a large proportion of the variance in behaviour. There are techniques for evaluating this type of exercise. These techniques of evaluating go throughout the Skinnerian work but complement other techniques. This is research which is going on but there is far too little of it which is clearly relevant to the teacher. No one, I think, in psychology would really want to make teachers research workers. Teachers have one job to do and research workers have another job to do but the two jobs can come remarkably close together, both in the techniques and in the aims which they have.

Mittler: Just one very brief thing I want to mention, although possibly this is better for discussion in the final panel. When I was listening to Dr. Gunzburg, and I support his basic position very strongly, I was still left just a little bit unclear as to precisely how the professional skills of the psychologist within the management team differ from those of other people in that team. One respect possibly, which he didn't mention, which I would like his views on, is that the psychologist in the team is probably better equipped than anyone else, to provide the kind of on-going evaluation of the way in which an institution is changing under the new management scheme, and I wondered if Dr. Gunzburg would agree with this? Otherwise, I'm a little unclear. The whole of the team can be agreed about organisation, about the sort of things he mentioned, whether nurses should wear uniforms, whether wards should be locked. I don't think that the psychologist has any specific contribution to make to this question, as a psychologist, but merely as a member of the team. The most depressing thing to me about Dr. Morris' book was her findings about psychologists, and I agree with the Chairman's pessimism. What psychologists do at the moment in mental deficiency hospitals is too depressing for words. I didn't realise it was as bad as it was, it left me feeling profoundly depressed. The reason why Dr. Gunzburg has been involved for the last few years in management is only, it seems to me, because his colleagues see that he has something to offer. What is it, precisely, that you offer as a psychologist that could not be offered by other members of the team? But maybe that's too big a question to answer at this stage of the morning.

Gunzburg: I simply deal with problems as they arise and as they have been found necessary to solve. Now whether PSYCHOLOGY, spelled in big capital letters is involved or not, I would not want to answer in detail, because really what it comes to is, I think, we have first of all to create a framework for ourselves, the working conditions for ourselves in order to put any of our ideas over, and until that framework is created we can't make this particular contribution for psychology. Now I think Dr. Kiernan just mentioned the conflict with hierarchy, if you do something on the ward which is pure psychology, like operant conditioning, you may run up against hierarchy, but if you are one of the hierarchy yourself, then you can, from the top, engineer things and do a lot to change the general outlook, which is your particular contribution on this management project. You may have consultants who have been there for years and years and who see the problems largely as medical problems. Then you may have a nurse who sees things as a nurse, and finally you have an administrator. Now all these people have got their view, a more or less constant idea of what a hospital should be like. Now I think if we come along with new ideas, we should help them to see their own contribution in a new light. That wards may not be locked all the time, that things could be done in different ways that have never been looked at, so it isn't only the question of evaluation but it is a scientific approach of judging a problem, seeing it differently and perhaps with less vested interest than in the past. This is the major contribution. I would not, however, say that it necessarily always works. But where it is possible, I think that a lot of those problems which one experiences on the front-line can be ironed out by having collaboration at the top.

Hodgson: I want to take up two points which you mentioned in your paper; organisation and multi-disciplinary teams and who should be at management level. It is rather interesting because the more people I meet, the more people I think ought to be on the team of management. Let me quote you an example. I've been at a subnormality hospital not so very long ago early in the morning and I saw an astounding sight—four cerebral-palsied children pushed up to a table which they couldn't reach because they couldn't get the chairs under it and, believe it or not, they had for breakfast porridge, followed by fried egg, and they were given a spoon. Now can you imagine what it is like? Cerebral-palsy trying to fight an egg on a plate, with a spoon. Now when we went into this it was interesting. 'Normalisation' was mentioned—they must learn to eat like everybody else and the same kind of food. The other comment I got was 'Ah, but this is what the Dieticians say they must have; this is a properly balanced diet; they need protein', and so on. When I asked the Dieticians, they said 'Ah, but we never go on the wards. We don't know which patients we're prescribing for. We are astounded at the amount of minced food we're asked for, but we can't query it.' Now should the Dieticians of the Catering Officer be in the multi-disciplinary team? And will it make any real difference to the outcome?

Gunzburg: First of all, an organisation as I defined it does not mean a definite number of members to be the norm, it can be adjusted. Secondly, as far as these other people are concerned, I don't think they are part of our multi-disciplinary management because these are questions which have to be investigated but the multi-disciplinary management is concerned with overall policy calling on experts for particular purposes. The third one is the question of the right hand not knowing what the left hand is doing. Now here again the psychologists can be useful not because they are better than others, but because they are the only people who have not a traditional role in the hospital set-up. What I do with my psychologists is get them out of the test situation and ask them to look at real problems in a new way. Some of them have started at 8 o'clock in the morning and finished up at 9 o'clock at night, living in the wards, and they bring back a lot of important information. I give you just one, a little example which we picked up the other day. The plated-meal service, the height of efficiency straight from a central kitchen, we saw it as not being normal, and not a learning opportunity, so the plated-meal service was abandoned, and we are back to the system where the nurse gives out the food, and, of course, it is less efficient, but we do a better human job that way. It is important that the management team gets information and works together.

Hodgson: I agree with you, but I still think we must look carefully at the team. You see, if I think I need somebody else's help, I ask them, but the crucial thing is, you need to know a lot before you know whose help to ask. It's marvellous to know that your psychologists are doing all this, but as somebody else pointed out, is it necessarily the job of the psychologist?

Chairman: I must close this as time is getting on. One thing that seems to have come out is that researchers and administrators should both be asking the questions together, not separately. Thank you very much, Dr. Gunzburg and Dr. Morris.

Session III

The Training of Teachers
and Their Attitudes to Research

The Training of Teachers of Mentally Handicapped Children

C. W. E. CAVE

Department of Education and Science, London

Introduction

In April of this year the education of severely mentally handicapped children became the responsibility of local education authorities. Up to then education for these children had been provided by local health and hospital authorities and the training of their teachers by a voluntary body until, following the recommendations of the Scott Committee, the Training Council for Teachers of Mentally Handicapped Children was set up in 1964. Under its aegis, and in a remarkably short period, a system of teacher training was established independent of the statutory system for training teachers of all other children. For young entrants the courses were of two years' duration; for experienced students, one year. Both types of course led to the Diploma of the Council, which was not recognised as a qualification in the rest of the educational system.

The courses were characterised by their markedly professional character. Older applicants were expected to have had at least five years relevant experience, young ones at least six months. Though the courses included some elements—for example liberal studies—designed to promote the students' own personal growth and development, the major emphasis was placed on those elements calculated to produce effective teachers, namely child development, the psychology and practice of teaching, the sociology of education and the characteristics of mentally handicapped children. These aspects of training had a good deal in common with the courses provided in colleges of education for teachers of young children, and it is perhaps worthy of note that at the time of transfer the Training Council was anxious to extend the length of its courses for young students to three years and to locate new courses not in colleges of further education but in colleges of education.

The Transfer of Responsibility to Local Education Authorities

The Education (Handicapped Children) Act of 1970 repealed Section 57 of the Education Act of 1944 and has brought into the education system all those children who had been or would have been determined as unsuitable for education at school. 'No child within the age limits for education, therefore, will be outside (its) scope.' (Circular 15/70). The characteristics of these children are familiar to all of you. The Department decided to designate them all 'educationally sub-normal'. This is not to suggest that the needs of severely mentally handicapped children are exactly like those of children whose degree of handicap is less severe: as the Working Party recently set up by the National Society for Mentally Handicapped Children (Under New Management NSMHC. Undated) recently put it, 'Evidence so far would indicate the probability that social pathologies, deprivation and cultural factors are predominant in esn school placement; biological, intellectual and developmental impairments the principal factors in ssn children.' But the division into severely subnormal and educationally subnormal seemed to us to have been primarily an administrative one; mental handicap is a continuum, with no clear cut educational or medical division. A single category of educationally subnormal children was therefore intended not only to bear witness to this fact, but to give the maximum flexibility in making educational arrangements for these children. For some time there have been experimental arrangements linking schools for the severely mentally handicapped with those for educationally subnormal children; in two cases these have now been fused into a single special school, and other local authorities are already making similar plans. I have no doubt that we shall see other experimental arrangements as 'Local education authorities . . . give early consideration to a broader strategy for the education of mentally handicapped children within their total provision for children in need of special education.' (Circular 15/70.) One or two authorities have suggested units for severely mentally handicapped children attached to primary schools; others may provide special classes in comprehensive schools for the less severely handicapped, and an extended range of mental handicap in their special schools.

I refer to these developments to show that mentally handicapped children will not for ever remain separate and isolated within the system of special education; they and their teachers are an integral part of it. If their teachers are to be sufficiently adaptable to meet these extended demands, able to meet the needs not only of the severely mentally handicapped but of other children less handicapped as well, they must no longer be isolated from the main system of teacher training. Nor would it be healthy, I believe, to envisage a teacher trained exclusively for a narrow sector of the educational scene and to remain in it for her whole life; if special education is to be truly a part of the wider educational system, then it must be enriched by an exchange of ideas and personnel.

New Training Arrangements

To end their former involuntary isolation it was therefore decided that 'the training of teachers of mentally handicapped children will be integrated as soon as possible into the ordinary teacher training system'; it 'will consist of three year courses in colleges of education leading to a certificate of education, and to qualified teacher status on appointment'. (Circular 15/70.) Conversion courses have been arranged for a limited period to enable holders of the Training Council's Diplomas to become qualified teachers without waiting for a five year period to elapse, and for a year or two a small number of one year courses under the Council will continue to be provided for mature applicants.

Six colleges of education in 1970 offered initial three year courses of training specially modified to meet the needs of students wishing to teach mentally handicapped children and by the end of 1971 six more colleges will be doing likewise. A number of other colleges are also anxious to offer optional courses for teachers of other types of handicapped children, and the Department is now anxious to see some extension of these to meet the needs of special schools and of ordinary schools dealing with handicapped children. The output from the specialised courses I have referred to is expected to exceed 300 teachers by 1973, slightly in excess, I believe, of the output of the Training Council's courses for teachers of children. But to guard against any shortages at a time when demands for additional teachers are likely to arise, the Department has given local education authorities permission for a limited period to recruit teachers without qualification.

Among the staff of the new courses are many of the tutors formerly in charge of the Diploma courses under the Training Council; they form a useful element of continuity, and will in large measure ensure that their accumulated experience is not lost.

In England, the content of courses of teacher training is largely under the control of the Area Training Organisations of the universities; not unexpectedly therefore the new courses differ considerably one from another, though there are elements common to all. The syllabus of one includes the following components:

Education, including child development and a child study.

The psychology of learning, a main course study with special relevance to the mentally handicapped and leading for selected students to a BEd degree. The course covers: the causes and types of mental handicap and associated forms of behaviour; primary and secondary handicaps; assessment procedures and observation; problems of language and communication and how to ameliorate them; sensori-motor and perceptual disabilities—problems and solutions; motivation, concept formation transfer of training, current psychological research and its implications for practice.

The Sociology of Education, including community responsibility and the social services, legislation, voluntary bodies, social and vocational competence, the case conference.

Health Education.

Educational Practice—organisation of the classroom and its environment, specific teaching, 'integration' in school and community, teaching aids, interdisciplinary co-operation.

Teaching practice in normal and special schools.

Courses in language, drama, movement, music, art, craft and mathematics.

The teacher successfully completing this course will be qualified to teach in any sector of the educational system.

The initiation of courses such as this constitutes something of a landmark in the training of what the Americans call 'special educators'. There are many, and I count myself among them, who believe that the ideal training for teachers of handicapped children is normal teacher training followed by some years of experience teaching normal children, to be followed by a course of specialised training. This was the pattern advocated by the Advisory Council on the Training and Supply of Teachers of Handicapped Children in its fourth report in 1954. It recommended that all teachers of handicapped children in special schools, and at least a proportion of those in ordinary schools, should be *required* to have taken a normal course of teacher training, followed by a one year's specialised course after a period of normal experience. Because of problems of supply, the Minister of Education at the time did not feel able to make such training a requirement, but the first one year courses of training were soon established which in the absence of any specialist element in initial courses, have been the principal source of supply of knowledgeable teachers in special education. But the output of all the 39 courses today is only just over 600 per year—far too few to meet the needs of special schools alone, and certainly nowhere near enough to meet those of ordinary schools as well. Now for the first time we see the establishment of a number of initial courses with a significant special education component, and others are likely to follow. The one year courses of in-service training will gradually have the opportunity of becoming advanced courses for experienced serving teachers. A number of these courses already provide opportunities for an intensive study of mentally handicapped children, and there is a likelihood that at least one other is shortly to be designed exclusively for experienced teachers of severely mentally handicapped children.

Changes in Teacher Training

These developments are occurring at a period of change in teacher training generally. The lengthening of the course of initial training some years ago from two years to three and the assumption by the University Area Training Organisations of responsibility for control of the content of courses has tended to place growing emphasis on the academic components of initial courses—the so-called 'Main Courses' designed to further the student's own education rather than his competence as a teacher. This trend has been further accentuated by the establishment of the BEd degree, which in most cases is awarded on a student's performance in academic rather than professional studies. This trend may not be unwelcome to secondary schools, where the emphasis on subjects is more pronounced; it has proved less attractive to primary and special schools, with their emphasis on children learning rather than on subjects taught. Mixed ability grouping is moreover now common in primary schools and increasingly to be found in secondary, especially comprehensive, schools; many young teachers therefore find themselves faced, in their first teaching post, with groups of children among whom there may well be a substantial minority who present learning problems calling for a greater than usual level of professional skill.

The James Committee

Developments such as these, changing patterns of school organisation, growing awareness of the substantial minority of pupils needing special help in ordinary schools, less willingness on the part of some young people to commit themselves to a teaching career at the age of 18 are among some of the considerations which led the Secretary of State to appoint a Working Party under Lord James to examine the whole question of teacher training, and it seems likely that substantial changes may be recommended. It has been suggested that the teaching profession in England should become a graduate one, as in Scotland; the present Colleges of Education should become 'liberal arts' colleges, providing a variety of two year courses in academic subjects or in social sciences, to be followed for intending teachers by a one or two years course of professional studies somewhat on the lines of current postgraduate teacher training. It is too early yet to be able to see what is likely to emerge. A two years general course followed by a year or perhaps even better two years professional training might afford teachers of handicapped children a useful opportunity of working during the first part of their course alongside others intending to take up social work or other courses; it might be that in this way we should begin to see a common core emerge that would give social workers, teachers, doctors and others some insight into the language and ways of working of other disciplines, leading us a little more closely to that elusive goal of genuine interdisciplinary understanding and co-operation. But any recommendations that diminish the professional skill of a teacher of handicapped children will render a poor service to special education.

In-Service Training

The pace of educational change increases; knowledge expands and fresh insights are gained into how children learn and develop. Initial training is now becoming recognised as such—the essential equipment needed by a young teacher to start his career. Initial training in fact should be only the beginning of a teacher's professional training; his knowledge and skills must periodically be refurbished by in-service training, and the development of this will probably be one of the most significant aspects of teacher training in the 70s. Short courses provided by local education authorities, often in conjunction with colleges of education, are increasing in number; a most significant development is the establishment of a large number of teachers' centres where working groups meet regularly to inaugurate and to assess curricular and other developments. The Schools Council, in which teachers themselves play a dominant role, has been established to inaugurate curriculum development, and has had considerable influence on the practice of responsive teachers. A current project is concerned with the curriculum for slow learning children.

Teachers and Research

One of the tasks of initial training (not only of teachers) should be to make them responsive to change and to the impact of new knowledge and ideas. At present I doubt whether we achieve this; but unless this is done then it is unlikely that in-service training will be successful in modifying attitudes and practice as new knowledge becomes available. Many teachers, perhaps the majority, are largely uninfluenced by research. Not long ago the Deputy Director of the National Foundation for Educational Research admitted that few teachers seem ever to set eyes on *Educational Research*—the major journal in this country to report new research in education—and practically none buy it. One reason often given is that the findings of research frequently seem either remote from classroom practice or to confirm the obvious; the dissemination of research findings in language intelligible to the layman may be another important factor. But some of the reasons probably lie in the attitude of teachers themselves. An article in the June 1971 issue of the *British Journal of Educational Psychology* examines 'Curriculum Research and Development Projects: Barriers to Success'. It sets out with the object of 'identifying obstacles to experimentation and implementation', and looks at 'the anatomy of innovation from the point of view of the pathologist'. Emphasis is laid on four points:

1. A researcher must understand the school situation. 'A new look at teaching, if there is to be one, seems to require us to move up closer to the phenomenon of the teachers' world.'
2. 'Teachers must participate in the management of their own development . . . Curriculum development will not be effective in the long term unless it is seen to be capable of being tailored to the circumstances and temper of particular schools and individual teachers.'
3. 'The head or principal of the school is such a key figure that effective curriculum development requires of him not merely goodwill but understanding'.
4. 'It seems that an experiment settles well in a school where teachers are confronting a problem and contemplating action. The experiment should extend the range of their strategies for dealing with the problem'.

The article seems to me to emphasise the key factors essential to success in implementing new ideas—effective communication at all levels, adequate support to those participating, and a sense of involvement. We must in fact seek more often to make the teachers themselves partners in research and innovation. I learned recently what seems to me an excellent research model lately carried out at Newcastle University.

The experiment (I doubt whether those involved would call it a research) was to evolve and assess the effectiveness of a language enrichment programme with severely mentally handicapped children in the North East of England. A large number of teachers from training centres were involved, and were given details of the experimental programme to be carried out in their own centres; throughout the winter they came together at regular intervals to discuss results and to plan modifications in the research pattern. I am not able to assess the value of the findings, which have yet to be published in detail. What I am quite sure of is the enthusiasm of the teachers involved, their readiness at considerable personal cost and inconvenience to take part in the experiment where they felt they were important members, and the beneficial effect it had on their professional development. The point was put clearly in an article (Beyond Inquiry No. 1. Dialogue Summer 1971) published by the Schools Council. 'There can be no effective long term curriculum development without teacher develop- ment; the strength of these Projects is that they start from the pupil but they depend on teacher understanding, and the extension of teacher confidence, expertise and resources.' Professor R. S. Peters put the point even more vividly in a recent article entitled 'What is an Educational Process?' (in 'The Concept of Education', Routledge & Kegan Paul 1967, page 6. Quoted in BJEP, op.cit.). 'The Spartans for instance were military (sic) and morally trained. They knew how to fight; they knew what was right and wrong; they were possessed of a certain kind of lore, which stood them in good stead in stock situations. They were thus able to comb their hair with aplomb when the Persians were approaching at Thermopylae. But we could not say they had received a military or a moral education; for they had never been able to understand the principles underlying their code. They had mastered the content of forms of thought and behaviour without ever grasping or being able to operate with the principles that would enable them to manage on their own'.

Some 'New' Teachers' Views

JEANNE M. CURRIE

County Education Committee, Durham

What follows is not a formal research report. Instead it is an account of a strictly local 'domestic' enquiry. We hoped that the response to our enquiry would provide some useful practical guidelines for the psychological service in planning future strategies in relation to special schools. It is at best then a means of providing a point of departure for further discussion.

On 1st April, 1971, the seven junior training centres of the local authority Health Department became additional special schools for educationally sub-normal children. The total teaching staff establishment for these (that is excluding welfare assistants and other ancillary staff who work with the children) is 32, of whom 19 already have qualified teacher status.

We were interested to gain a global impression of the attitude of the teachers in these newest schools towards the application of fundamental research to the teaching of mentally handicapped children. Each of the schools concerned was circularised early in the summer term 1971, before they had been involved in any of the review meetings and other staff discussions normally arranged in our special schools. These were considered to be relevant in determining the timing of the operation as follows. Past experience of such meetings shows that these are often occasions for some discussion of relevant research findings and their application to particular circumstances. It would therefore be reasonable to expect these to have an impact upon subsequent staff responses in this field of enquiry.

The enquiry was presented to the teachers in two parts. In Part 1 the teachers were invited to list not more than three research studies in the fields of subnormality or learning, the findings of which they had found to be valuable to them as teachers. In Part II they were asked to indicate not more than three areas relevant to subnormality and/or learning in which they felt a need for more research data to be available. Staff were free to make their comments at whatever length they wished.

The replies received are tabulated below.

TABLE 1

	Part I	Part II
Replies listing 3 significant items	14	13
Replies listing 2 significant items	7	8
Replies listing 1 significant item	2	1
Replies listing 0 significant items	0	1
Total Replies	23	23

It is encouraging to note the 72% response level and it is perhaps worth noting in passing that this was achieved including in the calculation one school which sent no reply at all. This means that among those schools from which replies were received, the response level approaches 90%. It is noteworthy that something approaching 40% of the respondents named less than three areas of relevant research which they have found valuable and a very similar proportion named less than three topics in which they thought further research was needed. How far this was determined by the wording of the enquiry is problematic.

Alphabetically ordered lists of topics in the replies are given in appendices A and B, with the frequency of responses listed.

TABLE 2

Frequency of mention of topics in Replies

	Part I		Part II	
		Total items		Total items
Mentioned on 1 occasion	27	27	20	20
Mentioned on 2 occasions	6	12	10	20
Mentioned on 3 occasions	3	9	3	9
Mentioned on 4 occasions	1	4	0	0
Mentioned on 5 occasions	0	0	0	0
Mentioned on 6 occasions	1	6	1	6
Totals	38	58	44	55

At first sight, the apparent diversity of the individual topics of research mentioned in both parts of the replies is striking. On inspection however the items can be grouped under a relatively few general headings. Additionally a high proportion of the references to specific works relate to general texts rather than to specific studies. This will result in some overlapping of references which cannot easily be quantified. However, allowing for these deficiences the following tabulation still appears to contain some useful pointers.

TABLE 3

Frequency of classified topics in replies

Class of topic	Part I	Part II
Developmental Studies		
(a) General	12	6
(b) Specific (i) Speech and language	10	6
(ii) Play	5	
(iii) Social	3	
(iv) Art	1	
(v) Mental Growth	1	
Specific Educational Topics	13	18
Mental Handicap	13	24

Considering the replies in this way reveals a preponderance of items in Part I concerned with developmental studies, while general educational studies and those related to mental handicap specifically run these a poor joint second.

It is tempting to speculate the reasons for this pattern of response. One explanation might be merely familiarity, implying that child development studies have been most frequently studied by the teachers concerned. Another interpretation could be that child development studies, producing as they do observations of patterns of development have provided teachers with useful frameworks within which to plan training programmes. This is perhaps an area of speculation which could be fruitfully discussed at this meeting.

The picture is very strikingly different when one considers the pattern of response in Part II. Here the teachers show a concern with matters specifically related to questions which they face in teaching severely sub-normal children. This suggests that the research which is most likely to be construed as useful by the teachers is that which arises in response to questions which they raise from their experience.

Perhaps some of the most useful general conclusions can be drawn from the responses referring in both Parts I and II to studies of speech and language development. This is the single area in which the teachers showed most frequent concern. However the bare figures mask what is probably a very important point to consider when planning research activities. Two of the replying schools had recently been involved in a research project on language development. The teachers themselves had been active participators in the research procedures. All the replying teachers from these schools listed the research topic in Part I of their replies. All of them were more eloquent on this topic than in any other of their responses. Two of them felt further research in this field to be needed.

Although in this kind of enquiry conclusions can only be speculative it appears not unreasonable to conclude that the implication of these responses is yet another manifestation of the wisdom of the proverbial "I do and I understand". It suggests that researchers who are really interested in practical application of findings would do well to carry their investigations into schools. It suggests additionally that it is likely to be more fruitful if they can involve teachers as investigators than it would be if they merely collected data in the field before retreating to base.

APPENDIX A

Topics given in replies to enquiry in Part I of enquiry
Authors listed alphabetically

Frequency
of mention

1	Boom (Ed.)	Studies of the Mentally Handicapped Child
1	Furneaux	The Special Child
2	Gunzburg	P.A.C. Charts
1	Hartley & Goldstein	Understanding Children's Play
1	Hollamby	Young Children Living and Learning
3	Isaacs, S.	The Nursery Years
2	Isaacs, S. & N.	Some Aspects of Praget's Work
1	Kellogg	Analysing Child Art
1	Kushlick	Community Services for the Handicapped
1	Laban	Expressive Movement
1	Lowenfeld	Creative and Mental Growth
1	Marshall	Experiment in Education
1	Nuffield (generic title)	Book I
1	Orff	Music Method
1	Pavlov	Conditioning

Frequency
of mention

1	Pestalozzi	Method
1	Piaget	Theories
6	Simpson	Language Development Stimulation
3	Sheridan	Developmental Progress of Infants and Young Children
1	Stephen & Robertson	Carshalton Experiment
2	Stevens	Observing Children who are Severely Subnormal
2	Tansley	Reading and Remedial Reading
1	Tansley & Gulliford	The Education of the Slow Learner
1	Thorndike	Conditioning
1	Tizard	The Mentally Handicapped and their Families
1	Tizard	The Brooklands Experiment
2	Woodward	The Earliest Years
1	W.H.O. Report	Maternal Care and Mental Health

Additional topics given without authors being specified by teachers, again listed now alphabetically

1	Activity Method
1	Autism
1	Causes of Mongolism
1	Child Development
1	Communication
4	Language Development
2	Play activities
1	Project method
1	Psychology of Play
1	Teaching Aids

APPENDIX B

Topics given in replies to enquiry in Part II of enquiry
Listed alphabetically

Frequency
of mention

1	Aids for spastics
1	Application of conditioning to severely subnormal children

APPENDIX B—*cont.*

Frequency
of mention

3	Autism
1	Behaviour problems
1	Brain-damaged children
1	Causes of severe subnormality
1	Childhood Schizophrenia
1	Comparative development
2	Constructional equipment
1	Deprivation and its effect upon development of severely subnormal children
1	Drawing skills compared with copying print
2	Elective mutism
1	Emotional effect on day-time maternal separation in nurseries
1	Employment services for the severely subnormal
1	Eradication of severe subnormality
2	Hyperkinetic children
1	Individual teaching methods
3	Learning processes in the severely subnormal
2	Maladjustment
1	Mental illness in the severely subnormal
1	Methods of educating the parents of the severely subnormal
1	Methods of encouraging community acceptance
1	Physical causes of subnormality
2	Physical development of the severely subnormal
2	Programmed learning for the severely subnormal
2	Remedial exercises for physically handicapped severely subnormal
2	Reading and number for severely subnormal
1	Severely subnormal 'savants'
1	Special care unit or mental hospital?
6	Speech and language development
1	Spina bifida
3	Teaching machines and visual aids
2	Toys and play material
2	Value of nursery school age attendance for the severely subnormal

SESSION THREE
DISCUSSION

Chairman: Mrs. Sheila Holden

Chairman: I think I am unique here in that I am an administrator and if Dr. Morris felt this morning that she was in a minority, so do I.

I work in the Department of Health and I am also Secretary of the Training Council for Teachers of the Mentally Handicapped and it is as the Secretary of the Council that I am down on the list here. Now the Training Council, as you may know, was set up in 1964 but it did have a certain amount of help and encouragement from the working of the previous courses of training of teachers of the mentally handicapped pioneered by the N.A.M.H. so it did not have to operate completely in a vacuum.

The many problems that arise in connection with the training of teachers of mentally handicapped children now rest firmly with the education service; that service has taken over a great deal from the Diploma courses and is making use of the experience gained, though perhaps not as much as some would have hoped. The courses are now the concern of Area Training Organisations and must conform to the pattern that is followed generally in teacher training. The Council, being concerned with the training needs of a special group, had a degree of freedom which is not so readily available in the much more highly organised set-up of teacher training. The Council could act without the same degree of restraint and it covered the whole country.

One of the interesting consequences of transfer to which Mr. Cave briefly referred in his paper and which interested me was the possible integration of mentally handicapped children into ordinary schools. This is being tried out in Sweden and its wider application raises all sorts of questions which you may like to follow up.

Mrs. Currie's paper restates what I have sometimes felt about psychologists; I must confess that I find their work difficult to understand at times, but Mrs. Currie has shown in the simple and clear words of her paper how psychologists can work closely with, and help, the teacher in the field. I cannot accept her description of the North-East as a quiet corner. At the Department of Health and Social Security we have the highest regard for what is being done there for the mentally handicapped. There are two well-established Training Council courses in the area, the children's one at Newcastle, now transferred to Durham, and the adult course at Durham. The research project at Newcastle University to which Mr. Cave also referred is another example of the positive attitudes in the North-East. This research has been supported financially by the Department of Health and a battery is to be made available commercially in a form which teachers in the schools can use to assess children's progress in language development. It should be remembered that, of the teachers who answered Mrs. Currie's questionnaire, fewer than half are likely to have had any training. About 42% of teachers in the Junior Training Centres had the diploma prior to transfer and a recent survey made by DES has shown that about 50% of all the teachers transferring, including those in hospital, either have or will be eligible for 'q.t.' status under the special arrangement that have been made.

Borkwood: To go back to what Mr. Cave said about the kind of initial training for the teachers, I recall my own career as an infant teacher with ordinary children. I hesitate to use the word normal, because I'm not quite sure what normal is, with ordinary children. From the very beginning I was partial towards the retarded child or slow learner, and I made up my mind that when the opportunity arose I would go further into this work. At a suitable opportunity I moved over to retarded children. Although I was exceptionally interested in them, I did find after a period of years I was getting bogged down with the subnormal child. I was in a position then to be able to choose where I taught, and I went back for a time to normal children to sort myself out, and I do feel that even in initial training students should teach the ordinary child first and then they would know better how the subnormal child deviates. In the past six years I've been in a position to be in very close contact with the very people that Mrs. Currie has been speaking about and I find that this is one of their problems. They don't understand what the deviation is because they've not taught the ordinary child and seen the ordinary child in the ordinary school. They've only had experience with the subnormal, and I think the work Mrs. Currie has started in Durham County is going to have repercussions and probably go a long way in getting them to see more of the ordinary child and how to have helped them to understand the subnormal.

Cookson: I don't know whether at this stage we've any clear indication that teachers who have had experience of normal children are more efficient, in which ever way we wish to define efficient, in teaching the handicapped, particularly severely handicapped, children. Certainly I don't know of any comparisons here. Also I think one must bear in mind the fact that the teacher who has had experience of normal children has virtually started her career with a level of child at the top end of the new Special School; that is to say we have some information suggesting that in terms of M.A., the top level of the Junior Training Centre has been dealing with children somewhere in the region of M.A. 5 to 6, whereas the teacher of normal children will start with children at this point. Therefore I offer a question—how much is there to transfer from children at one level to children at the other level?

Borkwood: A great deal depends on the teacher as a person. I think if the teacher has sufficient interest then she will find out about the subnormal child and I still maintain that her knowledge of the normal child will be a help, but she's got to have a real interest in the subnormal child to be able to use her knowledge.

Cookson: Would it not be better then that she had experience of the pre-school normal child in addition, in order to know not only about how a normal child functions, but about a normal child going through the same phases of learning as the severely handicapped child with which she or he subsequently wishes to be concerned?

Borkwood: I would agree, but I think that most Colleges of Education today do at least some pre-school work with their teacher training. Most of these I've come across locally, at any rate.

A. M. Clarke: Can I interject a point here? There is a general problem and a specific problem. The general problem which is relevant to Mr. Cave's question is in what way is the severely handicapped child like a normal child and in what way is he different? And here I'm afraid we're going to have to get back to methodological problems which we raised last night. Is it the C.A. match we're going to talk about or is it the M.A. match, and if you're going to take an M.A. match, in what way does a child of 12 with a mental age of 4 really resemble a normal child of 4? I think this is something which we have got to meet and face and develop. In connection with Mrs. Cookson's point about the experience that would be required of pre-school children I would like to suggest that this might not be appropriate to the teacher of the older child of this developmental level, if indeed he is at this developmental level in any really meaningful sense of the term. I don't know. Because until the normal child goes to school he is not supposed to be specifically taught or instructed and therefore, and I know Mrs. Borkwood is going to agree with me on this very strongly, if what is going to happen is that the teacher of the severely subnormal is going to be exposed to children of an age where our society has chosen not to teach them (this is not to say that they are not teachable—but we don't teach them, by and large until the age of 5) I think that the teacher of the severely retarded child might get an unfortunate view of what could be achieved with a child of 10, 11 and 12 who is severely retarded in terms of mental age on a psychological test.

Serpell: I would like very strongly to support what Dr. Clarke has said, because it seems to me that the primary assumption which underlies the clear suggestions in Mr. Cave's paper, that experience of normal education is a relevant qualification for teaching the severely subnormal, is that you know how to make the transfer between these two types of children. Dr. Clarke has said there are very good grounds for doubting that the M.A. match is the appropriate type of transfer to make, and presumably by the very definition of the subnormal population, the C.A. match is also not an appropriately simple transition. There is a problem here, and to pretend that an intuitively well-disposed teacher, who has got massses of goodwill and experience, can use adequately either of these possible comparison groups, seems to me to be very naïve at this stage. We must accept that there is a real technical problem and this is perhaps the major problem with which psychological study of the severely subnormal is supposed to cope. I don't think that any of the existing research can provide a definite answer but to imply that the problem does not exist seems to me to be retrograde.

Cookson: Can I come in again here and ask you to forget the immediately pre-school phase and go right back to the infant stage? We have some evidence to suggest that the severely subnormal child does in fact need the same stages of development as do normal children. Dr. Mary Woodward demonstrated at the Fountain Hospital a sort of hierarchy here, with children then classified as idiots. The value of using this sort of basis was simply to get a starting point for the kind of training or teaching within one institution, not to justify giving only the kind of free play or unstructured activity of the normal pre-school child, but as a definite basis for the sort of activities which one could present to that child and encourage in him.

Mittler: I would like to look at the same question, the question which Mr. Cave rightly put in terms of qualitative and quantitative differences between severely subnormal children and the rest of the school population. Of course, we have no answer to this and it is futile for administrators or anybody else to expect us to give a clearly definitive answer. But I think if one has to indicate the lines along which research findings can be produced, it would be to say that in all probability some aspects of learning and cognitive development will be found to be developmentally delayed (with all the implications for that statement) while others are likely to be specific deficits. Now the administrator has the problem of deciding what sort of lines of development the school system should take in relation to mentally handicapped children, and it's arguable whether or not the right decision was taken. I think probably the right decision has been taken, but it is very important that this should not be institutionalised because it may in fact obscure the differences between mentally handicapped children and the rest. Now I take the view, in terms of organisational developments, that the infusion of mentally handicapped children into the educational system is not only the best thing that has happened to the education system, but also the best thing that has happened to educational psychologists, because what mentally handicapped children do is to force one daily to reconsider the basis of one's whole educational work. The educational psychologist cannot do routine intelligence tests and think that it is a useful exercise. Neither can the teacher carry out what many of us admittedly caricature, as general stimulation activities. Mr. Cave is quite right to question this stereotype of teaching, it's just a personal extension of environment. But the specific problem which Mr. Cave asks us to consider is the implications for the initial training of teachers. My worry is that by insisting that the person is a teacher first and a teacher of mentally handicapped children second, we are in danger of obscuring some of the real differences which seem to exist. The contribution which the Training Council courses made has been that they've produced the young and the enthusiastic and, on the whole, extremely competent teacher who, as it happens, has not had experience of normal children and the specific way in which I think this is being translated into action is in terms of planning for the individual child. Now this is an exceedingly important concept, shared by psychologists and teachers, that by analysing in detail what sorts of difficulties the child has, not using rarified laboratory techniques, but some translation of these in the classes, it ought to be possible to discover how many difficulties he has that are basically developmental, and how many difficulties he has that are specific deficits. For example, there is a lot of evidence to show that these children have a lot less language than you would expect them to have and, therefore, this needs special attention, and I'm very interested that Mrs. Currie's teachers focus on this point. So here, and in other fields, the major problem is to achieve a balance between the developmental view and the defect view and, believe me, psychologists are interested in these problems and they are addressing themselves to them. But no simple solution is likely to come from research, and it's a long, slow, patient business, but I think the evidence is beginning to come in and one reason why we're here is to discuss how we can speed the development of this information.

Cave: It fascinates me that we are talking of mentally handicapped children and we are continuously talking of these as though we have one fairly defined group. But it seems to me that we are dealing with an extremely heterogeneous group of children and, putting myself in the administrator's shoes again, where does the cut-off line come if there is one? Who decides, if you like, which is the severely mentally handicapped child, is this a question of the environment which we put him in, I think this may well be? We're still tending to talk about a group of severely mentally handicapped children. Here is a group we can see has certain specific defined needs, if you like, and therefore we perhaps ought to train teachers specifically to meet their specific needs. One thing I'm quite sure influences our thinking is that there must be the maximum possibility of ease of transfer from one teaching situation to another, if the conditions for learning are not the right ones for the particular child. There is an enormous borderline, an enormous overlap surely between these mentally handicapped children and what we used to call the ESN children and between what are now called the ESN children and normal children. Secondly, I take Peter Mittler's point, we were very conscious of this in making decisions that there was a great fund of expertise in the Training Council's courses and I think a good deal of this has been preserved in the new courses. But there have been changes, I made the point in my paper that there may be even more substantial changes after the James' document on Teacher Training has been made public. It will have even more fundamental suggestions for changing the whole nature of Teacher Training. These could be a threat, a possible threat, to the teachers of severely mentally handicapped children, and I use the composite phrase.

Atkins: May I suggest that we need to look at how the environment of the subnormal affects that person and we need to look at how the teachers of the subnormal can influence that environment beneficially bearing in mind that indeed the environment can reinforce the subnormality, for example, by removing the child from many normal experiences which are stimulating.?

Dybwad: I would like to follow up what Mr. Cave has said by suggesting that perhaps it would be well to use less the term severely mentally handicapped and say severely handicapped, because as he points out there is a wide range, so many of these children are called severely mentally handicapped because of physical debilities which impair their functioning. Now this is not the only factor but this is one of the factors which underline what Mr. Cave said. We're really dealing with a group that is an administrative group, but in terms of the other important characteristics they vary.

Morris: I would like to develop something said earlier by Mrs. Atkins in relation to the environment. It seems to me that the trouble, or the danger, rather, with much psychological research which is too directly concerned with the actual learning process is, it doesn't pay attention to these wide differences. You tend to get a concentration on one aspect of the child only. People tend to develop a stereotypical image of a subnormal or a severely subnormal child, whereas while they may have these problems in relation to learning or other aspects of interest to the psychologist and teacher, they may react fairly normally in a social situation and need to be in contact with normals.

A. M. Clarke: I would like to support that very strongly. I think there could be a bit of a conflict of interest, which really must be resolved, between the desire to give the subnormal special education and the desire that they should be accepted by the community in general, and that their teachers should be accepted too. For this reason I am personally delighted that the education of these children is now going to proceed within the normal context of the general education service, and I think what Dr. Morris has just said about the importance of the mentally handicapped child having contact in school, in the social environment, with normal children and super-normal children is, in my estimation, very important. It is also important that their teachers should not be labelled handicapped along with them. On the other hand, despite the great diversity within the subnormal group, children of this kind do have certain very important characteristics in common. The mentally handicapped child is always a slow learner, and compared with the normal child (let alone the bright child) he is a poor incidental or spontaneous learner from ordinary life experience. These two things are very important for the teacher of the subnormal, and particularly of the severely subnormal, to understand, because they render inappropriate to teaching those methods devised for normal children on the assumption that the children will be spontaneously learning and discovering. There are two things which follow from the fact of slow learning and restricted spontaneous learning. One is that the ultimate repertoire of behaviours or skills which you can expect from them will be restricted with respect to the average person, and the second is that special techniques of teaching will be required. The first point presents the teacher of the severely subnormal with a number of decisions to be made which are not required of teachers of normal children. Are you going to teach them a little about a lot or a lot about a little? At what stage are you going to teach certain vital social or language skills and by what technique? I am not sure that experience with normal young children will be very helpful.

Atkins: May I suggest in fact that one must direct attention primarily to social skills. As a teacher of mentally handicapped adults I have had trainees, pupils from junior training centres, who can copy very accurately the alphabet but cannot tie their shoelaces and not only are they slow learners but they are limited in the amount they can learn. Surely one should put first skills which will make their lives, the lives of their parents, the lives of their teachers, easier. Even, I think, pure academic skills should take a really back seat until they are to a certain extent socially competent.

Herriot: I sent out some questionnaires to 120 Junior Training Centre teachers and about 100 Adult Training Centre teachers listing about 19 areas of skill and asking them to rate on a 5 point scale as to which they thought were most important and which a 16-year-old JCT leaver should have mastered, and one thing that came out of this was that both sets of teachers were in very considerable agreement about the order of importance in which they placed the skills. They all placed personal safety first, they placed communication skills fairly high, in the sense of expressing need or obeying orders, but both sets of teachers placed personal interaction skills, in terms of guessing what the other person is feeling about what you are saying, as very low.

Kiernan: I would like to bring in a point which Mr. Cave made in his paper and try to tie it up with the current discussion. Mr. Cave raised the point about the nature of free activity teaching and the problem of structured teaching. Indeed Dr. and Professor Clarke made this point in their paper. One matter on which I think Mr. Cave would agree, since he said it last night, is that if one took a close look at the activities of effective teachers in the classroom, one would find that, despite their particular adequacies, they were probably doing very similar things and probably operating on very similar principles. It stands to reason that if different viewpoints on education have any grain of truth in them, then there will be a big overlap between different systems. This could well be a worthwhile sort of research project of the type which Dr. Ryan was advocating. The other thing which might be relevant is that there are some experiments comparing the effectiveness of the different types of pre-school education which have been done fairly recently. These have some interesting results bearing on both Mrs. Currie's and Mr. Cave's remarks.

Dybwad: As a sociologist I have been watching the international scene in education with interest and I think we all realise it is not just a problem of the mentally retarded and mentally subnormal child but all exceptional children are clearly outside the main stream of education. It was not until 1968 that UNESCO had one single solitary worker concerned with the ten per cent of the world's schoolchildren who need exceptional services. To this very day, while it has a Department for Physical Education there is not a single department concerned with Special Education. In most countries teachers of special education are in separate organisations—they are not within the national organisation so, while we make progress, education is still primarily exlusive rather than inclusive. Educational Ministers worry more about children they can exclude rather than children they can include.

Kiernan: Could I go back to the point about subnormal children as slow learners? This is the important thing—they are slow learners and they do not learn by incidental use of information being fed to them and yet they are all going to leave the educational system by age sixteen or seventeen. Now this I think is a frightfully important thing, that a slow learner cannot pick up information just by looking around him, and it is our duty to recognise this. Education, in particular the Ypsilanti pre-school programmes run by Weikart compared highly structured pre-school programmes based on Bereiter and Engelmann, a Piagetian programme and traditional nursery school programme. He concluded that it really did not make much difference which teaching programme you operated with, that the I.Q. gains, which they were using as their initial index of effectiveness of the programme, were more or less the same across the three different types of educational procedure. Now there were common elements; they all used free expression periods and so on. Nevertheless, Weikart, in casting round for some alternative explanation for the effectiveness of the three programmes aside from particular components, came up with the idea that the particular active components might be that the teachers were really very involved. Because the teachers were involved in whatever programme it was, they were very careful to structure the day, they were very careful to think things out in terms of the need of particular children and the message which that particular research presents is that the fundamental problem is to get planning in terms of the needs of each particular child, of getting the teacher involved rather than to use a particular form of teaching. That's not the panacea, the panacia is the involvement. This, however, I think, seems to be really a long shot. The idea that you don't need a curriculum is rather bizarre. I don't think it's one which really could be supported for long, and, therefore, I think clearly we must go beyond this and start asking just exactly what you should teach the normal and the subnormal child and here we come to particularly Dr. Clarke's contribution and to Dr. Gunzburg; they argue from the point of view of their experience of subnormal children that there are various sorts of skills which have to be trained and these then integrate the child into society. In turn, the natural contingencies operating in society promote progress. But one thing we seem to be sadly lacking in the principles which the psychologist offers to the educator is anything which is derived directly from developmental research. Mrs. Cookson mentioned the Piagetian reformulations by Mary Woodward, but really these haven't been incorporated in any way into any educational programme and indeed a close examination of Mary Woodward's work suggests that it bears only tangential relation to what Piaget said and that its survival relies more on the fact that nobody has taken a close look at it than on the fact that it has anything practical to contribute itself. There does seem to be a great lack of any attempt to derive from a model of development of a normal child a scheme of education which could take into account that the subnormal child is a poor learner and that therefore he will not learn the things which a normal child will learn. Nor will he learn it spontaneously.

What, it seems to me, ought to be possible would be to draw up over a long period, but at least let's start working towards it now, to draw up a scheme of education which will take the subnormal child and educate him towards some sort of goal which we have to decide on. We've got to decide the aims and to educate him within this and to educate him not just in social skills, not just in occupation skills but to educate the child to become an adult human being.

Cave: It's a tremendously interesting problem, and what it's done for me is certainly to define quite clearly some of the dilemmas the teachers face where a great deal more knowledge is needed before they can make any really firm decisions. On the whole, this discussion suggests to me that the broad decisions made were probably right, but there are clearly some areas which we have got to look at very carefully. I think one thing that's been running through my mind, apart from the question which I put to the debate earlier, concerns the enormous diversity of these children, the other point is the way we look at the teacher's role. I think possibly we are tending to see this as a little narrow. There is a great transformation taking place on the context of the teacher's rôle in the rest of education over the last few years, moving well away from the emphasis on the cognitive development of children and more to the teacher functioning as an instrument assisting in the total development of the child. As several people have said, we must see the child as a whole and we are not certainly looking at mere cognitive skills, we are looking at the child as a creature of his environment, as a social being, we are certainly looking much more at his emotional development and also at his creative abilities. This leads me to some awkward questions. There have been some phrases used which suggest we see clearly the objective of some children. Now maybe that with very, very severely handicapped children we can decide on simple social objectives with which they can function socially at a better level, and these may be reasonable objectives. But I think what we have to do, and I think it is important in the role of ordinary teachers, is to create situations in which certain abilities can emerge. It may well be that some of these children may have creative abilities which we can only discover by putting the child in a rich kind of environment and provide materials so that these can emerge. But I don't think we are all very clear and can claim this in education generally that we can see our objectives so clearly and therefore we move quite certainly towards a clearly defined aim. I think this is dangerous.

A. M. Clarke: It might be more dangerous not to define an aim and, if we wait for things to emerge, I suspect we shall make little advance with the mentally handicapped.

Session IV

The Technology of Learning as Applied to Educational and Industrial Training

The Application of Educational Technology to Mental Retardation

C. C. CUNNINGHAM

*Hester Adrian Research Centre
for the Study of Learning Processes
in the Mentally Handicapped,
University of Manchester*

This study group is concerned with the application of fundamental research in the behavioural sciences to the practical problems in mental retardation. The manifestation of this application is itself a fundamental problem.

This conference represents one strategy for bridging the gap. Others commonly used are publications, lectures or lecture courses. Of the many characteristics of these strategies five appear critical.

1. There is an assumption that research findings will be put into practice if the practitioner is informed about them.
2. The direction of the information flow is from researcher to practitioner with little provision for a reciprocal communication channel.
3. Thus, the researcher normally selects the information which he considers should be communicated, and
4. The communication is phrased in reasearcher rather than practitioner terms.
5. Finally, and perhaps not suprisingly, these strategies do not appear to be particularly efficient or successful in affecting practice.

A common explanation is that the practitioners have deficits of cognitive ability, or training, or inappropriate attitudes, though the practitioners normally claim lack of opportunity for study and implementation and the unpracticability of the research findings.

Partial remedy of the above approach is provided by utilising the technology of education. It is generally recognised that science affects practice through technology and this is also true of behavioural science in relation to education. Educational technology provides the means for transposing behavioural science and research findings into evaluated teaching methods and materials (Anderson, 1967).

I suggest that a sound knowledge and application of current ideas and methods of educational technology can fulfil this function in the education of the mentally retarded.

If a researcher states that one of the aims of his work is to effect practice, he must be prepared to state this as an objective and demonstrate its attainment. Like any technology, educational technology is concerned with attaining a predetermined result or objective. An objective is a clear and precise description of a pattern of behaviour (performance) we want the learner to be able to demonstrate after completing the learning experience (Mager, 1962). It must be 'realistic' in that it is related to the learner's abilities and needs.

Modern educational thinking states that failure to meet objectives is the prime responsibility of the learning system (teachers, administrators, etc.) rather than of the recipient. Thus, as researchers trying to effect practice, we must neither blame the practitioners for our own failures, nor change or abandon our objectives, but look for a more effective technique of communication. Similarly, if we decide to educate the SSN, we should not simply blame our failure on their low cognitive abilities. Providing our objectives are realistic, we should continue to search for the techniques which will achieve them. Needless to say, the definition of what is realistic presents certain difficulties. Although it is now accepted that the main burden of treatment of the mentally handicapped must be educational, we have not satisfactorily defined which aspects of education are critical. Administrative advantages such as staffing and apparatus are frequently emphasised. Similarly, there is an increasing amount of literature on the positive effects of certain methods and techniques which derive from the main stream of education. But there has been little discussion of the aims of education with the severely retarded. Indeed, many researchers and practitioners, whilst agreeing that no person is ineducable, might consider that questions of aims and philosophy of education have little practical relevance for this population.

The SSN population was previously considered as trainable but not educable. This dichotomy has a long history in the field of education, and is still retained in many countries. Rousseau, considered that education, training and instruction were three different things with three different purposes. However, as Gunzburg (1965) states, 'it is an arbitrary decision to determine the exact point where a child ceases to be "educable" and is called "trainable".' Precisely what is the distinction between these two terms; are they mutually exclusive?

Peters (1967) states that 'training' is a learning process essentially concerned with the acquisition of skills and generally characterised by practice, instruction, correction and example. 'The concept of training has application when (i) there is some specifiable type of performance that has to be mastered, (ii) practice is required for the mastery of it, (iii) little emphasis is placed on the underlying rationale.' However, 'it also includes the inculcation of habits such as punctuality and tidiness . . . such habits cannot be learnt by practice and imitation alone . . . not just a kind of know-how.' (pp. 14-16).

Thus, whilst training is primarily considered as a process concerned with 'know-how' or means, education must concern itself with the application of this 'know-how', with the purpose and rationale for its acquisition, i.e. with ends. However, training and education are not mutually exclusive. When a teacher states that he educates not just trains, he means that his objective is not merely the acquisition of a skill, but a realisation of the reason for acquiring the skill and the development of other qualities, which are less observable, less easy to measure, yet considered essential to the goals of education.

Consider two examples; in training a retardate to use a knife and fork, the training objective—the manipulation of the implement—is easily observed and measured. But we cannot stop there. We must consider the rationale for the training. This is concerned with successful social interaction in the eating situation, with acceptability to others and conversely to oneself. Thus, from an educational viewpoint we must link the skill with its application to other situations.

Secondly, consider a 'low level' skill like reaching. The actual training of the skill is relatively simple. Take a sweet, attractive object, etc., and place it as close to the child's hand as possible. After the child has gripped the object, either retrieve or use another 'novel' object. This time hold the object at a short distance from the child. Repeat at longer distances and different angles. Thus we have reaching behaviour. Why? We are seeking to make the child interact with, explore and gain control over his environment, to learn that he can control through contingencies. So we now use reaching to do this: hang a string with one of the objects on in front of the child, so that when he reaches, grips and pulls something happens which he likes and will work for, e.g. a music tape will be switched on, a slide will be projected, bells will ring, mobiles will move. We now ask how we might utilise the music, slides etc. The slides, for example, might be a graded series of shapes or patterns to aid and develop visual exploration. Thus the skill of reaching is taught, not for its own sake but because it is part of the pattern of normal development, and also to give the child the means to explore his environment more fully.

By stating that the SSN population are educable rather than trainable we assume that the theories and philosophies of education are applicable to them. An important function of the philosophy of education is to determine the goals of education. Fundamentally, the goals of education are applicable to all. Ideally, they aim at developing the innate potential of the learner to as high a level of independence and autonomy as possible, to provide him with the means to think and decide matters for himself, in accordance with his culture and the nature of society. By accepting that the curricula for the SSN should include 'how to get on with people', 'how to accept the work situation and give reasonable satisfaction' (Gunzburg, 1965) we are, in fact, directing the retarded along this dimension, the final point reached being dependent upon his innate potential and the environment in which he is placed.

The same applies to philosophies of child-centred education, the principle that education must provide learning experiences in accordance with individual needs and abilities, in relation to the culture. This, too, applies to all children.

The importance of accepting that education in its fullest sense is applicable, not just adaptable, to the mentally retarded, lies in its influence upon the thinking and actions of the personnel involved in providing an educational system for them.

Blyth (1964) states 'Empirical scientific investigation of the factors influencing behaviour does not answer philosophic questions about the aims of education. Nor does philosophic inquiry about the aims of education settle any questions of fact regarding the most efficient method of attaining these aims . . . philosophy of education must go beyond the science of behaviour in formulating a concept of the subject to be taught to individuals.' For the retarded we do not mean subjects in the traditional sense but those tasks, skills, processes, etc. which we select as important to their development and needs. Thus, as indicated earlier, a prime function of the philosophy of education is to specify the aims of education, to establish the rationale for selection of educational objectives and so curriculum development.

Curriculum is a set of organised experiences provided by an educational system to realise the goals of education. These goals are the end point of the educational process. They are set in relation to the future needs of the individual and the nature of the present and future society in which he must live. Thus, it is important for the educationist to ask what ought the learner to be at the end of the process. The emphasis on long term effects is important in determining the other possible resources of the curriculum. For example, learning theory, focusing as it does on specific aspects of observable behaviour and behaviour modification is strongly influencing the structure of curricula in some SSN establishments. But learning theory is mainly concerned with explaining short term change, and seldom considers or analyses long term effect in relation to the aims of education.

The effects of this are apparent in much of the marketed programmed instruction material for the handicapped. These often concentrate on isolated aspects of reading without fully considering either the choice of one skill rather than another, reasons for using a programming method in the first place, or the relationship of the particular skill to reading in general.

Curricula are also frequently based on theories of child development. These theories are essentially descriptive of a particular state of affairs. Education, however, is concerned with changing the existing state and achieving some future goal. Developmental theory paradoxically enough tends to be static; it mainly informs the teacher what he cannot do at particular stages in the child's education. As a result many teachers cease to lead the child forward towards the goal in the apparent belief that they must wait upon the child's 'readiness'.

Thus fundamental principles and aims of education provide a base for determining educational objectives. Without concern for fundamentals, attention is attracted to and concentrated on the most observable aspects of the situation. Gilbert (1960) noted this with regard to teaching machines when he wrote 'If you begin with a device of any kind, you will try to develop the teaching program to fit the device.' In other words, there is a danger of programming to meet machine characteristics rather than learner and task characteristics in relation to educational objectives. We can also extend this to techniques. The technician essentially seeks the 'one best way' to achieve any designated objective. He is concerned with what is, whereas the teacher is concerned with what ought to be. In attempting to make the teacher more of a technician, and in making education more technological, we must beware of making the same error. We must view technology from the base of the philosophy of education.

Educational Technology

Just as science affects practice through technology, so philosophies of education also affect practice through technology. They determine the nature of the goals (Figure 1, next page) and the learning which is

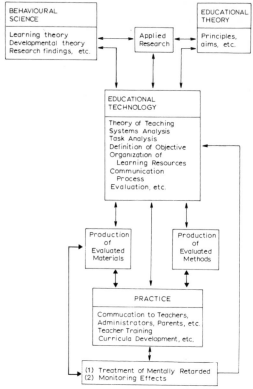

Fig. 1 The function of educational technology in relating theory of education and the behavioural science to practice.

expected to take place. The function of technology is to find the optimal way to achieve them. Davies (1971) makes this point, 'A theory of learning is essentially *descriptive* in nature, in the sense that it tells what has happened after the event. On the other hand, a theory of teaching is *prescriptive* and *normative* in character, in that it can prescribe how to proceed and how a learning experience can be improved, and, at the same time, yield a yardstick for evaluating any particular method or technique.'

Thus the concept of educational technology as a practical theory of teaching is a systematic approach to what we tend to call 'good' teaching. For educational technology 'good' teaching means optimal achievement of objectives considered necessary and applicable to a specific learner. Thus we are getting to a position where we can measure and evaluate what we consider is 'good' in teaching. Merton (1965) states, '...(technique)...converts spontaneous and unreflective behaviour into behaviour that is deliberate and rationalised.' In the teaching situation there is much 'spontaneous and unreflective' behaviour; the teacher might call it intuition. Unlike the researcher who can afford to decide not to decide, the practitioner is forced into making decisions often with little or no available empirical data. He uses his intuition. By intuition he normally means the sum of his experience, training and philosophy. Thus, if educational technology can make manifest this intuitive behaviour, it might function to bring researcher and teacher to a happier liaison.

Why do teachers place so much emphasis on their intuition? I believe that it is because their principal function is decision making—what method to choose, when to use it and with whom. In this sense the teacher is a manager controlling the resources of learning. His work is characterised by four broad functions:

(i) *planning*—establishing learning objectives
(ii) *organising*—relating learning resources to optimally achieve objectives
(iii) *leading*—motivating, encouraging learners, and
(iv) *controlling*—evaluating the success of his organisation and leading in achieving the objectives.

Thus, the concept of the teacher as a director or manager (decision maker) is fundamental to educational technology (Davies, 1971).

As the variety of learning resources increases, so do the number of decisions which have to be made. Add to this the heterogeneity found in handicapped populations and we have a very complex situation. It is no wonder that teachers rely on intuition, that they do not seek new methods or critically evaluate existing ones. Further, if the yardstick for evaluating particular methods and equipment—and so make decisions regarding their use—is rooted in the objectives, how can the situation begin to improve when administrators, educationists, educators and researchers have made little attempt to produce a set of educational objectives for the SSN population.

Thus, educational technology, in aiming at effective and efficient learning, has begun to define the function of the teacher, and the characteristics of the decision making process in relation to aspects of the learning situation. It is basically a framework used to gain control over the situation by directing the decision making process. It is concerned with the whole situation, applying the Gestalt concept that the whole is more than the sum of the individual elements. As such it uses a 'systems' approach to education. A system is a whole formed by a number of interrelated parts. To understand it we analyse the system by breaking it down into its products or objectives, its functions, and its inputs or resources (Bratton, 1969).

This system or wholistic approach has arisen primarily through the application of programmed instruction, perhaps as an educational reaction to the initial behavioural science emphasis. If we trace this development, starting with Skinner, we find an emphasis on behavioural aspects—small steps, overt responses, immediate knowledge of results, self pacing and validation, Skinner also emphasised machine aspects in relation to standardised presentation. We should note that, in the very few published studies which apply PL to the SSN, it is the above principles which are applied and found to be successful. The outstanding example is the work of Sidman and Stoddard (1966) which clearly shows the importance of small steps (i.e. near errorless learning), immediate and learner-oriented reinforcement, and especially validation. The behaviour produced was a fine circle-ellipse discrimination under automated conditions with the experimenter present. Unfortunately, this study is not applicable to practice. The teacher is neither given a rationale for teaching the task, i.e. a statement of behavioural objectives in relation to the learner's education, nor a set of conditions for its attainment which relate to the practical situation.

This 'application' problem is found by all programmers. Reid (1969) states 'even when the only intention is to produce an effective sequence of program items in a standard format . . . the (programmer) . . . is forced to make a series of intuitive decisions about matters that could and should be the subject of proper enquiry.' Thus, we find that by the early 1960's specifying behavioural objectives and carrying out a task analysis was pre-requisite to applying the basic 'principles'. By 1967 Unwin and Leedham were stating that 'programmed learning is basically a philosophy'. It was accepted that the principles and concepts were applicable to any learning/teaching situation whether or not they were using teaching machines or programs. This development can be seen as a progression from concentrating solely on the presentation aspects of the learner-teacher situation to an examination of all variables which affect its successful conclusion. It was to some extent an inevitable progression when its prime objective was successful teaching. Thus it now includes those variables associated with the learner, the task, the teacher, and the organisation, i.e. the total system. One of the most precise accounts of this development and the stage presently reached is that of I. K. Davies (1971) in 'The Management of Learning'. Figure 2, reproduced from his book, gives an indication of the present state of 'educational technology'.

This systems or wholistic approach is vital for teachers, researchers and administrators. The consequences of emphasising presentation

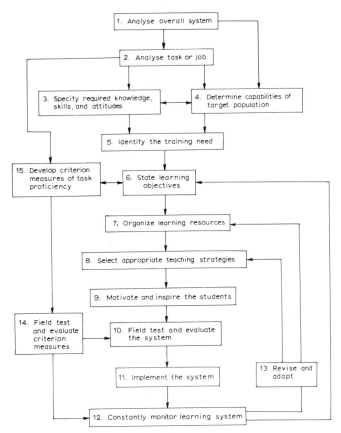

Fig. 2 The steps involved in developing a learning system. (From I. K. Davis (1971) 'Management of Learning'. London: McGraw-Hill.)

aspects at the expense of the total system, in particular the 'educational' aspects, is quite apparent when one examines the applications of PL to the retarded. Its effects are seen in research findings and programs which are not easily incorporated into schools (e.g. those of Sidman and Stoddard, 1966); reports on machine effectiveness and ineffectiveness which have limited value because the programs used were not validated, and not related to the educational needs of the learner; a concentration on reading, in particular teaching limited sets of unrelated nouns with little thought to their relevance. Machines are marketed without an adequate range of programs in relation to their purchase price, running costs and the curricula needs of the prescribed population. More seriously, perhaps, consumers, i.e. teachers and adminstrators, also appear to concentrate on the presentation aspects rather than on the intended objectives, evidence of successful application and relation to other available resources.

Educational Technology and the Education of the Mentally Retarded

When considered as a theory of teaching, educational technology has immediate and wide application to the treatment of the severely subnormal. The full potential of its usage will only become apparent when it is applied by the various personnel involved and it begins to feed back findings into the system.

This paper will conclude by indicating some more immediate and obvious uses. Researchers and teachers can create materials which will put methods and ideas into direct practice. These can be in the form of programs, with or without machinery, which do not depend critically upon the teacher or teaching situation. These programs are standardised instruments for attaining a specific objective. As such they constitute a set of predetermined decisions made in relation to a specific task, a specific presentation technique and a specific group of learners.

Since the subnormal population contains all manner of variability, so that even when the same learning deficit is shared, responses made, span of apprehension, personality, motivation, previous experience, etc. may all vary such that the method of communicating the task must vary also. Thus a variety of approaches is called for and this in turn requires a high number of decisions to be made by the presentation system. But most teaching machines and programs currently available are extremely limited in their decision making capacity. Even computers will not compare with the potential of the human teacher. If we are to build fluidity (i.e. the sum of the decisions which can be made) into our learning systems for the retarded, we must still rely on the human teacher. We can also treat the teacher as a resource in the learning environment.

The concept of 'programming' the teacher is particularly important to the researcher and administrator. For the researcher it means putting ideas into practice, for the administrator it means capitalising upon the teacher's function and thus defining the less important teacher functions which can be carried out by auxiliaries.

The heterogeneity of the SSN population also requires teachers to be capable of applying an experimental or prescriptive teaching approach. If teachers are taught the concept of educational technology, i.e. a theory of teaching, they are in a position to be experimental. They are more likely to evaluate techniques and so develop curricula and methods, but more importantly bring a system for evolution into their work. They will not be so dependent on outside influences for effecting change.

Another advantage lies in the teacher's internalisation of the philosophy or model such that it can provide 'informed intuition' for action. Let us accept that whilst the teacher must make on the spot decisions in a constantly changing situation, he will always need his 'intuition'. It also provides a common language and empirical approach for researcher and practitioner.

A Practical Example of Applied Educational Technology

It is common to see children in special care units lying on their backs in cots. Occasionally one finds a mobile hanging over the child. When asked why it is there, the answer is usually 'to give the child something to look at'. When was it put there? Is it changed? If so, what decides when it is changed, what is it replaced by? There are seldom, if ever, any answers to these questions.

Let us now apply a prescriptive approach. What are our objectives? We are aiming at independence. This is dependent upon the child's control over his environment. To learn about control he must interact with his environment. The initial stages of this interaction are responses to visual, auditory, tactile, olfactory stimuli, etc. We are here concentrating on visual interaction, but this is only one instance and we must assess its relationship to other parts in an attempt to interrelate and utilise them.

What are the components of the task? There is reaction to light (what intensities?), turning towards or away, sustained regard and focusing, following an object (how big, how bright, against what sort of background?), exploration, looking from one object to another (horizontally, vertically, diagonally?), etc. etc.

Let us assume that the child in the cot tends to stare 'blankly' into space or at a particular point. We decide to train eye movements and visual exploration.

Our learning objective is that the child will look first at one object then at a second object. The objects will be placed equidistant from the child's midline such that he must move his eyes but not necessarily his head to focus on them. We will set a criterion of four successive movements from one object to the other. Demonstration by the child of this criterial behaviour will call for a decision to change the learning situation.

How can we achieve this objective? What resources have we

available? Do we have a teacher available for a long enough period without distraction? Do we have slide projectors, or film cameras which might be used?

Let us assume that we only have card, glue, paint, etc. and limited teacher time.

One solution is to draw two faces on reasonably sized circles. We choose faces because infants tend to regard them at an early stage and for longish periods, we can consider them to be motivating. We draw them in black on white paper to gain the greatest contrasts. We hang them up to utilise movement which should also function to attract the child's attention. We will hang them such that each is just within the child's peripheral vision.

We will observe the child for the first few minutes that the apparatus is suspended to see if he immediately reaches the objective and then at set intervals over the day in an attempt to evaluate the system.

This outline is necessarily sketchy, but it may provide an example for the application of the system to aspects of treatment, and the nature of the system in analysing the learning situation.

REFERENCES

Anderson, R. C. (1967). Educational psychology. *Ann. Rev. Psych.* **18**, 129.

Blyth, J. W. (1964). In 'Trends in Programmed Instruction' (eds G. D. Ofiesh and W. C. Meier Henry). Washington: Dept. of Audio-Visual Instruction.

Bratton, J. E. (1969). In 'Media and Methods' (ed. D. Unwin). London: McGraw-Hill.

Davies, I. K. (1971). 'The Management of Learning'. London: McGraw-Hill.

Gilbert, T. F. (1960). In 'Teaching Machines and Programmed Learning' (eds A. A. Lumsdaine and R. Glaser). Washington: Dept. of Audio-Visual Instruction.

Gunzburg, H. C. (1965). In 'Mental Deficiency, the Changing Outlook' (eds A. M. Clarke and A. D. B. Clarke), pp. 417-446. London: Methuen.

Mager, R. F. (1962). 'Preparing Objectives for Programmed Instruction'. San Francisco: Fearon.

Merton, R. K. (1965). 'Introduction to the Technical Society'. London: Cape.

Peters, R. S. (1967). 'The Concept of Education'. London: Routledge and Kegan Paul.

Reid, R. L. (1969). In 'Media and Methods' (ed. D. Unwin). London: McGraw-Hill.

Sidmann, M. and Stoddard, L. T. (1966). In 'International Review of Research in Mental Retardation' 2 (ed. N. R. Ellis), pp. 151-208. New York, London: Academic Press.

Unwin, D. and Leedham, J. (1967). 'Aspects of Educational Technology'. London: Methuen.

Industrial Training: Problems and Implications

K. G. MORLEY*

*Department of Social Services,
London Borough of Croydon*

Introduction

Industrial training is not an endearing phrase. For one thing, many people seem to associate it with grimy factories, little boys climbing up chimneys and Dickensian working squalor. For another, it half hints at training in a particular craft or skill which, in the vocational sense, it patently does not set out to do. Perhaps *employment* training would be a better term.

Definition

Indeed, if pressed to define industrial training in the context of the mentally handicapped, my choice would be 'training towards the ability to undertake employment in an acceptable manner'. And I would define employment as any full time wage earning situation which confers national health insurance rights on the employee. Most people would not disagree with these definitions, yet industrial training is probably the least understood and most divisive issue among persons associated with the training of mentally handicapped adults.

There may be several reasons for this—the view that a broadly based educational programme will better equip a trainee for employment than specialisation, that community failures may be attributable more to social than work incompetence and perhaps most of all—the fear that industrial training may become an all-enveloping doctrine that is applied to the mass without regard to its desirability for the individual.

* This paper was introduced by Mr. A. D. Murray in the author's absence.

The uneven development of services for the mentally handicapped, the lack of in-depth planning and the scarcity of informed opinion may all have contributed to the general uncertainty, but whatever the reasons we need to look more closely at this sector of training.

Composition

It would be as well to enumerate some of the basic elements which one sees as the essentials of industrial training. They should include:

Continuous assessments on graded and varied work processes to determine levels of ability;

Observation over a period of time of speed and accuracy of performance, judgment and reliability, physical and mental limitations;

Training for as long as is necessary in processes in which aptitude is shown and which will have significance in future employment opportunities, together with relevant aspects of social and educational competence in the workshop situation.

We accept the importance of considering each trainee as an individual, with his own special needs and the right to lead as full and rich a life as his disability will permit. It is equally important that he should be considered as a potentially useful member of society, so that he can lead as productive and independent a life as possible.

But industrial training does not imply that trainees should undertake pressurised work processes indiscriminately in order to meet external production commitments. It can, and often does, imply application for a period which may extend into years but the length and pressure must be determined by the trainees' requirements.

In short, the total training needs of the mentally handicapped must not be overridden by commercial considerations. This is easier to postulate than to implement because the management implications of providing industrial training in centres have yet to be adequately researched. The prime necessity is the control of production so that it can be geared to the training programme, but usually this immensely complicated aspect is evaded altogether or left to the manager to sort out as best he can.

Application

Industrial training should be applied 'according to need' but one of the great difficulties lies in determining what this phrase means in practical terms. Who of the mentally handicapped require industrial training and what criteria should govern the extent and intensity of its application?

At one end of the scale is the person who may need little or none and at the other the person who may require it almost full time. The comparison is roughly between school, where the subject is one of many, and a kind of apprenticeship, where it is the major speciality.

It seems reasonable that near full time industrial training might be desirable for those who have reached acceptable levels of social competence, but this involves subjective appraisals which have to be flexibly applied and vary according to the skill and expertise of the persons carrying out the assessments. Equally, at the lower end of the scale, few of the very severely handicapped will reach any sort of employment and one would see them getting relatively little industrial training.

In between are the numerous trainees, probably the largest single section, whose potential may only be revealed as training proceeds.

Nevertheless, any unit which attempts to use and evaluate industrial training will find eventually that trainees can be categorised into four groups:

1. Those who will obviously benefit from industrial training;
2. those who may possibly benefit in the forseeable future;
3. those who appear unlikely to benefit, but should not be overlooked;
4. those who are clearly unlikely ever to benefit.

It would be possible to use this breakdown as a guide and say, for example, that industrial training will range from 80% of the syllabus time with group (1) to none at all with group (4). However fallible this might be, it would instil a sense of purpose, encourage staff to devise imaginative programmes and give them some sort of framework within which to plan them.

The proposition would need to be flexible, as the proportion of unit population in each group would vary according to the quality of input, the standard of training given and the external employment opportunities. It should also vary according to individual progression from within.

It is important to recognise at this point that industrial training and industrial processes are not necessarily synonymous. Selective work processes can be used in a variety of ways that may not be linked with industrial training at all—for example, as a group occupational activity, for language development, to improve perceptual skills, co-ordination and judgment, or even to foster creative interests.

Effects

There appears to be little information available on the consequences of allowing industrial training free scope for development and it may be relevant to consider the experience of my own authority.

In 1960 Croydon opened its first adult training centre with a declared policy emphasis on purposeful activities, the stimulation of production potential and the graduation to employment of as many mentally handicapped persons as could be occupied happily there.

From this start emanated the 'open ended' concept in which, when prevailing resources had been fully explored, additional facilities were introduced to meet exposed shortcomings.

In 1965 a second centre materialised which was an approved sheltered workshop under the Disabled Persons (Employment) Acts and in 1970 a further unit, functioning as a stepping stone between the other two.

Thus, at this moment of time and in graduation sequence the local authority has an adult training centre, an advanced adult training centre and a sheltered workshop/assessment centre. Each centre is open ended. Any trainee able to benefit can progress upwards so that there is constant movement between the three units and, as far as the sheltered workshop is concerned, between that unit and open employment.

Patterns of Training

The advent of each new centre has had a marked impact on training trends elsewhere. The adult training centre has a much higher proportion of very severely subnormal persons who are unlikely to move on than formerly and its programme is based on a much broader syllabus in which industrial training plays an important, but relatively minor role. At the advanced centre industrial training has the majority role, whilst at the sheltered workshop the emphasis is entirely on work.

So that we have a three tier system in which each tier is different in character and functional emphasis, yet together they form a logical sequence of training media through which a mentally handicapped person can progress on the way to realising his full potential.

On 31st January, 1971 mentally handicapped persons were attending the centres in the following numbers:

	Mentally Sub.	Severely Sub.	Totals
Adult Training Centre	24	74	98
Advanced Adult Training Centre	26	9	35
Sheltered Workshop	29	16	45

Twenty-eight mentally subnormal and three severely subnormal persons have been placed in open employment since 1965.

For purposes of classification an intelligence quotient of 50 has been taken to represent the upper limit of severe subnormality.

Conclusions and Implications

There is nothing particularly earth shattering about the direction of the Croydon Service's expansion and in a way the analyses have a certain inevitability. If one sets up a realistic target there will always be some people who reach it, with wide gradations of partial success among the remainder.

The most significant statistic relates to the 45 mentally handicapped persons employed in the sheltered workshop. Of these 18 were originally ascertained as unsuitable for education at school and attended junior training centres, 6 were patients in subnormality hospitals for periods ranging from 3 to 18 years and 19 attended special schools. Fourteen of the total number have physical disabilities in addition to mental handicap and 5 are mongols.

It is worth re-emphasising that all these persons are *employed*—men over 21 years receiving a basic wage of £14 per week and the women £10.29 plus free mid-day meals, reimbursement of fares to and from work, two weeks paid annual holiday and full trade union representation.

In most other areas these are persons who would be fairly representative of an adult training centre population. Whether or not they would have reached sheltered workshop status without industrial training is arguable. Probably some would and others would not, but, in Croydon at least, the results are there to be seen and it is reasonable to assume that any authority which sets out similarly to develop its services will identify comparable groups of persons who are employable.

The implications here could be considerable. If we take the number of mentally handicapped Croydon residents who are employed either in the authority's sheltered workshop or Remploy and project it on a national scale the need for sheltered employment places for community sources would be in the region of 6,500 probably equivalent to a productive capacity of 6,000,000 man hours a year. This is likely to be a conservative estimate bearing in mind Croydon's low unemployment figures (1.2% compared with regional average of 2.8% and the national average of 3.4%), its excellent school careers service and close links with the Department of Employment's services. These factors coupled with the drive towards rehabilitation makes it likely that many of the mentally handicapped who are in open employment in Croydon might have to be provided with sheltered employment in less favoured areas.

About 9,700 sighted disabled persons are employed in sheltered workshops in Britain. Nearly 7,500 of these work for Remploy and in that number only 579 (7.8%) are classified as mentally subnormal. The remaining 2,200 work in factories run by voluntary societies and local authorities, most of which cater primarily for the physically handicapped. Over the whole of the country the total number of mentally handicapped in sheltered employment may not be much more than 1,000 of whom relatively few will be severely subnormal.

At the present rate of growth the Croydon projection will in five years time indicate a need for as many sheltered employment places for the mentally handicapped alone as the country now has to cover the total needs of all the disabled.

It follows that administrators responsible for services for the disabled must urgently review adult training centre policies. Clearly, no mentally handicapped person should be retained in an adult training centre if he is capable of sheltered employment, nor even more so if he can be placed in open employment.

Then there are the less obvious implications. The logical extension of a policy of training for employment is *placing* in employment. And this means more than searching vaguely for 'sympathetic employers'.

It means seeking out and investigating every employment possibility and evaluating it in a way that takes into account not only the trade or type of work, but the environmental factors on which, for the mentally handicapped, success or failure so often depend.

The absurdity of spending vast sums on training without providing an efficient, professional placing service which understands the needs and problems of both the mentally handicapped and prospective employers and keeps pace with the manpower output from that training demands little further comment. Except to say that, in general, such a service does not exist.

It means too the introduction of a new kind of rehabilitation specialist to liaise with employers, to provide a follow-up service for the handicapped and to be immediately available to employers for advice and practical help. Industrial training cannot anticipate all the manual skills, adaptability demands and other stresses that the mentally handicapped person may encounter in employment and the onus is on the placing agency to recognise these areas of vulnerability.

For reasons of simplicity this paper has concentrated on mentally handicapped persons in community centres, but the general points would, of course, apply no less to those in subnormality hospitals.

SESSION FOUR
DISCUSSION

Chairman: Mrs. Winifred M. Curzon

Chairman: If ever there were a time when advisers and organisers needed help of a positive kind it is now. It is no longer valid to say 'we don't know enough about severe mental handicap ... we are only on the fringe of things' there is already information to hand, a sufficient base from which to work. There are existing gains in teacher education and in the educational upbringing of severely mentally handicapped children. Involved leaders are interested and anxious to obtain clear guidance, to be given a more precise lead on how these children learn. Without this guidance now, quickly, opportunities will be lost, none of the gains will be left to us as the system begins to take over.

Too many valuable child years have been lost already because we have not been bold enough to cut out the dead wood and to plan priorities in curricula, for the children and for the teachers in training. We should do well to capitalise on the existing expertise, and begin to assess the changes that must be brought about to assure increased success to this group of children. Education departments now have full responsibility, and this is a splendid move, but there is some constraint and uncertainty; Universities cannot accept mental handicap as a main subject. Teachers in special courses of training are becoming so anxious about other training demands that they may be in danger of finally taking up their work without sufficient specific background help in the management of children with special difficulty. Priorities include (1) Parent collaboration. The more the parent is involved from the beginning the greater the understanding of educational programmes; which may not be what was expected for their child at this time, (2) Expectations. What are they based on by parents and by teachers? Everybody expects growth and change but at what levels for this group? A positive look at achievement is needed. Mr. Cunningham attempts a definition of aims in special education, he considers the 'how' and 'why', he selects priorities and makes unique reference to the human teacher; this helps to balance his other more provocative statements. He offers a new awareness of programming and pattern, the result should be a more able adolescent. This has tremendous impact socially and economically. The worthwhile lies in attacking quickly, along the lines Mr. Cunningham suggests.

A. D. B. Clarke: I would like to rise to Mr. Cunningham's challenge but before doing so, say that this is a very important paper. I liked in particular his distinction between aims, and the technology for pursuing these aims. I want, however, to comment on his feeling expressed when he introduced his contribution that maybe we haven't given the free approach a fair trial. If he is right, it has implications, if he's wrong it also has considerable implications. I think one can tackle it from two ways. Of course, the free approach is very seldom as extreme as the words imply and like free association, isn't really free. Nevertheless there is one well-known study employing the free approach and that is the Brooklands Study. Half the results are well-known, concerning the improving verbal abilities in those who had been placed in enriched surroundings. What is not always appreciated is the other half of the story, comparison of the development on non-verbal abilities in the same enriched surroundings showed no difference between experimental subjects and controls. There was, I repeat, no difference whatever between those living in the stark confines of hospital and those living in enriched situations at Brooklands. So this is one study which shows that while the 'free' approach, provided it includes a lot of language, does aid development in verbal abilities, it does not have an effect in other areas of intelligence which were not taught. There you have a test of the so-called free approach, but I would like to place much more reliance not on this single study buried in the mists of ten years past, but rather on an almost logical approach to the learning problems of the SSN child or adolescent. I would put it to you, perhaps in an overstated form, that the most obvious defect in the SSN child or adult is a relative inability to learn anything spontaneously and incidentally, unless directed. Now if I'm wrong about this, I hope people can give me evidence; if I'm right about this then it has very considerable implications for practice. My evidence is that on Trial 1 of any new task the child who has lived in the same kind of environment as a non-SSN child is often pretty hopeless. So much so, that for fifty years observations which were absolutely accurate for Trial 1 in any new situation were taken not only as being an indication of Trial 1 but as an indication of prognosis on Trials X, Y & Z.

Ryan: Could I say something about what Professor Clarke has said? I think one has to be very careful about interpreting literature on what you call incidental learning. One interpretation is that subnormal children are simply unable to learn in the way you suggest, the other interpretation being more concerned with motivation, and it seems to me that a lot of Zigler's work is relevant here, suggesting that very often subnormal children fail because they don't respond to the motivation of the task provided, and also that they are much more competent in their own solutions to problems and tend to wait on external cues and are much less prepared to disregard cues which turn out to be misleading.

A. D. B. Clarke: I think there's something in this. But why is motivation weak in such children? I think you probably agree that motivation is not an independent entity but results from an intimate interaction between the constitution of the individual and the experiences that he has had. I would suggest motivation is weak partly because of the succession of failure experiences, which brings me back to my first point that there are usually failure experiences on Trial 1 simply because the spontaneous learning hasn't taken place. So I don't think that if you hang it on to the hook of motivation, you are out of the wood from the point of view of your argument.

Ryan: I take your point. We have to maintain a distinction between inability and disinclination.

A. D. B. Clarke: Surely. And there I would agree with you, as some of the work of O'Connor and Hermelin shows very clearly. I'm sure you're right, motivation is something which all too often is put on one side by behavioural scientists. But as I say, I don't think it all together destroys the general argument about the poverty of spontaneous learning, the poverty of retention, or the poverty of awareness of stimuli.

Cunningham: Can I come back, Ladies and Gentlemen. I didn't mean this to be too much of a red herring. First of all, what I'm saying is that the so-called discovery method was there to develop children's ability to control their environment, to become autonomous, to get away from the former principles where we believed that children should be trained to fit into their social class. And these are the concepts which are held. Now, if this philosophy of principle that a child should, through his sort of discovery technique, arrive at our objective of controlling his environment better, then if we say the subnormal child cannot use this discovery technique, presumably we are saying his needs are different and this is where we come back to spontaneous learning. I don't know if this is true. But until you've taught the child how to learn from his environment you don't know if he can do it. You've got to achieve your objective and therefore you're bound to structure to achieve this end, but what you don't do is to structure to prevent the child becoming independent, an individual learning how to solve problems for himself. My answer is that perhaps with the subnormal we want to concentrate more on teaching him to concentrate his abilities on incidental learning, not just sort of side-step it and say well he can't do this let's just train him with these skills and leave it at that. Does that make sense?

Cave: I'm not quite sure what areas of child development we are talking about. If I remember the Brooklands Experiment there were some areas where there seem to be very positive gain. For example, I think I'm right that these children moved very much better, there was considerable motor development. They were certainly very much happier children at the end than they were at the beginning and I think this may be something which we might take as one of the aims of education. They were a lot easier to live with, and I've never been really clear how it was that if they gained in speech, they had not gained intellectually. These two seem to be so closely aligned. There seem to be certain areas where in fact there were very positive gains, now are we discounting these when we indulge in the argument against the unstructured free approach?

A. D. B. Clarke: May I come back on this? Frankly speaking, the Brooklands Experiment, looking back with the wisdom of hindsight over ten years, was less than satisfactory. There were statements that these children were better adjusted, were emotionally happier, and I would take this to be true, but I wouldn't go to a Court of Law and swear it. These reports depended on the impressions of experimenters. It is a pity these workers didn't have some measure of social competence or stability before, during and after the intervention. The only measures they had were cognitive measures. Therefore, the only thing one can talk about with any precision, seems to me to be these latter, the cognitive measures. The two published cognitive measures depended on the Minnesota Pre-School Scale over a two-year period. There was a considerable pull-away by the Experimental Group on verbal ability as measured by that scale, probably due to the good staff–child ratio as opposed to an inadequately qualified, changing staff for a much larger number of children in the Fountain Hospital. I take this, therefore, as a response to being talked to, not being talked to by other damaged children but being talked to by normal, educated and enthusiastic adults. The other measure was the scale of non-verbal abilities. These children had been exposed to a wide variety of apparatus and toys which they used, as far as I can gather, in a free situation, and the result showed no difference whatever between the two groups, the grossly deprived group on the one hand, the group in the enriched surroundings on the other.

Cave: May I raise a different point? Mr. Cunningham's paper suggests that even when the only intention is to produce an effective system of programme items in standard format, the programmer is forced to make a series of intuitive decisions about matters which could and should be the subject of proper inquiry. Now Mr. Cunningham goes on to suggest that this type of proper inquiry falls within the realm of educational technology and it would seem that a large part of his contention is that we have to leave in the hands of the teacher, the task of making a lot of decisions about the particular form of teaching which is going to be given to the individual child. This, in fact, is the process of bringing to bear those general principles of programming, of structuring of materials as Professor Clarke would put it, on the particular needs of the individual child. I would like to ask Mr. Cunningham if he could tell us here what sort of technology would serve to guide teachers in this regard, and to what extent he feels that the existing tradition of intuitive decision taking by teachers is already a sufficient process by which to do this?

Cunningham: Well, I don't think the existing situation for teachers is adequate. I think we have to give the teacher this programming model, this descriptive or experimental model, because basically it says 'decide what you want to do, find a technique to do it, examine it when you've done it and by meeting your objective this tells you whether the technique has been adequate or not.' And if the teacher has this approach which is basic to teaching generally, not just in subnormality, I think they will have a better system for deciding which resources they're going to keep or throw out. You accept that? At the same time, as the number of resources becomes available, for example, the number of reading schemes, the number of fixed apparatus like teaching machines, tape recorders, the number of techniques they can use, they have to start to make decisions on which one they're going to use in which situations, and why they are going to use them. Then they are going to be in a position of analysing the data given about those things and at the moment it's nominal. The educational technological model which is inferred in this paper demands that you provide the foundation, the apparatus you're putting out. The teacher is going to have to be able to understand and use this validation, or conversely, he is going to have to be in a position to evaluate it himself. So what I'm saying is that if the teacher can be given this model, can be taught this descriptive way of trying to teach, of evaluating, then the key thing is to know his objectives and measure to establish whether these have been reached. At that stage, intuition is going to change into the more objective mode of decision making.

Borkwood: There are two points. First, Mr. Cunningham has said that the task of the pupils will be made easier if the master, when he teaches them anything, shows them at the same time the practical application in everyday life. So I was delighted to read in connection with the practical example of the application of the educational technology, you say 'do we have a teacher available for a long enough period without distraction?' This brings me to the point of teacher training and I would like to ask the researchers this question. Apart from the obvious answer, of a one-to-one relationship, what pupil/teacher ratio would the researchers consider ideal and how far the Department of Education and Science would be prepared to accept their recommendations?

Cunningham: Actually, I was just thinking of the ratio. It depends on the task, doesn't it? If I were teaching mass choir singing then the ratio could be 2000 to 1. If I were trying to teach a child an individual skill, which needs constant immediate reinforcement, I have to be in a room on my own probably, across a table. Now, when we ask for the ratio we then have to ask how the function of the teacher is seen by the administrators. If the teacher's function is well defined and with adequate auxiliaries, you have one situation, but if a teacher still has to collect dinner money or whatever, chase after Johnny, go and see the headmaster and wait twenty minutes before he can get in there, write reports on things which are perhaps not really needed, you have another. If you give him a telephone so he doesn't have to leave the classroom, it is different again. This determines then how many children he can work with. Also, the apparatus. If the teacher has apparatus in his room which can simulate some of his functions, like teaching machines, he must have a smaller ratio than if he's got these, providing he can use them. So this problem of a teacher/pupil ratio is complex and must not be too glibly considered.

Borkwood: You speak about the teacher as a manager. This interests me very much. Would you, perhaps, consider the best teacher training course should have something included in it under management training? For example, where the teacher was trained in decision making, considering the problems which confront him or her, formulating the questions which they wish to ask themselves, systematically writing down the answers, the pros and the cons, sitting back and looking at it, weighing up the information and then making the decision. Would you consider teachers should have some sort of training in this, because to the best of my knowledge, it isn't done in basic training courses.

Cunningham: The whole function, as I see it, of the teacher is as a director and manager. Not just somebody to slap out information all the time.

Mittler: These questions put by Mrs. Borkwood have brought us very much down to earth and, since they've been raised, and Mr. Cunningham has carefully stated the complexities of the issue, I hope I can be forgiven for oversimplifying, because the question was asked in a very direct sense. Some of the things we have been talking about in this Study Group have been concerned with planning for the individual child. This does not by any means exclude working with groups and using discovery and activity. To my mind, you can be absolutely dogmatic about this—the difference between the special school and the normal school is that in the special school there will be more planning for the individual child. It happens in normal schools as well, but less so. I agree with Professor Clarke that if a child is not as able as a normal child to learn incidentally from his normal environment, you have to think very carefully about how much he's picking up from the elaborated Bernstein codes which the teacher is using, how much he's learning from the labelling of the door as a door and the window as a window. How much he is learning from the sound of water flowing and so forth. The next step is to plan for the individual. The basis for this is undoubtedly careful assessment. I think I said last night and I'm going to repeat it dogmatically, that in my special school for the immediate future there will always be one individual who is competent in newer methods of diagnostic assessment. Having diagnosed we mustn't leave it at that, but we must go on to provide the form of education which we think suitable for that child. That may sometimes mean doing nothing very special for certain children, but this must be a conscious decision which is taken, rather than one that goes by default. The next step is that if you're going to provide individual programmes for at least some of the children, somebody has to do this. It therefore seems absolutely axiomatic that in every classroom (assuming we're going to have classrooms in the future) for handicapped children you must have at least two adults. Whether there are 10 children in the class or 15 or 20 the absolute minimum is two, and this is not just because it is hard to teach handicapped children, but because planning for the individual, and executing the planned programme for an individual, is quite impossible for one person. The second person is there to hold the fort, to keep up the stimulating environment, to see to the needs of the group, to go on speaking in Bernstein's elaborated code sentences, to make the necessary catalytic remarks, 'Oughtn't you to make it again, Johnny?' and so forth, while the teacher goes and does individual teaching for five minutes per child, perhaps. There is another implication of this and this is architectural. If this is a classroom for handicapped children it is no use expecting the teacher to do individual teaching in a corner with the hurly-burly of free activity method going on all around her. We must build our special school in such a way that off each classroom there is a small room for the individual teaching. I have said this before but it is architectural anathema to many people. The reasons, I'll just borrow cheap sociology here, but the reasons why we build special schools to look exactly like normal schools is primarily political. We want parents and the public to feel that the kind of school their child is going to looks just like the school that normal children are going to. But I don't care what the building looks like on the outside, it's the inside that matters. So planning for individual needs at least two adults, it needs a diagnostic expert, it needs a room off each main classroom for individual teaching, and, of course, above all it needs a teacher who is trained to do just that.

A. D. B. Clarke: Now, can we stop there and consider Mr. Murray's paper?

Chairman: I wonder if we are not going to have to pay much more attention to preparation of the adolescent for adult status and productive work. I wonder whether we've got this strategy and whether we should in a sense be preparing children early on, if there isn't something in the notion of preparation for work running through the whole scheme of education. I wonder, too, importantly, if we can develop a broadly aimed educational option up to 19 years in association with the schools. Won't this step alter the internal organisation of the present and existing adult training centres? Since at the moment we are thinking in terms of carefully extending our education, may we not then be thinking narrowly in extending education in the school and not sufficiently broadly in preparation for work? We could then be taking on vocational training programmes that we have at the moment, somewaht retarding the retarded by our continual babying. I'm sure that Mr. Murray would agree that many of the trainees going into his centre have to be taught again the most basic things.

Gunzburg: Could I please sort out one question which I'm not quite clear about from the paper. Mr. Morley describes a three-tier system which makes it quite clear that it is one step after the other, and he differentiates as far as I can see very clearly between training and employment. Employment after leaving this community will often be in sheltered conditions and training, as far as I can make out, is the stage which leads towards employment either outside or inside the community. And then I find here that this same centre has a much higher proportion of relatively severely subnormal persons who are unlikely to move from it, and also I gather that in the training stage, there are a lot of very profoundly retarded people who cannot be employed but who probably are occupied. Now I just wondered how this started, did you simply put your very profoundly retarded eternally into a training situation when in fact you are not intending to offer training? Shouldn't they logically be in a sheltered situation as another function of your sheltered workshop rather than keeping them in a training situation?

Murray: Really, I suppose this boils down to the name that we have given to the adult training centre. Obviously we hope that all the people who start in the adult training centre will graduate to the advanced training centre, or sheltered workshop, or even open employment. But we know that a large proportion of the severely subnormal aren't going to graduate even one step up the ladder so really what we have created in the adult training centre itself is a sheltered occupation. In other words, a very large proportion of the severely subnormal in our work centres have been there for a fair period of time and it really is more occupation rather than training for these people, although they have gone through a clearing house, if you like. They have been assessed and, as far as we are able, we have decided that these are people who will not progress beyond the training centres.

Dybwad: I think this paper brings out rather clearly how as we talk about the practical application of research to practical problems of mental retardation we will need to involve many professional groups who have been in the past non-existent in our field. The economist is simply a necessary colleague of ours. Around the world, there are hundreds of thousands of people in either sheltered workshops or some other kind or form of sheltered employment without involving the economist. The thing is, how to get work for the workshop and that's where, throughout the world, they are breaking down and becoming ridiculous enterprises. There is even more idleness than occurred in the classroom in the training centres in the past. So we need the economist. Furthermore, our whole relationship to labour unions and to management needs examination, and to the insurance industry, and this brings us to the third professional group, the legal profession. As we deal now with adults living in the community, their rights and also the rights of the team that work with them, are becoming an ever more important question. It therefore seems to me that as we go into the practical problems we really have to admit very quickly that we can outline what we see as potentials of the handicapped people for whom we would like to care, but very quickly we are aware of a situation where we have to look to other forces we haven't even learned to involve nor have they learned that we want eventually to involve them. I think we have a great unfinished agenda.

Mittler: I think we have to distinguish here between long- and short-term objectives. The points that Professor Dybwad has made, with which I completely agree, are essentially long term goals but we mustn't forget the immediate problems. The immediate problems as far as we know, and we know very little from objective information, is that, sad to say, the impetus created by the Clarkes at The Manor in the early 1950's, seems to me to have largely vanished. My evidence for this is taken from Pauline Morris' book which shows that in the late 1960's 50% of adult patients in hospitals, spent their entire day unoccupied. That's problem number one which is a problem for hospital management. Problem number two, which is at the local authority level, is that we have no published evidence of what actually goes on in adult training centres. We know that many adult training centres are very work orientated and the paper very clearly brings out the problems here. So the first thing we need is a very thorough study of what in the educational sense we can call curricula. I would like to draw a parallel here between remarks which Professor Clarke made in relation to Brooklands and a study which is better controlled but which has also been misinterpreted, namely Professor Clarke's own work. Going round adult training centres and hospital workshops it is quite clear that the basic principles which were laid down 20 years ago have been largely forgotten. I've been doing this exercise recently and rather than talk in terms of very fine and precise analysis of skills, we see situations where there is no grading of work, there is no training of patients and where this is justified by recourse to half-baked educational philosophies that the trainees are happy in this way and we mustn't make demands on them because, of course, they are severely subnormal. So we have this curious parallel here of work being quoted which is in fact not properly used and this seems to me to be the prime objective and I would like to register my very strong approval of the one paper in the conference which has talked about adults. Again, this is a side issue from a sociological point of view, but whenever a group of experts get round a table and start talking about mental handicap they invariably talk about children and very little about adults. We have a vast number of adults still in mental subnormality hospitals and I think out of sixty thousand or so patients who are still in hospital, something like six and a half thousand are children and the others are over sixteen. So we really do need to address ourselves to the problems posed in this paper and I was a little bit unhappy that we were starting to discuss this paper in terms of adolescents—this is important but I think we have to consider the problems of adults as adults. There are problems of transition from junior to adult training centre but I have been in too many discussions where the problem of the adult in the training centre has degenerated into a problem of how do we prepare children for the adult training centre. I would be very interested in what people have to say about the specific points made by Mr. Morley. Firstly about the need for assessment which in my limited experience is non-existent in adult training centres. People are 'sitting next to Nellie' just as they were 20 years ago. The need for a fine-grain analysis of behaviour. I think we could now, if the Clarkes' studies had been implemented, we could now go further and look at the precise skills which are needed to carry out industrial operations. But first of all we have to get Clarke & Clarke findings implemented and I am sorry that we should be so many years behind.

A. M. Clarke: Clarke & Clarke have been horrified at discovering, after many years tucked away in the University of Hull, what has happened to the impetus which we and Gunzburg and others tried to create, and the unfortunate state of affairs which we now perceive at some adult training centres, of a kind which was never projected. Not only do we not see the findings implemented, but we do not see new research undertaken to take further the whole question of the social habilitation of the adult mentally handicapped.

A. D. B. Clarke: This business of taking things further is enormously important, and it seems to me the scheme at Croydon was an attempt to do so. It's one of these natural laboratories which is bristling with data but anyone who has worked in rehabilitation knows one is too damned busy, to be quite crude, to collect all the data one ought to. We know, for example, from some American studies, that the open employment rate for the SSN, for the better SSN in this country, is vastly below their possible potentials. I don't say it is necessarily right to place SSN people in open employment. This I think is itself an open question until we know what the consequences of such employment are upon these people, upon society and upon their families. But it strikes me, looking through this interesting paper, just to take one paragraph, it's worth emphasising, re-emphasising, that all these persons in the sheltered workshop are employed men over 21 years at a basic wage of £14 per week and the women, (perhaps a bit of women's lib is needed)—at £10.29. All right, now this is enormously important. What are the effects on the individuals, what are the effects on their families? Going back to Dr. Dybwad's point, this is something in the economics of mental retardation we need to know more about. On the question of the outside employment just to quote some figures, old figures now by Saenger in New York, taking the upper group, those whom the World Health Organisation and the Americans call the moderately retarded, they show that something like 27% were in employment at the time of the survey, a wide range of employment, and a further 9% had been employed. Well, British figures are nowhere near this. Now maybe Saenger and his colleagues were wrong. Maybe they're right. We don't know. It's a question of value judgment again until you have more information about the consequences of open employment or sheltered employment. We know of the very interesting scheme in the Middlesex area produced by Dr. Guy Wigley which was right in the mainstream of the 1950's research and still going on. SSN people were placed in normal factories in groups under the supervision of local authorities' staff. To me, according to my bias, this sounds splendid, but we don't really know whether it is splendid until we've studied the people, the factories and their families. And this to me would be the logical move ahead from this abortive impetus (as it now turns out) of the 1950's. I'd like to just finish this peroration by asking Mr. Murray whether there is anyone in his setup who has the time to document this natural laboratory at Croydon, because the more information we have on it the more likely we are to be able to persuade other authorities to follow suit.

Murray: We are in the process of analysing data on the people that we have placed in open employment over about the last five years, not only the mentally handicapped, but the physically handicapped and mentally ill. We are looking at this, seeing how many of them are still in the employment we arranged for them in the first place, how many aren't, and where they are. But when you work for a local authority, you do find that if a person does break down and has problems, he comes back to you anyhow. So this really isn't a too difficult job. We are right in the middle of it at the moment and I think Mr. Morley does intend to publish something on it in the near future. I would emphasise that in placing people in open employment—disabled people generally—it is essential to have a tailor-made placing service, that is probably the best way to describe it. You don't just send a person out for a job. You must find out the type of firm you need for placing the person, and try and fit each individual to a particular job, and also the follow-up is most important. You must also give support after they are placed in employment. Support to the person and to the family and to the employer, which a lot of people tend to forget. The employer above all people, is the person, if we're going to put people in open employment, that we must get on our side. So you've got to give the employer some form of reassurance and help. If the trainee doesn't come up to the grade they will at least come back into our system and it won't be the awful experience of just being kicked out. The indications are, (we are half-way through this survey), that a very large proportion are still employed, if not the same job, in open employment. The family's perception of these people seems to have improved because of their employment.

Chairman: Could I go further back and say why was there this failure? Why do you think your research work hasn't been implemented? We have got representatives here from the Training Council which trains the people who work in these centres. Is there then something lacking in the training? I now belong to a large institution which provides teachers for your Adult Training Centres. Is there a place then for teachers in the Adult Training Centre? And if we're not going to look at the link between the top end of the school, which is the adolescent of 19—and moving on into the Adult Training Centre, and then to the sheltered workshop where shall we look for this build up that we're so anxious about? We're leaving a lot unsaid here when we've got people to say something, please.

Borkwood: It wasn't on this point I wanted to speak but on a point of

Mr. Murray's in which he said he was very careful what type of employment he looked for. Having this in mind, I designed a project for students who were taking the Training Council Diploma for teaching mentally handicapped adults and I sent them out into a factory of their own choice. First of all to go and look around the various estates and various areas then decide on a factory of their own choice, and find out all they could about everything that went on there. They then had to come back to college and analyse the skills that would be required to train a person to do a specific job. They went thoroughly into it and then produced for me a study on this. We got some very interesting ones. Some really honest students said they'd chosen the wrong type of employment; there was nothing whatsoever for mentally handicapped persons. Some of the others came back and said they'd rather shattered the personnel officers when they had realised just how many jobs in their factory could be done by a mentally handicapped person. The other thing I asked the students to do, was to make the jigs which were required, or sketch the jigs, to train the person in this particular job. Apart from going into the actual analysis of the skill, we also went into how they trained them in this particular skill. For example, if you want to take a flat pattern and translate it into a piece of three dimensional wood then the handicapped person has got to understand spatial relationships in order to do this. Another outcome, and I've met a number of industrialists particularly on this, many of our people and many of normal people are left-handed and nowhere did we find a left-handed machine. A person who is ready for sheltered workshop, inserting a piece of wood into a chair would have to round and work backwards because he is left-handed and he couldn't set it as he needed to. Now Mr. Murray what would you like to say about this?

Murray: Fortunately, there are not many left-handed people. But certainly this is a problem not only for left-handed persons, but more generally adapting a machine to specific disabilities. If you're running a sheltered workshop you've got to have a decent toolmaker who can adapt machines, make fittings and fixtures to suit the individuals. It's as simple as that. Even in an adult training centre I would certainly have an engineer with a decent workshop and at least give him the basic machine tools to provide these things. Not only for industrial but for any of the other training methods that you use, even in making your own teaching machine, it's handy to have a chap who knows something about electronics and can use a machine to put into practice what the educationists want.

Atkins: I am a little bit worried about the prime motives that seem to be appearing. We seem to think it's a good thing to develop the subnormal's potential as far as possible when they're in a junior training centre, or a junior training situation. At 16, when they enter the senior training centre, it seems to be that they are still inadequate, most of them, and they still have a lot to learn. Now, fair enough, if you can put a person in outside employment, this seems to me an adequate criterion. They are then full human beings in one sense. But, the subnormals who cannot go out into full employment are left in a 'training centre' and I think the emphasis on training is important. I've spent many happy hours and many unhappy hours, putting stamps into little cellophane packets and folding them up. I've done the same with fitting aerosol caps onto jars and if I do that for a very long time, I feel my I.Q. diminishing. I'm pretty sure that some subnormal people, rather than being trained in these training centres, are having retardation reinforced. We can retard the retarded. Are we justified in replacing training with occupation? Are we justified in training in saying 'Oh, they're earning £14 per week, they are occupied.' It seems to me that while they can learn, and while they are inadequate in any way, the emphasis should be upon developing their skills and if it's possible to find an occupation which can combine amelioration this is important. In fact this should be our priority. As I say rather than be contented putting caps on bottles, can we not find variations, can we not find stimulation through the industrial training because it is supposed to be training.

Dybwad: May I just come back a moment. May I, in the presence of representatives from two ministries, point to one factor. You can hardly expect industry to develop great ambition in employing the handicapped if the government doesn't This was an insight which came to us rather belatedly in the United States because our government has set the pace now in employing mentally retarded individuals. And therefore this has provided a tremendous stimulus that the government, federal government first, state government second, has discovered for themselves, how many jobs they have in which fairly definitely retarded people, not just the so-called slow learners can be placed. For example, some can very effectively distribute mail without being able to read. I agree with you that we can upgrade all work once we have the work. The other thing I think, a much more definite involvement of industry is needed. I believe this is now almost an application in practical problems. We have 'employer of the year' awards in every region of my country and when the public's attention is drawn to the successful experience of employers in employing the mentally retarded this is very important. You might like some day to acquaint yourself and possibly even repeat in this country the exploits of the secretary of the President's Committee on Unemployment who went out as an handicapped person and had himself hired and worked as an ex-mental

patient and a retarded patient and found out for himself, posing very
successfully, what happens to such people. I think we could do a great
deal more in the practical area of getting work because unless we get
more work opportunities, our training ends as you say, in these
absolutely inane, deadening and retarding occupational tasks.

Cookson: I would fully endorse this. My own observations of adult
training centres being that the prime need has been to occupy, the
second need has been to make money, the third need has been to train.
This is in practice, not in principle.

Chairman: I just wondered if the Clarkes could answer the question
they never did answer about why they felt their impetus had never been
carried on, for I think it's very interesting.

A. M. Clarke: It is a very difficult question to answer, and I think part
of the answer has been given by other speakers. We turned our
attention to other research problems, and were unaware of the misuse
of our work. Perhaps we wrote too much about industrial skills, and
not enough about other aspects of our training programme. But one
difficulty is that of obtaining and retaining an adequate supply of
varied sub-contract work. In our ideal set-up, when it ran ideally, there
were difficulties through the year because we were constantly faced
with the problem of getting suitable contracts in sufficient numbers.
Paradoxically, we were happier when the workshop was virtually empty
of people, because everybody was out at work, but the manufacturers
supplying the contracts were very unhappy because it wasn't getting
done. The other situation which pleased us was when we had sufficient
work so that the minute trainees were skilled in one job, they were
never left on that, but put on a different one, so that they were being
extended. I think if I were asked to choose one particular point of
which there are many, this would be the one: there is this tremendous
temptation to turn a training centre into a sheltered workshop where
the contract becomes of overriding importance and a human being is of
less importance.

The other thing I would like to ask Mr. Murray is, what provision is
made in your training centre in Croydon for further education or, even
basic training in skills like reading and arithmetical problems? Now this
is something that vexes many of my colleagues at the Adult Training
Centres and, I am sorry to say, I personally believe reflects very
unhappily on what has gone on in Junior Training Centres. I would like
to ask the participants of this Study Group, who have expressed
caution in prescribing what should go on, since we know the principles
of training, what should the educational aims be? I would like to
suggest that if any retarded child is capable of learning either to read in
a normal way or to use a social sight vocabulary, he should be

programmed to do so at the junior school level. It should not be left to the Adult Training Centres to receive an adolescent, who has been doing, goodness knows what, for these many years, and who is completely ill-equipped in basic skills which are essential to successful placement in the community. I would so like to hear your comments on this. This was part of our rehabilitation scheme, not just industrial training.

Murray: This problem that you are talking about is one of the very many problems we came up against in Croydon, and in fact our Adult Training Centre could have become a 'sweatshop' with production just overriding everything. We realise that this shouldn't be. This is why we introduced a centre with higher levels which is the sheltered workshop, where the people who, having spent a period of time in the training centre, a certain number could graduate to the sheltered workshop, leaving the Adult Training Centre to concentrate on social training and education, the work being found by the sheltered workshop. Now one of my jobs is finding the work. I have something like 800 disabled people to find work for. Because of this, I can command huge contracts with large firms of fairly complex work. We do aerosol tops on bottles occasionally, but we can also get the very skilled tasks, television assembly, capstan lathe operating, this type of work now we can get this work at the sheltered workshop, we are being paid a proper wage. We would then sub-contract it to any centre who needed work for any reason, the physically handicapped simply for occupation, but for the training centre, for training purposes. I don't say to the manager, 'look I want that out in a week.' He says to me 'well this is the type of task I want' and I give it to him to suit his particular training programme so the pressures of work aren't on the training centre, the manager hasn't the responsibility of finding contracts, I don't think the manager should have these responsibilities, he should be managing his centre as an Adult Training Centre. As far as education is concerned, when a person is in a sheltered workshop, admittedly he is there doing a full day's work, he may still need education, basic education—reading and writing—and this we have introduced now in conjunction with our education department in adult evening classes. We have managed to convince the Chief Education Officer that this is vital, and this year, for the first year, in a small way, we are introducing evening classes. We had been doing this teaching ourselves at our clubs, but now we have convinced the education department there's a need. We've just done a survey with all our disabled at our centres and all our voluntary centres on what is needed. Not only basic education but also leisure activities, and a new programme will be put into practice this year. So this covers to a certain extent the further educational needs rather than a full-time job.

A. D. B. Clarke: Since there has been some question about why a particular piece of research has provided considerable impetus at the time, and then later gradually was extinguished, I think the short answer is we don't fully know, it's a matter of guesswork but propaganda wasn't very high in our priorities. Talking about Piaget someone said earlier that there had been a great deal of preaching; we were too busy to preach. However, I want to make two points. First, it was a long experiment, and when it was going on, it acted as what the Americans call a demonstration pilot experiment. We had vast numbers of visitors of whom incidentally Mr. Morley was one of the earlier ones, planner as he then was for the Croydon scheme, and while that was going on, there was something one could show in the flesh, and this was worth lots of Study Groups, far more than Study Groups, far more than words, far more than articles in obscure journals or books. What we need today is a national demonstration centre, perhaps at Croydon, where people can go and study an ideal situation. Reading Mr. Morley's paper and listening to Mr. Murray, however, indicates that some of the early ideas have been splendidly put into practice, but there is a lot more to do, some of them exciting. I have in mind social training for semi-independent living in the community.

My second point is that from the very first steps in mental retardation, namely 1800 to 1805, from Itard onwards, there have been two conflicting schools of thought concerning mental handicap. One said 'here is severe or moderate handicap, in what way can this behaviour be actively modified, and if so, what are the desirable methods?' There has also been that school of thought which is governed by an equally humane motivation, 'these poor handicapped people, we mustn't put pressure upon them, this is very wrong.' In brief, as put so beautifully, the 'maypole dancers' versus the 'sweat-shops,' these being the extremes, rarely found incidentally, but both movements exist: the challengers of handicap and what I call the sentimentalists. I feel at the moment that the sentimentalists have gained some ground and I believe at the expense of the development of retarded people. So these are the sorts of very complex and interacting reasons that cause us now to do a post-mortem on this kind of research which partly failed to be implemented. I would like, however, to extend it away from that and say that obviously while in Professor Dybwad's country one can get government support for employment of the mentally retarded, this sort of thing must make an enormous difference to the development of services for the handicapped. I imagine that this type of support in fact came originally from the observation and careful description and documentation of demonstration pilot projects. I would like perhaps later to say more about this because, to me it has a lesson for anyone who is doing work which might be thought to have practical implication.

Dybwad: I would like to underline what has been said. I think that if more educators would see mentally retarded adults in action, see what they really do, who they are, it would have the most profound effect on changes in education. My wife and I have been privileged to travel in 35 countries. You name me any job, I will tell you one country where retarded and including those who are severely retarded, are engaged in that enterprise. Whatever machine you think of, whatever process, they have even, I've heard reported on one project, they've even been engaged in the demolition of buildings which involves considerable skill, caution and care and so on. All the cherished prejudices will fall by the wayside when you see in various places and in various ways what retarded adults can do and far too little research has been undertaken to find out the processes by which they got from there to here, from then to now, so I would merely like to underline what Professor Clarke says, more attention to the adult retarded and his problems but also his accomplishments and his place in society would help us.

Borkwood: If managers of training centres would get into their hands the international classification of work and go through it, they'd know where to start looking for contracts because this would tell them job prices and what must be done must be done. If your training centre is in an area of heavy industry, there is very little which the handicapped person can do and very little the manager can get. If your training centre is in the back of beyond, then the matter of economy comes in because the cost of transport is added to the cost of the goods. But if your training centre is near light industrial areas, either the manager is very fortunate and gets plenty of work or all the managers are cutting each other's throat and undercutting the costs. Now this happens but what should happen is they should ask for the proper rate for the job and there should be no undercutting in this way. I think what we need is liason between managers both on rates to be charged and how work may be shared out fairly.

Mittler: Can I just mention the scheme in the North-West which is still experimental. There is an organisation known as M.E.R.I.T., whose job it is to oversee the soliciting, if that is the word, of work from employers over an enormous geographical area. I think everyone would agree that getting work from employers is a highly skilled business. At the moment, each manager or each area manager, is responsible for this and while he's getting work he is away from his centre. Now this organisation takes this task over on a regional basis, they do it with tremendous resources and they then inform all the sheltered work-

shops, all the training centres in their area of what is available, so there
is a process going on which saves the manager an enormous amount of
time and regionalises and rationalises this problem.

Session V

Psychological Models in Research and Practice

Assumptions Underlying the Use of Psychological Models in Subnormality Research

P. HERRIOT

*Hester Adrian Research Centre for
the Study of Learning Processes in the Mentally Handicapped,
University of Manchester*

Model-making and Defect-discovering:
Definitions and Relations

Before discussing the assumptions of others in conducting their research, the writer would like to outline his intentions in writing this paper. They are, briefly, to deal with that part of research into subnormality which has the aim of formulating theories about subnormal function. This excludes research having the aim of discovering more about human intelligence in general (Haywood, 1970), and also research using the subnormal to reveal aspects of learning and motivation in general by means of comparative research (Heal, 1970). It furthermore excludes research having the primary aim of devising remediation. Of course, all these aims may in fact be fulfilled as by-products of theoretical research into subnormality *per se*. Furthermore, some of the techniques suitable to attaining the excluded aims (e.g. comparative research, methods of improving performance) are also applicable to theoretical pursuits. No implication is intended that theoretical research is in any way more valuable than other sorts of research into subnormality. Rather, all that is being stressed is that aims should be stated explicitly and not confounded.

However, it is also part of the intention of this paper to show that the creation of a model for subnormal information processing should in fact have considerable implications for remediation. For any activity benefits from the existence of a model, providing that it is a description of what is known, and providing also that it can adapt to new evidence. The benefit derives not only from the fact that the model presents in shorthand form the state of knowledge in the area concerned: it also derives from the fact that most people have unspoken assumptions logically underpinning their activity, and model-making forces such assumptions to be made explicit. Of course, there is always the danger that a model becomes a canon, and in fact limits rather than expands the development of further work, including remediation.

A basic aim underlying most theoretical research is that of producing a model. A model is a theory in the sense that it adequately accounts for existing evidence and generates testable hypotheses. Recently, models have tended to be process models; that is, they imply a temporal *sequence* of sub-processes subserving a *function.* The temporal sequencing feature is usually expressed by means of a flow-diagram. The functional feature is indicated by the existence of a terminal point of a flow-diagram and of alternative sub-processes available to show how the terminal point might be reached.

There is usually, in other words, more than enough adaptive capacity to fulfil the required function. While the system as a whole may have adequate capacity, individual parts will of course be inadequate on their own. Thus, for example, in the case of currently popular models of memory (Tulving and Madigan, 1970), one of the functions of short-term memory is assumed to be the relief of pressure on the limited capacity channel to long-term store. The latter would be inadequate on its own.

Alternatively, some sub-processes may serve two functions in order to subserve the overall function; thus for example, rehearsal in short-term memory may serve both to retain items in short-term memory for as long as possible and also to effect their more efficient filing into long-term store (Atkinson and Shiffrin, 1968).

Clearly, malfunction of an overall system (as evidenced by inferior overall performance either of a sub-group relative to the population as a whole or of an individual relative to a sub-group) may be the result of defects in subsystems *or* of properties of the whole system. Taking the latter first, one basic property is whether the system permits parallel processing or not; that is, are there alternative channels for flow of information if one channel malfunctions. A second property, granted that parallel processing is possible, is the flexibility of the system in switching from one channel to the other; is the system *capable* of utilising alternative capacity? Finally, the channel capacity of the system as a whole, given presence or absence of parallel processing and flexibility, is important; for spare capacity after any specific defect in a subsystem is allowed for may still permit a degree of adequate function.

Defects of subsystems, on the other hand, may differ along the following dimensions; the degree of malfunction of a subsystem; the number of subsystems which are malfunctional; and the position of the defect in the flow diagram.

Clearly the systems analysis proposed above bears certain conceptual similarities to current theoretical positions in the field of subnormality. System characteristics are related to developmental theories of retardation, in the sense that developmental delay would be likely to refer to the system as a whole. Defect characteristics relating to subsystems within the overall system are obviously similar to defect theories of retardation, in the sense that they both presuppose that certain subsystems are underfunctioning compared with others.

Systems analysis differs from defect and developmental theorising, however, in the following important ways. Firstly, it does not necessitate experimental procedures which support either one case or the other; if a difference with controls is found, the defect theorist considers his position supported, while if one is not found, the developmental theorist considers himself vindicated. He then searches for experiential variables to 'explain away' defect findings. In a systems theory, this mutual exclusion of alternatives does not operate; for firstly, experimental procedure need not necessarily result in either one or the other conclusion; and secondly, system characteristics need not all be considered developmental in nature. Indeed, it is the interactions of system and defect characteristics which offer most power in explaining malfunction.

It is clear how individual system and defect characteristics could result in overall malfunction; the lists of characteristics presented above will clearly translate into individual variables resulting in an overall performance deficit. The number of possible interactions, however, is considerable and their effects on the overall function illuminating. Degree of defect could interact with overall capacity of the system; it could also interact with the degree of parallel processing and flexibility within the parallel alternatives available. Number of defects, too, could interact with degree of parallel processing, since the more defective subsystems there are, the more flexible parallel processes will be required to compensate for them. Position of the defect in the flow diagram will also interact with degree of parallel processing, since if a parallel process is not available near the beginning of the overall system, then a defective subsystem there will prevent any subsequent passage of information.

Not only does the systems analysis offer many more possible and logically compatible explanations for overall malfunction; it also resolves the logical problems which result from the (false) opposition of defect and developmental theories. Briefly, the problems are as follows. At what stage of theorising does one stop positing separate defects and start suggesting overall deficiency? And at what point of development does one start calling a developmental delay a defect? When the subnormal individual appears to have stopped developing? The evidence for defects at present is derived from findings from detailed experimental tests which show that a subnormal is worse in the specific area tested than would be predicted from the general test of ability used to equate him on mental age with a normal control group. Clearly, if the detailed experimental tests and the general test of ability are measuring the same things in the same way to the same degree of accuracy, then it is logically possible for only some areas to be considered defective (the interesting corollary is that in other areas the subnormal must be superior to his mental age matched control). However, there is an increasing number of specific defects being discovered. This leads to two possible conclusions: either subnormals are superior to normals in a considerable number of areas of functioning leading to a completely different profile of abilities; or general and specific tests do not measure equally relevantly or efficiently. If the latter conclusion is justified, then one is faced with the dilemma of deciding whether the discovery of a specific defect is evidence of a defect in a particular subsystem under and below the functioning of other subsystems; or whether it is merely a reflection of the fact that all the subsystems are underfunctioning, and the detailed experimental tests of this area are particularly sensitive. Thus one is left with the possibility of interpreting a defect result in terms either of particular subsystem or of overall system characteristics. And the overall system characteristics are assumed to be those typical of the normal population and evidenced (indirectly) in intelligence tests.

The alternative is to create overall models of subnormal systems. If such a model were complete, then its degree of parallel processing, its adaptability, and its overall capacity, would be known. Given that it would be capable of representation by a flow diagram, interventions might be experimentally carried out at different points in the flow. Thus, for example, interventions in a memory model might be made at the point of storage into or at the point of retrieval from long-term store. Such interventions would determine whether or not the stage immediately preceding the intervention in the flow diagram was particularly defective. This decision would be made relative to the expectations derived from the *model* of the system as a whole. *Thus the model of the system takes over from a test of general ability as the criterion for postulating a specific defect.* Then the interaction of the system characteristics and the defect characteristics can be used to explain overall malfunction as evidenced by poor performance on a general test of ability. In sum, the chain of inference is (a) creation of a model of the subnormal system, (b) inference of defects relative to the overall system, (c) explanation of poor intellectual functioning. It is worth noting that such a chain of inference nowhere presupposes the need for the prior existence of adequate models of normal function.

Clearly, the logically prior task, if this analysis is correct, is to create a model of the information-processing systems of the subnormal. The major proviso is that the experimental tests used to create such models must not differ in degree of accuracy and validity from any that are used later to test specific subsystems for defect. Only if this proviso is met will the logical difficulty of the use of intelligence tests as the criterion of normality and specific experimental tests as evidence of defect be avoided. However, a difficulty remains; which detailed experimental tests are to be used as evidence for the model and which as evidence for defects? Or, putting it another way, how can one distinguish systems from subsystems? The example of cues in free recall, cited later, shows that the same technique can be used for both purposes depending on the experimenter's aims. Perhaps the answer to the difficulty lies in a reconsideration of the definition of defect when considered in the context of system theory. A defect is said to exist in a system when that system is not fulfilling its function to the fullest extent of its capacity. The model will provide details of the extent of parallel processing and specify the degree of adaptability. If evidence suggests underfunctioning, this may be due to a lack of capacity throughout the system; or a defect can be suspected in those parts of the flow diagram which do not fulfil these expectations; as has been suggested, it can be evidenced by sampling at different points in the system.

A second proviso, then, in model-making, is that it is not only the actual subsystems of the model which require elucidation, but also the characteristics of the information flow; for example, it is not only important to know whether or not the subnormal can use rehearsal to aid short-term store; it is also important to know whether more information than usual can be shunted into short-term store when limited channel capacity to long-term store becomes overloaded. Perhaps such 'characteristics of information flow' or 'adaptability' are better described as the results of control processes. This amounts to saying that control systems must be available to respond to the feedback from the system and regulate the nature of flow accordingly in such a way as to maximise capacity. Thus a model of a process must include a control system.

A third requirement is that the model is complex enough to reflect any differences from the normal model which might be required to account for the facts. It should also be complex enough to permit discovery of defects, as just defined. Thus any model incapable of differentiating between the functions of humans and pigeons is unlikely to differentiate between normals and subnormals. Clearly, however, a limiting factor is whether experimental techniques are available to support such complexity. A fourth requirement is that the model should be evidenced by different experimental techniques; otherwise the model and any defects will be in danger of being artefacts. A final requirement is that the model should remain compatible with physiological evidence; the likelihood of the need for a different model for different aetiological groups is a corrollary. The writer has no evidence so far that the normal information-processing model is inappropriate to subnormal non-mongols, but has considerable hesitation about its application to mongols.

Granted that the above requirements are fulfilled, however, there is still the actual task of making the model; or, in other words of ensuring that the model is not simply inadequate to 'explain' the function with which it purports to deal. In fact, most systems require control processes which respond to feedback concerning whether the system is functioning adequately or not. Thus, for example, current models of memory postulate control processes to explain why some items are jettisoned from short-term store while others are selected for long-term storage. Even supposing that the problem of control is dealt with, however, there are other difficulties in the memory-model. For example, there is doubt whether storage and retrieval rely on the same organisation, or whether organisation in memory continues while the material is in long-term store. Moreover, the modes of organisation applied are apparently incredibly varied; the fact that the learning of a list of 15 unrelated items interferes with the learning of a list of 20 unrelated items containing the original 15 (Ehrlich, 1970) shows that a list is organised as a whole unit (Wood, 1971). The tidy picture of categories being sorted and retained is largely a product of the experimenter's tidy mind (Tulving, 1968). Perhaps one should be concerned instead with stressing those features which make models flexible enough to account for the multiplicity of different types of organisation which subjects can apply given suitable material (Cofer, 1966). Even supposing that adequate models can be devised, the very length of the task is a final difficulty. For example, different series of experiments would be required to elucidate degree of parallel processing available, and its flexibility given that it was available.

Thus, in conclusion, it is being recommended that new models are required to describe subnormal functioning. This is because, firstly, it has to be discovered whether the components and flow are the same or different for subnormals and normals; supposing it was found that they are the same, overall capacity and flexibility might still differ. Secondly, because if any defects are to be found, they must be found relative to the subnormal's system. And third, because system characteristics and their interaction with defects multiply explanatory power. However, most defects so far discovered have been derived from experiments using normal controls. It is instructive to consider the relative difficulty of this latter form of defect-discovery and of model-making. For despite the requirements of models just described, defect discovery appears far more difficult.

Model-making and Defect-discovery: Technical Difficulties

The above argument has assumed that the provision of a model is a necessary addition for the discovery of defects. However, when no model exists, all the well-known problems of obtaining adequate normal controls have to be faced (Heal, 1970). Many variables other than mental age have to be controlled (Zigler, 1969); indeed, the task itself may be different for normals and subnormals, in the sense that, for example, asymptotes may differ or differential learning and experience may be operating (Baumeister, 1967). Further, any defect hypothesis has to be tested by all the experimental methods available; otherwise positive results may be merely a methodological artefact.

The building up of psychological models for subnormality is a long process; research may begin with a highly specific experimental paradigm, such as paired-associate learning (Baumeister and Kellas, 1971), free recall (Herriot and Cox, 1971), or more general models such as the Piagetian account of cognitive development (Woodward, 1963) or transfer of training (Clarke and Clarke, 1967). A great deal of research has been required before comparable models have been built up for normal function (Tulving and Madigan, 1970). However, the technical difficulties have largely been solved by these previous workers; the task remains to create models of subnormal function (instead of assuming they are identical with those of normal function).

A specific example may indicate the difference in difficulty between the defect-discovery and model-making tasks. Consider the case of the use of experimenter-provided cues to facilitate clustering in free recall. Free recall is a task in which subjects can recall items presented to them in any order that they wish. Items may be categorically related—out of 16 items, 4 may be articles of clothing, 4 means of transport, etc. If they are presented in random order but recalled clustered in category order, then the inference must be that subjects have imposed organisation upon the material. A defect theorist (Spitz, 1966) wishes to say that the subnormal have a defect in organising input. Free recall is one of several techniques he will have to use to support this hypothesis. On finding that subnormals did not cluster significantly above chance, he provided a cue to organisation; he presented (auditorily) all the items belonging to the same category consecutively. This blocked presentation did lead to significant clustering in recall. Spitz inferred that, since cues had to be provided for clustering to occur, the subnormals were deficient at organising input. There are many objections to this inference (similar, incidentally, to Flavell's hypothesised 'production deficiency' in young children, Flavell, Beach and Chinsky, 1966).

The first objection is that which faces all defect theorists—to what extent does the finding depend on specific experimental conditions? Later research has shown that clustering with random-order presentation can occur, given simultaneous visual presentation and few items (Herriot and Cox, 1971). One cannot, furthermore, use the failure to cluster significantly above chance without cues (even supposing it is well-attested) as evidence of a defect in subnormals. Normals of the same mental age must cluster significantly, not only above chance, but also above the subnormals, for such a defect to be evidenced. Nor indeed can one use the facilitatory effect of cues to support a defect position. If subnormals are to be shown to be defective in comparison with normals of the same mental age, then the normals must improve significantly less with cues than the subnormals; ceiling effects make such a finding technically difficult, and it has not been evidenced to the writer's knowledge. Further, it is always worth questioning whether the experimental manipulation (in this case, the cue) does in fact compensate *in a one-to-one way* for a function lacking in the subject who is benefited by it. It seems likely, on the contrary, that the cue benefits the subject because it allows him to exercise a function he actually possesses. In this case *any* beneficial effect is to be treated as evidence of ability, even though the benefit derived may be less for the subnormal. A real absence of function is indicated by inability to benefit by these or any other cues.

A final caveat concerning Spitz's inference of deficit *at input* must also be entered. It is quite possible that cues are important for retrieval purposes rather than for storage purposes. It might not matter whether cues are explicitly available at input so long as they are available at recall. In this case, the blocking could have led to codings which were important because they were retained and facilitated retrieval rather than storage. Thus even if the facilitatory effects of cues *is* to be taken as evidence of deficit, that deficit still cannot be allocated to the input part of the flow diagram.

No such theoretical difficulties face the model builder using the same experimental paradigm. He may use cues to reveal the existence of processes which were not inferrable without their aid. Thus, for example, if cues such as category names or functions facilitate clustering and amount recalled (Herriot, 1972), it may be inferred that storage and retrieval by means of category cues is an available strategy. If subnormal subjects exhibit positive transfer from a situation in which they have been trained to organise material to be remembered to one in which no such help is given (Clarke and Clarke, 1967), then it may be concluded that they can learn this strategy.

Thus an entirely different picture emerges of the relative difficulty of defect-discovery and model making in the particular case of cued free recall. In particular, it has been shown that diametrically opposite inferences have been made from the positive effect of cues, the defect theorist treats them as showing a defect, the model-maker as revealing a sub-process.

Models and Remediation

The different experimental strategies of research described above imply different strategies of remediation. This section is intended to crticise remediation derived logically from one or other of the experimental strategies; it is realised that most remediators are eclectic and therefore that the writer is knocking down straw men. Possible differences in aims as well as in rationale also apply; one possible aim is to change the system or subsystem, another to compensate by placing more emphasis on well-functioning parts of the system and less on the defective subsystem.

Consider the experimental strategy of defect-discovery, using normal controls. The defect-discoverer might infer that he should either remedy the defect or compensate for it. However, exactly the same difficulties arise in remediation as in theory. That is, just as one cannot always explain overall malfunction by means of defects alone, so, when remediation is successful, it does not follow that this results from the defect alone being remedied or compensated for. On the contrary, those who benefited from the remediation may be those in whom a defect interacts in a certain way with a system characteristic. The corollary of this is that those who failed to benefit failed because the defect interacted with a different system characteristic in their case. Thus immediately an alternative explanation for failure to benefit becomes apparent; failure need not be due to the fact that the defect is too great or the teaching inadequate.

A further difficulty facing a defect rationale for remediation is to decide upon the order in which defects are to be remedied. It was noted that one important feature of defects was their position in the flow diagram. Thus it follows that the remediation of some defects (e.g. attention) is logically necessary before other defects later in the flow diagram (e.g. retrieval systems) may be effectively remedied.

A second basic experimental strategy is to deduce from the null results of defect theorists that there is a developmental retardation, and to try to explain their positive findings in terms of other variables (e.g. degree of social reinforcement). One strategy of remediation implied by this theoretical standpoint is to ensure that the retardate reaches the optimum level of development of which he is capable. This strategy accepts that that level is fixed, and is primarily concerned to remove performance obstacles so that cognitive competence may be fully realised at the stage which the retarded person has reached. To this end, experience in many different aspects of, for example, conservation, is now provided. An alternative strategy might be to endeavour to hasten the transition from one stage of cognitive development to the next in the hope of finally reaching a higher asymptote.

However, just as the defect position omits the possibility of remediation based on defect-system interactions, so does the developmental position. For both positions largely ignore the existence of one of the partners in the interaction. Further, the developmental position has the added disadvantage that it assumes that a model applicable to normals also adequately describes the subnormal; it in fact does not try to elucidate the essential system characteristics described earlier. Thus, once again, success or failure to benefit from 'developmental' remediation have no clear explanation. Success might be due to the fact that the system characteristic at which remediation was aimed was in fact interacting with a defect; failure might be due to the fact that a defect existed where none was allowed for. Thus there is an alternative explanation for failure to the conclusion that the retardate was further back in the developmental sequence than had previously been thought.

Another strategy of remediation is to provide specific training to remedy certain aspects of behaviour. In this case, the criteria for choice of area of remediation are extrinsic rather than intrinsic. Ways in which the individual's behaviour does not meet some criterion of social adequacy are discovered, and a specific teaching programme, together with tests of its efficiency, is initiated. Such teaching may or may not explicitly use operant procedures. Its continued use is based on the empirical criterion of whether it achieves its specific aim or not. Clearly, it may achieve its specific aim but have no effect whatever, or even deleterious effects, on other behaviour, or on subsystem or system characteristics. Further, since it has no theoretical foundation, it has no theoretical pay-off in terms of confirming or infirming a model.

It is worth distinguishing the use of operant techniques alone from the use of an operant model in conjunction with operant techniques. In the latter case, it appears at first sight that a very strong theoretical assumption is employed to justify a certain area and technique of remediation. The assumption is that the behaviour to be remedied is the product of the reinforcement history. The remedial inference is that every behaviour is capable of being taught if properly shaped and reinforced. There is no refuting this hypothesis, since failure to learn can always be attributed to bad teaching. The nature of the system or defects of subsystems need never be considered when remediation is being devised, since assessment is in terms of behaviour rather than inferred models. Thus the same criticism must be made as in the previous paragraph—remediation may be successful according to external criteria, but random or deleterious according to internal criteria.

It seems, therefore, that the existence of models would be beneficial to remediation. Such benefit would be due to the fact that their existence males it possible to postulate several more reasons for overall performance malfunction than are available otherwise. Developmental theorists tend to ignore defective subsystems, defect theorists tend to ignore system characteristics, and operant conditioners ignore both. The result is a multiplicative decrease in the number of potential explanations, since possible interactions are always ignored. The increase in the number of explanations resulting from the existence of a model should help remediators. For it should make the programming more specific, since it is aimed at remedying or compensating for a more defined description of the malfunction of the process. As a corollary, it should decrease the number of possible explanations for failure.

Of course, a model of the subnormal is not tailored to fit the individual. It is by definition a generalisation resulting from experimental results derived from samples of a population. But it is a first approximation to a description of what one might expect a subnormal's functioning to be. It therefore justifies the making of certain prior assumptions when remediation in general is being devised.

Summary

The activities of model-making and defect-discovery are defined, and some relations between them are explored. It is suggested that the existence of process models of the subnormal is a necessary condition of discovering defects, since it is proposed that defects should be defined by reference to the systems of the subnormal rather than to models derived from normal functioning. Model-making and defect-discovery are contrasted in terms of their technical difficulty, and an example from the area of free recall is provided. Finally, ways in which remediation might benefit from the existence of models are suggested.

ACKNOWLEDGEMENTS

The author would like to thank Dr. Peter Mittler, Dr. Robert Serpell, Roy McConkey and Josephine Green for their helpful comments.

REFERENCES

Atkinson, R. C. and Shiffrin, M. (1968). Human memory: a proposed system and its control processes. In 'The Psychology of Learning and Motivation: Advances in Research and Theory' Vol. 2 (eds K. W. Spense and J. T. Spence). New York: Academic Press.

Baumeister, A. A. (1967). Problems in comparative studies of mental retardates and normals. *Amer. J. ment. Def.* 71, 869.

Baumeister, A. A. and Kellas, G. (1971). Process variables in the paired-associate learning of retardates. In 'International Review of Research in Mental Retardation' Vol. V (ed. N. R. Ellis), pp. 221-270.

Clarke, A. M. and Clarke, A. D. B. (1967). Learning transfer, and cognitive development. In 'Psychopathology of Mental Development' (eds J. Zubin and G. A. Jervis), pp. 105-139. New York: Grune and Stratton.

Cofer, C. N. (1966). Some evidence for coding processes derived from clustering in free recall. *J. Verb. Learn. Verb. Behav.* 5, 188.

Ehrlich, S. (1970). Structuration and destructuration of responses in free recall learning. *J. Verb. Learn. Verb. Behav.* 9, 282.

Ellis, N. R. (1970). Memory process in retardates and normals. In 'International Review of Research in Mental Retardation' Vol. 4 (ed. N. R. Ellis), pp. 1-32. Academic Press.

Flavell, J. H., Beach, D. H. and Chinsky, J. M. (1966). Spontaneous verbal rehearsal in a memory task as a function of age. *Child Dev.* 37, 283.

Haywood, H. C. (1970). Mental retardation as an extension of the developmental laboratory. *Amer. J. ment. Def.* 75, 5.

Heal, L. W. (1970). Research strategies and research goals in the scientific study of the mentally subnormal. *Amer. J. ment. Def.* 75, 10.

Herriot, P. (1972). The effect of category cues on the free recall of retarded adults. *Psychonomic Science, in press.*

Herriot, P. and Cox, A. M. (1971). Subjective organisation and clustering in the free recall of intellectually normal children. *Amer. J. ment. Def.* 75, 702.

Spitz, H. H. (1966). The role of input organisation in the learning and memory of mental retardates. In 'International Review of Research in Mental Retardation' Vol. II (ed. N. R. Ellis), pp. 29-56. New York: Academic Press.

Tulving, E. (1968). Theoretical issues in free recall. In 'Verbal Behavior and General Behavior Theory' (eds T. H. Dixon and D. L. Horton). Englewood Cliffs, N. J.: Prentice-Hall.

Tulving, E. and Madigan, S. A. (1970). Memory and verbal learning. *Ann. Rev. Psych.* 21, 437.

Tulving, E. and Pearlstone, Z. (1966). Availability versus accessibility of information in memory for words. *J. Verb. Learn. Verb. Behav.* 5, 381.

Wood, G. (1971). Organisation, large memory units, and free recall. *J. Verb. Learn. Verb. Behav.* **10,** 52.

Woodward, M. (1963). The application of Piaget's theory to research in mental deficiency. In 'Handbook of Mental Deficiency' (ed. N. R. Ellis), pp. 297-324. New York: McGraw-Hill.

Zigler, E. (1969). Developmental versus difference theories of mental retardation and the problem of motivation. *Amer. J. ment. Def.* **73,** 536.

Applications of Attention Theory to Teaching in Schools for the Severely Subnormal

R. SERPELL

*Hester Adrian Research Centre for the Study of Learning
Processes in the Mentally Handicapped,
University of Manchester*

The Problem of Application

That the teaching of children in SSN schools presents a distinct problem was bluntly indicated until April, 1971 in Britain by the official designation of these children as 'unsuitable for education'. Apart from the social rejection implied by this now abandoned formula, there remains the important fact that the criteria for admission to these schools are predominantly negative. The decision is arrived at by a process of elimination: the child is not acceptable in a normal school, an ESN school, a school for the maladjusted, a school for spastics, a school for the deaf. If he is to live at home and is to attend school at all (the only two positive criteria) he can only attend a school for the SSN. A major assumption of the present formulation, therefore is that education as currently practised, including a flexible application of the methods used successfully with normal children of the same 'mental age', has either been tried and failed with the children under discussion or else been judged by a suitably qualified person as doomed to failure.

Given that unconventional teaching methods are called for, why choose to apply attention theory to the problem? The systematic elimination of alternatives described in the previous paragraph finds no parallel here. It is a commonplace in modern psychology that the fragmentation of theoretical analyses divides behaviour somewhat arbitrarily into categories or systems which are interdependent. Characteristically the children under discussion display deviant or defective behaviour in so many ways that almost any process is fair game for the theorist wishing to pin-point a deficit. A specific bonus for the present analysis is, of course that such outstanding research in the field of attention theory has been conducted by Zeaman and House with SSN children. But it can also be argued that the field of learning in general has logical priority in the search for psychological principles relevant to a teaching problem. And within this field an emphasis on selection of perceptual input has rather wide support among recent theories.

The design of schools for the SSN tends in many ways to be modelled on the prevalent style of infant school education. An implicit assumption of this style appears to be that intense and varied stimulation is a necessary and almost sufficient condition for cognitive progress. Because attention selects stimulation, an awareness of how it operates in SSN children is essential if teachers are to make effective use of the classroom environment with which they are provided. In this paper I shall use the expression 'attention theory' to refer to a broad range of theoretical views which are consonant with the general idea that some kind of active perceptual selection mediates between sensory stimulation and discriminative responding in learning tasks. In this way it will be possible to draw on many of the studies reviewed by Wolff (1967) and Serpell (1969, 1970), which are not explicitly related to particular models. Certain differences among models are discussed at the end of the paper, but the discussion is throughout confined principally to the mediational aspects of attention rather than the arousal aspects.

So far, I have argued that teaching in schools for the SSN presents by definition a practical problem, and that within theoretical psychology it seems appropriate to look for relevant principles in the field of learning in general and of attention theory in particular. The topic of this paper will be how to proceed from there. It is conventional to express caution about simple extrapolation from experimental psychology to practical education. 'Many of the principles that have been observed in the laboratory have yet to be put to the test in a practical learning situation. A considerable amount of intermediate research remains to be conducted.' (Baumeister, 1967,, 181). The function of such intermediate research can be defined in various ways:

1. *Simplification:* To make available the distilled wisdom of psychological science in a form comprehensible to unsophisticated teachers.
2. *Reality testing:* To bring psychological theorising down to earth by confronting those who engage in it with a problem as it arises in the real world rather than the artificially restricted conditions of the laboratory.
3. *Translation:* On the one hand, to present what is usually defined as an 'everyday, practical, classroom problem' in a form which is perceived

by the experimentalist as a legitimate empirical question free from loose terminology and prescriptive overtones; and, on the other hand, to present what is usually defined as a 'complex, abstract, theoretical idea' in a form which is perceived by the educationalist as a useful teaching method free from technical jargon and impractical requirements.

The views caricatured as (1) and (2) are so obscurely related to one another that we appear to be dealing with a case of 'paradigm clash' (Katahn & Koplin, 1968) or 'mud-slinging' by rival ideologies, such that the reconciliation defined as (3) would be practically impossible. In my view this pessimistic conclusion would not be in order. Rather it is essential to bear in mind the conflicting orientations in choosing the criteria by which to define 'intermediate research', and to make concessions on both sides.

Thus if psychologists are to claim educational 'relevance' or 'applicability' for the results of a study of learning, it is not sufficient that the experimental Ss be SSN children. The experimental learning tasks will also have to be demonstrably related to tasks which educationalists can resonably justify including in the curriculum, and the experimental methods will have to be clearly related to methods potentially available to teachers on a realistic scale. On the other hand, educationalists asking for technical research on a practical problem cannot expect adequate returns from psychologists simply because the problem concerns learning. They will have to be prepared to consider and explore various detailed formulations of their problem. They will have to accept that in research, convictions based on intuition are not adequate substitutes for empirically established fact. And in evaluating the recommendations they may ultimately be offered they will have themselves to use scientific, as well as intuitive criteria.

Since this conference is peopled mainly by psychologists I shall concentrate on the concessions which their side are required to make in 'intermediate research' according to this scheme. I shall also try to show that the results of making such concessions are not necessarily without payoff even within the value system of theoretical psychology.

Changes in Procedural Paradigm

The great majority of studies on which attention theory is based fall within a narrow range of procedures conventionally used in studies of 'discrimination learning' or 'concept attainment'. Within this convention we can distinguish two strands.

Critical features. In certain basic respects the procedural paradigm defines the structure of the theory: a fixed number of alternative response categories are available to the Subject; criterial behaviour is related systematically in terms of these response categories to a fixed number of stimulus variables; samples of behaviour are taken repeatedly over time in a stimulus situation which is constant in respect of the critical variables; 'feedback' or 'reinforcement' is provided according to a predetermined schedule. If any of these structural characteristics of the procedural paradigm is dropped, it becomes very difficult to generate predictions from any of the tighter models of attentional learning.

Incidental features. There are other uniformities, however, which are dictated by considerations of lesser intrinsic importance to the theory. Response categories are usually (for human Ss) a very simple manipulative response (such as lifting a cover, pressing a lever, pointing at a picture, dealing a card) or a very brief verbal response. Critical stimulus categories are usually small, visual and simultaneously presented. Irrelevant stimulus variation is usually confined to patterned repetitive variation of a small number of discrete alternatives. Feedback is usually in the form of stereotyped verbal responses by an unfamiliar adult, and/or small tokens or sweets.

Each of these 'incidental features' can be justified on general theoretical or methodological grounds, but it may be suggested that their abandonment would be less crucial to attention theory than any of the 'critical features'. Yet they contribute cumulatively much of the appearance of artificiality which is so striking for the uninitiated comparing laboratory learning situations to those of 'real life'. If we could relax these restrictions without violating the requirements of theory, we could demonstrate greater generality for the models than is usually apparent, and spell out their exact relevance to practical issues confronting the teacher. It is therefore worth examining in some detail what theoretical consequences their abandonment would have. In most cases it seems there is probably as much to be gained as there is to be lost.

Response Categories

Historically, cover-lifting and lever-pressing would seem to have made their *début* in human studies largely as close analogues for responses studied in primates and rodents by the pioneers of discrimination learning theory. Mazes were probably unpopular because of their expense and inconvenient size—still more so jumping-stands. (In another field salivary conditioning has been tried, but ethological intuition has so far apparently forestalled any attempts to train children in discriminative key-pressing with their noses.) Finger-pointing is, ethologically, a natural response to pictures for children, as is dealing in response to cards for adults. Pressing and pointing lend themselves to latency measures much better than lifting and dealing, and can activate automatic sweet dispensers. On the other hand although slot-machines are widely known in Western urban enviroments, lifting a cover seems the response most naturally related to sweet rewards for most children.

Educational priorities would surely suggest quite different criteria by which to choose response categories. The child is about to be taught something. How much he will learn is something we cannot prejudge. But if we are about to invest time and effort in trying to teach him, presumably the responses he is required to learn had better be of some use beyond the immediate confines of the experiment. Depressing a door-handle, turning a tap and spooning sugar into a tea-cup are likely to feature higher on this list of priorities than the responses most commonly required in discrimination experiments.

Baumeister (1967) states that 'the experimenter, in attempting to control as much of the behavioural variation as possible, often deliberately attempts to use a task that is divorced from the subject's experience' (op. cit., 181). This would seem to apply to the choice of stimulus categories and feedback contingencies but not of response categories. Here either the choice is based on rather crude analogy with animal experiments, or else a universally familiar and natural response is sought. Clearly the latter approach is much more consonant with the educationalist's criteria, and there is scope for much improvement in this field. An interesting apparatus is described by McConnell (1964) which departs radically from tradition, yet gave results fully consonant with the main body of discrimination learning data. The task was to 'feed' into the mouth of a model clown the stimuli which he 'likes': success was signalled by a blink of the light inside the clown's nose as well as the delivery of a sweet at the base of the model. The rationale for the design of this apparatus was mainly concerned with motivation. But it should be clear that quite other criteria intrinsically related to curriculum development might suggest equally drastic changes in response requirements. Far from resulting in loss of experimental control, such modifications to the standard paradigm could if carefully implemented yield valuable theoretical information.

A latent restricting influence on the traditional choice of response categories is probably the idea of maintaining spatial contiguity of stimulus, response and reward. An interesting study with monkeys suggests paradoxically that gross separation of the discriminandum from the manipulandum may be as effective as close contiguity in facilitating appropriate attentional behaviour (Otteson, Sheridan and Meyer,

1962). The insight leading to the formulation of that study would have been less startling if the literature on discrimination learning included a wider range of response conditions. It is not implausible to suppose that the elaboration of procedures advocated here on educational grounds might bring to the notice of experimentalists other latent theoretical assumptions safeguarded by the narrow traditional range. For instance, it is commonly posited that position habits are evidence for the salience of spatial cues in the hierarchy of visual dimensions attended to by SSN children. Yet one possible interpretation of House's (1964) study of 'the effect of distinctive response on discrimination reversals in retardates' implies that position is utilised largely as a proprioceptive rather than a visual cue. Studies departing from the conventional response category paradigm could usefully throw light on this issue.

Verbal responses are no doubt among the most natural categories of response for most humans. But this may not be so for SSN children. Certainly where induced verbal labelling is used as a procedural technique, there are grounds for doubting whether a high level of conceptual mediation is involved (cf. Jeffrey, 1968). Shortage of space precludes an extensive discussion of language in this paper. Attention theory has little positive to say on the subject.

Stimulus Categories

A certain amount of research has been devoted to the comparison of visual with other modes of stimulation in discrimination learning. One attentional learning theorist has even suggested that the salience of 'dimensions', like height and brightness, may be organised hierarchically within 'modalities', like vision and touch (Sutherland and Andelman, 1967). O'Connor and Hermelin (1963) report striking data to the effect that non-mongoloid imbeciles score more highly on stereognostic recognition of unfamiliar shapes than normals of comparable M.A., while the reverse is true when the problem is presented visually. The result has been replicated by Mackay and McMillan (1968). This phenomenon may be related to other features of attentional priorities in discrimination learning by SSN children—the greater discriminability of 3-D than 2-D forms, and the salience of spatial position (Serpell, 1969, 1970 sections 3.ii and 4.iii). There is also some evidence that aetiology is significantly related to the salience of haptic cues, mongoloids performing significantly worse on stereognostic recognition than non-mongoloid imbeciles, and indeed than normal M.A. controls (O'Connor and Hermelin, 1963).

It is thus possible to argue, with greater confidence than in the previous section, that substantial theoretical payoff may be expected with a departure from the traditional emphasis on vision in discrimination learning studies, specifically in work with SSN children. Moreover in this case the type of departure called for is quite closely related to that indicated by educational priorities. On the theoretical side we need to know more about how far the generalisations of attention theory hold good when the mode of stimulation is changed from visual to haptic, while on the practical side there is a need to explore in the haptic medium teaching methods which are less than optimally effective with SSN children using visual materials.

One of the earliest discrimination learning studies for which an attentional explanation was offered used successive as well as simultaneous presentation of the discriminanda (Lawrence, 1949, 1950). Yet, since then, the majority of relevant experiments (particularly with human Ss) have used only simultaneous procedures. One of the stimulus variables which seems to be exceptionally effective in influencing the attention of SSN children is novelty (Serpell, 1969, 1970, sections 3.iv and 4.ii). The exact mode of operation of this factor is interpreted differently by various models, but the evidence suggests that stimulus change is in itself a favourable condition for precipitating changes in behaviour of SSN Ss. Since this contingency is inherent in successive discrimination procedures, it would appear that they offer a good opportunity for exploiting this aspect of SSN children's behaviour. Needless to say, the generality of attention theory would be enhanced by demonstrating the validity or limitations of its conclusions within this less used procedural paradigm.

The small size of the stimuli traditionally used in human discrimination learning studies is probably largely determined by considerations of economy. One cannot but be sceptical of the validity of cross-species comparisons of dimensional hierarchies when the extremes of brightness are presented for rats as the colours of whole areas of a maze, while for children they are confined to a pair of 5 cm. squares. Likewise one may speculate that if the form discriminanda had occupied a similar proportion of the visual field as they did of O'Connor and Hermelin's (op. cit.) Ss' manual grasp, a less striking modality difference might have been observed. This seemingly trivial variable could thus lead one away from a theoretical position concerned with the phylogenetic and ontogenetic priority of different sensory projection areas in the brain to the issue cited above of general sensitivity to variation.

On the practical side, in dealing with Ss for whom, according to Zeaman and House (1967), the essential handicap in learning is attending in the first instance to the relevant dimension, the idea of making visual discriminanda large has obvious attractions. We should not, however, underestimate the theoretical complexity of this variable. In the case of shape discrimination, gross receptor orientation as an additional mediating process increases in significance relative to implicit attending responses as the size of the discriminanda increases, while the opposite is true of brightness. As with the question of modalities, this is a promising area for demonstrating the detailed relevance of attention theory to the practical problem of devising effective methods of teaching.

Irrelevant Stimulus Variation

The paucity of irrelevant stimulus variation in most laboratory learning tasks stands out, perhaps second only to the restricted nature of the response, as an indication of their remoteness from the real world. Here too a consequence of abandoning the traditional paradigm is likely to be a greater emphasis on the importance of receptor orientation. At one stage in the emergence of non-continuity theories of discrimination learning, it became a hotly contested issue whether mediating responses were confined to receptor orientation (cf. Mackintosh, 1965, 142-3). Those who favour the contrary view can perhaps nowadays afford to relax the requirement that appropriate receptor orientation be guaranteed by the stimulus situation, and turn to an examination of the more fruitful questions concerning how this type of mediation interacts with implicit dimensional responses.

A distinction must be drawn between loss of simplicity and loss of control. For instance, with regard to irrelevant stimulus variation, the classroom situation is both more complex and less controlled than the traditional laboratory task. We may consider it useful in an experiment to borrow from the classroom the feature of complexity, in order both to enhance the practical relevance of our results and to gain new theoretical insights into the nature of attention. But to borrow the feature of lack of control would, of course, prohibit reliable interpretation of our results. This is not at all an insuperable difficulty. It involves more work, but not all that much more (cf. Fellows, 1967), to equate the background distraction of a classroom level over Ss and/or conditions, than to equate the sequence of positions for the discriminanda in a standard W.G.T.A. Certainly the problems are not different in kind.

A striking example of unwanted side-effects due to a rigid adherence to the convention of restricting stimulus variation is provided by Brown (1966). Not only in experiments, but also clinically 'in cases of assessment and examination children are generally taken to unfamiliar environments, often by people they do not know. It appears that certain forms of distraction are more likely to set in under such circumstances' (op. cit., 259) than in the apparent chaos of the classroom. It seems likely that unfamiliarity is the critical factor giving rise to the 'global gazing' observed in this and a later study with young, normal children (Brown and Semple, 1970). But remarkably little is known in detail about the price the experimenter pays in terms of emotional disturbance for the often specious simplicity of his laboratory environment. My own feeling is that the tradition of conducting learning experiments with individuals rather than groups is probably worth adhering to, not because it constitutes a 'critical feature' in terms of attention theory, but rather because interaction between Ss in a group task is likely to prove prohibitively complex to analyse theoretically or to control. The value of giving individual attention in the classroom is, moreover, widely accepted by educationalists, however difficult it may be to implement in practice.

Feedback

Probably as a reaction against the excessive emphasis on this parameter by other learning theories, research in the field of attention theory has shown little concern for the effects of various kinds of feedback. Attention theory's greater emphasis on stimulus control will probably be useful in counterbalancing the almost exclusive concern with 'reinforcement' of the currently popular applications of operant techniques. Nevertheless, a simplistic approach to feedback is likely to jar with educationalists who are traditionally much concerned with motivation, and attention theory will doubtless benefit from elaboration in this respect as with types of irrelevant stimulus variation. A promising line of direct theoretical interaction between attention and motivation is Tolman's suggestion that the range of cues attended to is narrowed under high incentive or drive and becomes broader when S is less intensely motivated (Bahrick, 1954; Bruner, Matter and Papanek, 1955).

Interacting Objectives of Research and Education

In discussing some possible changes in incidental features of procedural paradigm, I have tried to show that much of the unintelligibility to educationalists of experimental research in the field of attention theory could be eliminated, not only without loss of theoretical interest or experimental control, but even to the positive advantage of theory itself. The kind of study I have had in mind is one designed to test specific hypotheses derived from attentional learning theory, where the small print under the heading 'Apparatus and procedure' would describe a task meaningfully related to criteria of curriculum development, and methods of instruction geared to the capacity of existing manpower and equipment in schools for SSN children.

In addition to the specific openings of theoretical interest I have described, there is also inherent in this approach an opportunity for revalidation of the experimental psychologist's conception of learning. While it is clear that psychology can afford to be more analytic than education about the process defined as learning, there is room for doubt as to whether the science can afford in the long run to rely exclusively on definitions which are not susceptible to 'translation' into terms meaningful to teachers. As with the concept of intelligence, there is a need for dialogue so that education can refine its methods to take account of experimental results, and psychology can define the relation between the constructs of its models and the broader, philosophical concepts which link the various social and behavioural sciences with one another and with the humanities.

A major assumption of the argument has been that in the definition of experimental method a distinction can be drawn between the guiding principles of research stategy and the detailed tactics of its implementation. The concessions which I have advocated have all been changes of tactics. As regards strategy, a further distinction can be made between methodology and objectives. If research is to lead to scientifically reliable conclusions the stringency of methodology (precise definitions, exact measurement and statistical evaluation) cannot be relaxed. Different objectives may, however, without such relaxation, radically alter the character of research in the field under discussion.

A contrast is drawn conventionally between the objectives of remediation and assessment. But if the criterial task chosen for an 'assessment' study of learning is closely related to the requirements of curriculum it thereby qualifies equally to be classed a 'remediation' study. A distinction which cuts across this sometimes dubious contrast concerns 'what is learned' (or, alternatively, what is taught). The theoretical literature on age and intelligence differences in performance on discrimination learning tasks contains a controversy (discussed by Eimas, 1965, Wolff, 1967 and Serpell, 1969, 1970 section 3.v) on whether these reflect primarily qualitative differences in capacity for mediation (Kendler and Kendler, 1962; Tighe and Tighe, 1966) or quantitative differences in the hierarchy of dimensional preference or cue salience (Zeaman and House, 1967; Jeffrey, 1968). In the second camp it is difficult to avoid the theoretical implication that the hierarchy is always susceptible in particular instances to modification through training. Prolonged discriminative training on a S's non-preferred dimension makes it effectively the most salient cue for that S in the context of that task.

Views differ within the other camp about the nature of mediation and the scope for intervention to improve it in deficient organisms. Clearly a non-verbal organism cannot, on the strong version of the Kendlers' model, be trained to mediate. But perceptual pre-training is seen by the Tighes as making available to young normal children previously undifferentiated component dimensions. It would appear that this type of intervention differs, in the kind of objective it is aimed at, from overtraining on the Zeaman and House model. The Tighes seem to conceive of the change effected as analogous to what Piaget describes as cognitive adaptation, in that the cognitive structure of the organism is reorganised. In educational terms the difference between these objectives is perhaps between attempting to raise the pupil's intellectual level and attempting to impart a particular skill. Attention theory, as opposed to verbal mediation theory and differentiation theory, would seem to have more to say at present about teaching skills than about raising intelligence.

More specifically, the main type of contribution which SSN education can expect from attention theory comprises manipulations of the environment designed to increase the effective salience of non-preferred stimulus dimensions. In the first section of this paper, it was stressed that the category of children we are concerned with is defined primarily by exclusion. From this seems to follow the commonly expressed view that the population in question is heterogeneous. It might appear futile, therefore, to try and generate, from any theory, principles appropriate to the population as a whole. It is interesting in this context to consider a paradox about the nature of attention as defined by currently available models.

Attention is said to be selective: it restricts (at some point along a flow diagram) the ammount of stimulus information processed by the organism. A dimension is a category of stimulus information which can be selected in isolation to pass through this kind of filter. A dimensional preference would thus appear to be a tendency for the filter in the particular organism to give priority to that dimension of stimulation, and conversely to exclude other, less preferred dimensions. But consider an experiment by Shepp and Zeaman (1966). SSN children were presented with a single-dimension, two-choice, visual discrimination problem (either brightness or size) with position irrelevantly variable. The greater the difference between the discriminanda along the critical dimension, the more rapidly did the Ss learn; but this effect was entirely due to decreases in the length of Ss initial phase of responding randomly to the relevant dimension. Inspection of backward learning curves showed that the slope of acquisition once Ss ceased responding at random did not vary with the magnitude of the difference to be discriminated. Theoretically this finding indicates that the magnitude of the difference presented affected the probability of Ss attending to the critical dimension. But in order to be affected in this way the organism logically must process information from a dimension before its behaviour indicates that it is attending to that dimension.

Shepp and Zeaman (1966) meet this problem by postulating 'a search mechanism'. The S may attend to a particular dimension, and, if the cues of that dimension are not very different, attention may be redirected to another dimension before a choice is made. Cue differences of a dimension control the probability of stopping at the dimension'. (op. cit., 59) A different, parallel processing, possibility is suggested in the case of selective listening by Treisman (1966); 'unattended signals are not blocked completely. Instead, the filter only damps them down—attenuates them or makes them in some way less likely to get through'. (op. cit., 110). Mackintosh (1965) speaks more generally of a 'modified non-continuity theory' which states 'simply this: that animals do not classify their stimulus input with equal effectiveness in all possible ways at once, and it should be possible to influence what an animal attends to by appropriate training procedures' (op. cit., 130).

The relevance of this widely agreed position to the doubts raised above about broad applicability to a heterogeneous population is as follows. Even a non-preferred dimension sometimes gets information processed and its effectiveness can be enhanced by using widely different values on it. Therefore the organism's particular hierarchy of dimensional preferences does not necessarily call for individually-tailored shaping before training can begin on a low preference dimension. As Jeffrey (1968) points out, 'flexibility in adult problem-solving behaviour probably reflects hierarchies of both cue-utilisation strategies and cue silence' (op. cit., 324). The possibility of remediation applicable to a whole group is more plausible for cue salience than for strategies, which are more probably of an all-or-none nature. If it is true that 'a hierarchy of cue salience is more fundamental' (op. cit., 324), valuable educational returns may be expected from experiments (with SSN children as Ss and task procedures relevant to a socially desirable curriculum) designed to reveal other more radical ways of enhancing the salience of critical dimensions. From my own reading of the literature, the most profitable lines of enquiry will involve exploiting susceptibility to stimulus change, to familiar compounds of several dimensions, and to haptic cues, in establishing preliminary stimulus control, followed by gradual fading into the criterion task.

ACKNOWLEDGEMENTS

I wish to thank Mr. Cliff Cunningham, Dr. James Hogg and Dr. Peter Mittler for their constructive criticism of an earlier draft. Such errors and obscurities as remain are, of course, due only to me.

REFERENCES

Bahrick, H. P. (1954). Incidental learning under two incentive conditions. *J. exp. Psychol.* **47**, 170.

Brown, R. I. (1966). The effects of varied environmental stimulation on the performance of subnormal children. *J. Child Psychol. Psychiat.* **7**, 251.

Brown, R. I. and Semple, L. (1970). Effects of information on the overt verbalization and perceptual motor behaviour of nursery school children. *Brit. J. Educ. Psychol.* **40**, 291.

Baumeister, A. A. (1967). In 'Mental Retardation: Appraisal, Education and Rehabilitation' (ed. A. A. Baumeister), (Chapter 8), 181. London: University Press.

Bruner, J. S., Matter, J. and Papanek, M. L. (1955). Breadth of learning as a function of drive level and mechanization. *Psychol. Rev.* **62**, 1.

Eimas, P. D. (1965). Comment: comparison of reversal and nonreversal shifts. *Psychon. Sci.* **3**, 445.

Fellows, B. J. (1967). Chance stimulus sequences for discrimination tasks. *Psychol. Bull.* **67**, 87.

House, B. J. (1964). The effects of distinctive responses and discrimination reversals in retardates. *Amer. J. ment. Defic.* **69**, 79.

Jeffrey, W. E. (1968). The orienting reflex and attention in cognitive development. *Psychol. Rev.* **75**, 323.

Kendler, H. H. and Kendler, T. S. (1962). Vertical and horizontal processes in problem solving. *Psychol Rev.* **69**, 1.

Katahn, M. and Koplin, J. H. (1968). Paradigm clash: comment on some recent criticisms of behavorism and learning theory with special reference to Breger & McGaugh and to Chomsky. *Psychol. Bull.* **69**, 147.

Lawrence, D. H. (1949). Acquired distinctiveness of cues: I. Transfer between discriminations on the basis of familiarity with the stimulus. *J. exp. Psychol.* **39**, 770.

Lawrence, D. H. (1950). Acquired distinctiveness of cues: II. Selective association in a constant stimulus situation. *J. exp. Psychol.* **40**, 175.

Mackay, C. K. and Macmillan, J. (1968). A comparison of stereognostic recognition in normal children and severely subnormal adults. *Brit. J. Psychol.* **59**, 443.

Mackintosh, N. J. (1965). Selective attention in animal discrimination learning. *Psychol. Bull.* **64**, 124.

McConnell, O. L. (1964). Perceptual versus verbal mediation in the concept learning of children. *Child Developm.* **35**, 1373.

O'Connor, N. and Hermelin, B. (1963). 'Speech and Though in Severe Subnormality'. London: Pergamon.

Otteson, M. I., Sheridan, C. L. and Meyer, D. R. (1962). Effects of stimulus-response isolation on primate pattern discrimination learning. *J. comp. physiol. Psychol.* **55**, 935.

Serpell, R. (1969). Selective attention in children: a study with special reference to Zambia. Unpublished D. Phil. Thesis, University of Sussex, Chapter I.

Serpell, R. (1970). Selective attention: a mediating process in discrimination learning by children. *Human Development Research Unit Reports,* 14, University of Zambia, Lusaka: cyclostyled.

Shepp, B. and Zeaman, D. (1966). Discrimination learning of size and brightness by retardates. *J. comp. physiol. Psychol.* **62**, 55.

Sutherland, N. S. and Andelman, L. (1967). Learning with one and two cues. *Psychon. Sci.* **7**, 107.

Tighe, L. S. and Tighe. T. J. (1966). Discrimination learning: two views in historical perspective. *Psychol. Bull.* **66**, 353.

Treisman, A. (1966). Human attention. In 'New Horizons in Psychology' (ed. B. M. Foss), Chapter 4, p. 97. Harmondsworth: Penguin.

Wolff, J. L. (1967). Concept-shift and discrimination-reversal learning in humans. *Psychol. Bull.* **68**, 369.

Zeaman, D. and House, B. J. (1967). The relation of I.Q. and learning. In 'Learning and Individual Differences' (ed. R. M. Gagne), p. 192. Columbus: Merrill.

SESSION FIVE
DISCUSSION

Chairman: Mrs. Gail Hawks

Chairman: It is clearly a main function of a Study Group like this to encourage attempts to develop practical applications in other fields of fundamental research. While completely agreeing about the need for immediate application of all relevant research findings, especially to the educational training of subnormal children at this particular time, it is clearly also necessary to encourage research activities which show promise of producing applicable results in the longer term. This Study Group is a more direct channel of communication than the usual ones we have to deal with. The normal channels are particularly diffuse and unreliable in conveying information from theoretical research sources down to the practical applications and maybe we can extend our ideas on how to improve these. Dr. Herriot's paper on psychological models, and the application of these to practical problems in mental subnormality, indicates how the use of these might prove to be of value in subnormality research of a descriptive nature, and also in remediation. Various points for discussion arise from it, some theoretical and some particularly relevant to the activities of educational and clinical psychologists, especially in remediation, and also in the assessment of patterns of intellectual functioning in the individuals. Clearly our functions in assessment have to change a great deal at this time but I think these will extend rather than be reduced. Assessment will have a broader scope, and it will need to be of a more continuous nature and in line with the educational system as it is now. Dr. Mittler has already pointed out that in this connection we shall probably need to involve teachers and this would seem to be a very valuable approach. Appropriate theoretical bases for assessment would be a great help in assessing the functioning of the subnormal, if these models were available. As it is, assessment is rather a haphazard procedure on occasion. In the remediation areas specifically, for instance, in the application of operant techniques, the use of models might allow us to decide on priorities for attention and so make for greater efficiency of operation. It might be possible to predict which stimulus situations and reinforcement techniques could be most appropriately used to facilitate specific types of response categories. This is also very much awaiting the model or models which might be appropriate. I find it rather difficult myself to conceptualise the sort of form models of this nature will take, theoretical formulations which would allow such variety of application; we will clearly be needing rather more computers than we have at the moment, won't we? I also wonder about the type of model mentioned, the temporal process model, which I don't know very much about, and whether there are any alternative forms which might be applicable in these practical areas. This analysis of the possible use of theoretical formulations in model form rests on various assumptions, however, which I do feel we should examine in this discussion. Previous contributors have already critised matching in terms of chronological and mental age and Dr. Herriot has now extended this. Clearly from this it follows that the way we now discover deficiencies in functioning in the subnormal is quite often on a rather shaky methodological basis. Can we really visualise, however, that using certain theoretical formulations, psychological models will enable us to do this more appropriately? Will we indeed be able to construct sufficiently complex systems to begin to hope to do this at all, and with systems with sufficient flexibility, to account for the inter- and intra-individual variation which has been so widely emphasised? I should like to throw this open for general discussion.

Cave: Might I ask a naive question? I would feel more confident to enter the discussion if I could have the word 'model' defined for me.

Herriot: A model is theory in the sense that I'm using it. It's a description of a process, the description being based on experimental results. It doesn't necessarily have to be a model of a temporal sequence of events but the specific one I've been talking about in the paper, is one that expresses a process in terms of how it begins, how it carries on and how it finishes. The process supposed is, of course, the process in the brain and the temporal sequence is (in parts of the process anyway), extraordinarily rapid, but it nevertheless seems possible to talk now in terms of models, at least in some areas of psychology. Because so much work has been done on these problems, models of normal functioning are available and are generally agreed on in some areas as being adequate. When one has a model, I think that benefits are considerable because one isn't saying that everybody should follow the model in the same way, one is saying that here is a model, a generalised model, of the sort of processes that occur; people may differ at different points in the process because different events are occurring at different stages within it. Variance to me isn't that much of a problem because if I find that an independent variable, for example, the time manipulated on experiments, has an effect despite considerable individual variation, I'm very pleased, because it shows that the effect that I've produced by manipulating the independent variable has a reliable influence over a wide variety of subjects. Obviously one is then left with the problem of accounting for the variance. This opens the way for further experiments.

Chairman: In using the model to identify defects in individuals, would it not still need to be very flexible to account for the possible variance in individuals? Could you explain it in terms of the model?

Herriot: I think, of course, that nobody actually works with the sort of model that experimental psychologists aim at providing. People work with their own models and incoporate into these materials from a great number of different sources. The point I made at the end was that such models should be made explicit, whatever they are, and all the experimental psychologist hopes to provide is simply something that practitioners might care to incorporate into their own model.

Ryan: I would like to make three points. First, I wonder if we could clarify the distinction between systems and sub-systems? While I absolutely agree with your criticism of developmental lag versus defect theories, I don't really see what advantage your distinction between systems and sub-systems has. And you go further and say, quite rightly I think, that it's always possible that both these sorts of explanations could be appropriate in any one case. But we know of the dangers of multiplying explanations in any one instance and of over-determining the situation. That really leads on to another point which you said, namely, that there is always an implicit comparison involved with something or other. The implication is that what we must do is just to describe subnormal functioning in itself and compare it with normal functioning. I agree with this. You said we are still implicitly comparing the behaviour of subnormals with something else. I wasn't quite clear whether you were implying that we compared the behaviour of a group of subnormals with some task we had decided it was a good thing to investigate and if so, how do you choose that task as a basis for saying there's a defect in a particular system or sub-system? Already you are only referring to treatment paradigms or not, and that really leads to another point which is, you say at the end of your paper, that you don't see what's wrong with trying to generalise about subnormal behaviour, about a group of subnormals. You don't actually see the danger in what you said, which is that it would prohibit you from working much more closely to individuals; that's to say, if you are just looking at subnormal functioning, I don't see why you should have several different models for different sub-groups of subnormals when you've been trying to generalise about subnormal behaviour as a whole, because this has in a sense been what you were saying.

My last point is really a criticism of both the kind of model you are putting forward and also of most psychological work, which is that it is a very static kind of model. I think this is a bit curious because after all, subnormality is primarily developmental and it seems to me we need descriptions of subnormal behaviour in more developmental terms.

Herriot: Experimental psychologists can't do everything. I am trying to investigate memory function. This is largely a cognitive phenomenon. I'm not saying that the sort of model that I'm proposing is a model that deals with all subnormal functioning. I'm just saying that here is one which describes a certain area of functioning, which we can call information processing. The first point concerns the difference between systems and sub-systems. The reason I made the distinction was that when one has a model of subnormal functioning one may well be concerned to find out why it produces the behaviour that it does, what particular parts of it are responsible for the end behaviour being perhaps not of the quantity that you might expect, of the quality that you might expect. Now such explanations are not possible if you distinguish, or if you place in contradistinction, developmental and defect theories. They are only possible if you are prepared to look at systems as a whole and then parts of the system and then admit that there may be facets of both of them, aspects of both of them, that are determining behaviour at the same time. That's why it's important that both of them should be looked at. Of course, this increases explanatory power, that's why I'm suggesting it. If you look at most of the theories of subnormal function, they stress one defect. People have spent their lives discovering one defect and they then try to explain overall malfunctioning in terms of that defect whenever they can. Alternatively, people say 'well, the person is at the mental age of five and because of the way children function at the mental age of five, that's why the subnormal person functions the way he does'. Both explanations are impoverished because they exclude the possibility of the other.

Your second point concerns what you say about description involving a model and I think I was concerned to state that any form of observation or remediation, or any activity concerned with the subnormal involves a model in the head of the person who is dealing with them. They contain certain assumptions which they may or may not have made explicit.

Your third point concerned the generalisation aspect, and you said that it would be important to discover not necessarily models of subnormal functioning overall but models of sub-categories of subnormal functioning. Agreed, and that would follow from investigating the variances that are involved in experiments on subnormals as a whole population. However, I've done such experiments separating, for example, mongols from others and I found that in one experiment the variance among the mongols was significantly greater than the variance among all the non-mongols together, so I think perhaps variables such as excitatory versus inhibitory aspects of personality functioning, such as James Hogg is investigating at Hester Adrian Centre, may well prove useful here in discovering just what the variance may be due to.

Lastly, you said that this wasn't a developmental theory. Well, precisely not, because that's making the assumption that the subnormal is developmentally retarded.

Ryan: I'd just like to come back on two points. You keep on referring to the behaviour that's not of the kind one might expect. I'm afraid I'm still not very clear by what you mean by that. The very last thing you said was that to think of developmental theory is to assume that the subnormal is developmentally retarded.

Herriot: If you have a model, then you expect that the model will be able to do such-and-such. If this is a model of subnormal functioning that one has, then one says 'well, this looks pretty efficient but it's not producing quite what one might expect given the nature of the model'. Look closely, therefore, at its sub-part to see why it's not producing what one might expect from it. So that's the origin of my expectations.

Kiernan: The whole point which Dr. Herriot makes, and which has come up a couple of times in this discussion, is that whatever approach one takes to the behaviour of subnormals or normals for that matter, you always have a model. In his discussion, or in his answer to Mr. Cave's question about what a model was, it seems to me that he didn't emphasise one point which I would have thought was worth emphasising, and that is that many of the models which we carry around are rational constructs. Many, however, are irrational constructs and contain massive inconsistencies. At one stage, we make one prediction from one part of implicit models that we've got and at another stage we make a direct contrary prediction. One function of the type of operation involved in making a model explicit is to try and throw up these inconsistencies so that they can be ironed out and experimented upon. Having said that, I think there's another point: I am not sure that Dr. Herriot is going in the same direction as I would feel appropriate. The value of any theory in psychology or any other subject is the use to which it can be put. Immediately that comes up, you've got to ask 'useful for what?' In the area of subnormality, and in particular in a discussion of the type we have been having the last couple of days, this question is obviously paramount. At two extremes, I think that one can say that a model may be useful for organising data derived from experiments conducted in the laboratory and that this model may be of the nature of a crossword puzzle or some interesting game which is given to rather intellectual people in order to occupy their time. Now this sounds very unpleasant, but I put it like this in order to point to the extreme. The difference between the experimental approach and real-life approach is that in the laboratory situation you can 'control out' and *do* 'control out' many of the variables, which in the real-life situation, control behaviour. So you can, because of this, end up demonstrating the influence in your laboratory situation of variables which may be compensated for very adequately in the real-life situation. Now the example which comes to mind is this one of the all-figure telephone numbers where the finest flower of British short-term memory research could have predicted, did predict I'm sure, that the all-figure telephone number would provide considerable human problems because a lot of research has demonstrated that—well we already know what the research has already demonstrated. I don't know of any survey, but I would suspect very strongly that the response of most people to the all-figure telephone number was to develop almost immediately compensatory mechanisms like, for instance, writing it down on a piece of paper, and so on. Now in this case, I think the question arises as to whether or not the mass of distinguished research from the APU and all the other distinguished centres in this country was really worthwhile in any meaningful sense outside of the crossword puzzle system. At the other extreme, you've got the strict practical situation, and here again I think there's an important point to be drawn from Dr. Herriot's paper, particularly related to the idea that you always carry around a model with you. To my mind, an important problem is that much assessment seems to be assessment without a clear idea of where the assessment is leading to and that in many cases, what is measured in the assessment procedure, is behaviour which is a correlate of a behaviour which reflects some fundamental defect, if you like. Again, I think the close instance of this would be the consequences which one might feel able to draw from an I.Q. test. If you do an I.Q. test, you'll find that the child fails on this, that and the other item. I don't think there are many people who would seriously argue 'well the thing to do now is to train that child to do those items' because the nature of the I.Q. test is that it produces correlates of what we see as the capacities of the child and the incapacities, rather than reflecting the real processes. On the other hand, let us take a developmental theory and assume that you've got some sort of programme built on that. The theory is such that it ought to argue that if you train a child to get through such a stage of development, that it ought to change its behaviour. So you've got a much stronger prediction but what is often apparent is that people don't come down one side or the other, they won't commit themselves and say 'my theory, my model, is a strong model' or 'my model is a weak one' and if this were done, I think it would create a better situation.

Kiernan: Well, I feel myself bound by my past history to strike a blow for the operant analysis of behaviour. Skinner, way back in 1950, pointed out that models often closed options, rather than keeping options open, that models often blinkered people who carried them around with them to such an extent that they produced ameliorative programmes which, when they were unsuccessful, caused them to say 'right, nothing can be done'. Dr. Herriot's point is that, if your model is complex enough, you keep your options open for a long time. This is an interesting point, but I would ask him whether or not, given that you've got such a complex model, you can really handle it adequately, whether you can conceptualise the situation clearly enough to allow you to use a complex model and whether it wouldn't be better in many cases to take up the type of line which Dr. and Professor Clarke mentioned in their paper, of investigating much more thoroughly the independent variables in the situation and trying to see whether the rational analysis which you have taken to the laboratory is not one which has missed out on important variables which need to be brought in and also explain the behaviour.

A. M. Clarke: There are two points I would like to make. One is that I so completely agree with Dr. Herriot, in fact, I would go further and say that I don't think it is possible for anybody to do any experimental research, or indeed any other kind of research, without a model. I think it's important, as has been said, that the model should be explicitly stated in order to iron out the inconsistencies. However, (I'm going to announce a truism, now, but I think it's an important one) the careful scientist exercises systematic doubt, not only about other people's work but also about his own. He is aware always that the model he has built is probably too simple, too crude, and is leaving out a number of variables, and he is therefore aware that his model is not just possibly going to have to change, but is almost certainly going to have to change, in the light of incoming information from colleagues and in the light of his own developmental process, as he refines his techniques and gets in more data. One of the fascinating things, to my mind, about work in the field of mental subnormality, is precisely this question of the variation, not just within the population but within the behaviour of any single individual you have been studying over a period of time which makes it highly unlikely that you are going to have some kind of a static model which is inflexible and unchangeable. This is an important point to remember in thinking about the models and the hypotheses that one has, the hypotheses, for example, that one erects about the strategies that a subnormal or indeed young normal children whom I've been studying, may be using in a given situation.

Chairman: May we now turn to Dr. Serpell's paper? I don't want to say very much at the moment because there seem to be so many very interesting possible practical applications of this area in terms of Dr. Serpell's formulation, I should just like to raise the question of its application to two particular problem groups of retarded children as I see it, in my field of work, the physically and mentally handicapped who have to be educated within the new system as well as ordinary mentally retarded children. This more individually-tailored approach appears to have much of the possible relevance here. The other group is the group of children, usually within large institutions, who don't have any sort of preferred dimension to external stimuli, who are more-or-less inaccessible at the moment to stimulation, how are we to approach them, the profoundly retarded, who have not previously had any training? I know that this is explainable in many formulations of past reinforcement and other approaches but it may be that this area can offer quite interesting applications for these children. Any comments?

Serpell: I wonder if I could take up your question of profoundly retarded children? I have no experience of working with them as yet and I can only make a general theoretical point. It does appear from the literature that in almost all imbeciles, and I take it profoundly retarded children are not an exception, there is a reaction of some sort to intense novelty or to intense change and this, as I say, is one of the techniques which seems to arise from attention theory for beginning to get an interest in stimulation. I'm sure this is already used in the clinical approach to the profoundly retarded; sometimes I clap my hands to get some reaction; the idea which one would like to see developed is to combine this in some way with a variable which is of relevance to a task which you would like the child to learn, the sort of very limited task which Mr. Cunningham spells out in the end of his paper, some elementary focusing on stimuli and then, to use the traditional fading procedure, having once established some sort of effective stimulus.

Carr: Perhaps I could just expand on that a little. In Hilda Lewis House, we get some very profoundly retarded children indeed and our problem has been not only to get them to attend to some stimulus, but in fact to find some channel which is rewarding to these children at all. The usual reward with retarded children is some sort of food but we've come across a good many children to whom no food is rewarding and in fact it can be actively unpleasant, so that's another channel that is closed. We have also had several children where it seems almost impossible to do anything whatever for them because there appears to be nothing that they find pleasurable, all they want is to be left alone. There is another characteristic, that if you disturb their vague, passive or even self-mutilating situation, this will be seen as so unpleasant, it's very difficult to find something that will be rewarding. However, what I really want to say is that we've never yet failed to find something eventually and sometimes it can be quite bizarre. One of the more normal ones that we've used extensively is music, and we have three children who were in fact able to respond to commands and to learn command training, using music as a reward, sometimes the music would be gramophones which we had to put on and were very clumsy and time-consuming, but nevertheless it worked and even sometimes we could even make them respond and apparently enjoy our own singing and so it hasn't yet proved impossible, although it does very often look as though it's going to be.

Mittler: Can I just make a parallel here between work with the kind of child we are talking about now and such information as we've got from experimental psychological studies of the newborn baby. I think here there are parallels with attention theory which have not been developed because most of the experiments haven't really been done within that kind of framework, but the point arising from this is that one reason why it's taken so long to make certain types of discovery about newborn babies and their quite extraordinary capacities, is that we've lacked the technology to ask the right questions and to induce them to behave. This is also true I think of the profoundly retarded child with whom very few people have worked, but it appears that when you can produce some channel of communication, that the newborn baby, some two or three days old, is capable of extraordinary complex discriminations both in the visual and auditory field. In the auditory field, I am thinking of work which is summarised and partly carried out by Friedlander who shows that the newborn baby can, in fact, be given a choice between listening to different types of stimulations and in some very crude way can be induced to express choice for say high tones versus low tones, the mother's voice versus somebody else's voice and so on, and this sort of work has been going on with babies up to twelve months. We have here to battle with the same stereotype about the normal baby that we have to deal with when thinking of the profoundly retarded child that in some sense these are inert, passive organisms. There is an old medical stereotype that for all practical purposes the newborn baby is functionally blind and deaf for the first days and sometimes even weeks. Well, I think it's absolutely clear now from research done in the last ten years that this is not so, we have yet to discover what the response repertoire of the neonate is. There are very few children who are so profoundly retarded that they are below the developmental level of a baby say of two or three months old, or even one week old, so in a sense, I feel fairly optimistic because while, as I said earlier, attention theory has not been invoked directly to look at newborns, there is a wealth of experimental material on salience which is one aspect, if not the whole story, which can be used, but a lot of this work does involve complicated apparatus.

Dybwad: With regard to Dr. Carr's remark, I would like to make reference again to the danger here in the use of the term profoundly retarded. I wonder, and I think some research has gone on a long time, to give substance to this query, to what extent we are often dealing with severely mentally ill children who are referred to us because psychiatrists just don't know what to do with them and who then get marked as retarded? In a 1954 study of a psychotic child who had been just rescued at the New York Psychiatric Institute at the last moment before being deported to an institution for the mentally retarded, it seemed the child would have behaved as a profoundly retarded child and it was discovered that this three or four-year-old girl, who had undergone a profound emotional shock, which had closed up everything, she was inaccessible to food, tube-fed and so on. But it was a reaction, you see, where she did not respond because she withheld response and so I think we do have this problem which doesn't again clear the problem of finding the proper proportion of mentally retarded, but some of our research findings are obscured by the fact we are trying to find an answer to a mechanism of mental defect when in fact we are dealing with a profoundly mentally ill or emotionally disturbed child.

Cookson: I would endorse this. I think Dr. Mittler has made this point that it is useful to use the behaviour that we are learning about concerning the newborn infant as a basis for helping to develop, to make contact with, to stimulate, this type of extremely withdrawn and unresponsive child. I would also like to say that I think the position with many of these children is worse than that of a new baby, partly because of the defects that we've already mentioned may be apparent, that he may in fact be technically blind, or deaf, or something of this kind, that he may be unable to perceive for example movement, or something in this way which would naturally stimulate a normal baby of a day or two. But apart from this, he has become inaccessible as you've already said, Madame Chairman, because of possibly of years of failure to get stimulation from his environment and failure on his own part to be able to respond in any way and so perhaps he resorts to this somewhat inert behaviour, possibly to self-damage, but this has been in a sense an adaptive thing and it's made him a greater problem for dealing with than a child with the capacities even of a two-day old baby.

A. M. Clarke: May I change the subject a bit? I believe that Dr. Serpell has made an extremely important summary of what I believe to be an extremely important area of experimental evidence and theory. I would like, however, to question, but may I say very sympathetically, the statement which he makes when he says: 'my own feeling is that the tradition of conducting learning experiments with individuals rather than groups is probably worth adhering to, not because it constitutes a critical feature in terms of attention theory but rather because interaction between subjects and a group task is likely to prove prohibitively complex to analyse theoretically or to control.' Now my deep fellow feeling with Dr. Serpell is there in that last statement. Having attempted myself to conduct discrimination experiments and look into hypotheses of attention to dimensions of tasks and the strategies which are being employed both by the subnormal and young normal child, I am entirely sympathetic with what he says. However, recently I have attempted myself to switch strategy a little bit for two reasons. Firstly, I have become very sensitive to the problem which often comes out in discussions with my teacher colleagues. It is all very well for you to know what to do with an individual child in a quiet room all alone, but you come in and try doing it in a classroom. A classroom is a group situation even in Dr. Mittler's Utopian classroom, which is ours as well. You may have a one-to-one situation with an individual child, but in the meanwhile, if we are not going to continue with the situation which is general uncontrolled activity, with, as he put it, the elaborated code being used by the teacher, we will have to address ourselves, whether it's complex to analyse and difficult to control or not, to the problem of how we control behaviour in group situations. I would like to ask Dr. Serpell whether he really doesn't feel that the time is ripe now to explore ways of conducting first of all, controlled psychological experiments outside the classroom with groups, and at least have the stimulus input in a group situation? Have you considered this, have you thought about it? Even if you then take the response individually and analyse it. The practical problem is the one that the teacher faces, you know, lots of children, (it's no good us saying we know all about how to handle one child) and the second thing is that in fact human beings are rather rarely alone, and so there is the matter of theoretical importance. We need to know in what way, if any, does perception, selective perception, change from the individual situation to the group. I don't know whether it does or not, but should the question not be raised?

Serpell: Dr. Clarke is positing a particular dimension of difference between the traditional individual laboratory study and the classroom situation where you have a group of children, and suggesting that, in order to make a systematic transition from the information which is fairly reliable in the laboratory situation to the very difficult situation in the classroom, what we should do is take the group out of the classroom and put it in the laboratory where she supposes that we can control it better. My feeling is that possibly the laboratory strategy is better, and that in fact we should take the well-established methods of control in the laboratory situation with the individual child into the classroom. Indeed I do quote in the same paragraph a study by Brown in which he did this and found that the effect of emotional shock at being taken into an unfamiliar laboratory—this is probably what the effect was—was so powerful that it was no less effective to be doing the experiment under all the distracting conditions of the classroom with an individual child than it was to take him out into the lab. Since we can get reliable results in the lab. even with that difficulty, it seems to me there's a good case for putting up with the practical difficulties of taking a child into the corner of the classroom. I'm not even sure that I agree with Dr. Mittler that we have to have a separate quiet room off the classroom, I certainly think we ought to have two teachers, one who controls the group and one who controls the individuals. Secondly, I do go along with this bit which you pick out, and I'm glad you did pick it out, it's very controversial, the point that the value of giving

individual attention in the classroom is widely accepted by educationists. The teacher does after all accept in the normal classroom
situation that she's got a heterogeneous group of children. It's not
enough just to stand there at the front and expect them all to listen, she
has to pick out individual children and say 'Johnny, what's the point of
that I've just said?' or 'Jimmy, can you do this?' and presumably she's
going to put the question somewhat differently to the different
children because she knows them and frames the question at their
individual level of understanding. I see this, and the shift from that
situation to actually removing the child into the corner of the room
advocated by Dr. Mittler, and I agree, for the subnormal child, as the
sort of qualitative difference in educational methodology which at this
stage it ought to be obvious that we have to adopt. If I may, I would
like to broaden this point to include a question which Mr. Cave put
yesterday: 'does the research on basic processes indicate that the
severely subnormal is qualitatively or only quantitively different from
the normal child?' I think there is a curious difference in the answer
one has to make, according to what we were talking about here. All the
theoretical psychology on the process of learning that I've read seems
to move towards the position that the differences are quantitative
rather than qualitative. I have indicated in my paper that there are two
outstanding groups of research workers, who believe otherwise and they
have some support, but on the whole, I think the balance of the
evidence is in favour of the quantitative difference in particular
processes. But, this evidence is only made possible by a fine grade
analysis of the kind which Dr. Herriot has shown can be done with a
complex model. What is quantitatively different is a particular
component in a very complex system, namely, for instance, in this
particular theory, the hierarchy of dimensional salience. Now, first of
all, we have to have a model which postulated dimensions and
hierarchies at all, and having got that organisation of the information,
then it's possible to see that the differences were quantitative, not
qualitative. The second point which is curious is that, in spite of the
fact that the differences are quantitative, I think they call for
qualitative differences in teaching methods.
Carr: I think that's very important.
Serpell: Well, I hope this paper does show how psychologists can begin
to demonstrate in an acceptable way to teachers that they have got
qualitatively different methods which are derived from the laboratory
and which could be really useful to teachers in the classroom situation,
not I think in the group situation, but I would be willing to accept that
research could show me to be wrong.
A. M. Clarke: Well, I'm just wondering whether we ought to try it, as

experimental psychologists, to see if it's a rather more sympathetic way than we have done in the past, try to have some new thinking on experiments. You see, I'm not just calling for practical applications of findings, I'm thinking in terms of new experimental techniques which incorporate groups of subjects, rather than individual subjects, because I'm not sure that one might not have to modify the theory a bit, or extend it to incorporate findings in this situation, and I had hoped that you might have considered this as a possibility.

Serpell: If I could come back briefly on that last point of how the theory considered this, I think that Dr. Ryan was questioning just now the value of the sort of models which Dr. Herriot has been advocating on the ground that it is too rigid. I have a feeling that there is a misconception here about the function of models; I didn't altogether agree with some of the statements made about them. It seems to me that one of the qualities of a model is the fact that it is rather rigid, it is a way of making rigid what sounds very flexible until we try and build a model. One of the values of model building is to find out whether one is guilty of slovenly thinking or not. Another purpose is to define different areas of behaviour. It seems to me that the answer, if a model leaves lots and lots of variance in your data, is not that this model must be more flexible but rather that we've got to have other explanations for other components of behaviour. If we start making our models flexible, then I don't think they are any use as models. I would like to stick to attention theory in a fairly rigid form because it's a very small theory; I can look beyond my blinkers at lots of other issues like motivation and see that we need to have models of that as well, which will explain whole ranges of variation which are not within the scope of attention theory. Likewise group behaviour, I'm sure that theories of group behaviour will, in the long term, be necessary for complete explanation of the classroom situation. I doubt if they will have much to do with attention theory as such.

Carr: Back to Dr. Clarke's point, isn't it possible that the models you are using in attention theory which, as Dr. Kiernan says, are basically useful in organising experiments, would be different if your experimental evidence was taken in a group situation? The model would have to be different to explain the data you were getting; for instance, the sort of non-preferred dimensions of attention that you are talking about might be actually different in an interactive situation.

Serpell: We could get into a theoretical discussion but I think that would be wrong. I think there's a very good case for believing that it's not so. We are talking about the relation between somebody's eyes and a piece of paper and I doubt that the question of a group context is relevant.

A. M. Clarke: So what you are really saying is that attention is always an individual matter, it's a question of the interaction between the stimulus and the individual. Well, this was the thought that occurred to me, but I wondered if I had missed something.

Carr: I still think it's worth saying that the actual structure of the situation can affect the sort of relation between the eyes and a piece of paper.

Cookson: I, also, was a bit surprised that you excluded motivation at that point from your consideration because this seemed to be extremely relevant. It seems to me that a particular piece of apparatus that we may wish a child to attend to at a given moment may attract a child because in itself it is bright, it is moving, perhaps it is novel. It may attract because it appeals to that child in a very individual way, because, for example, it happens to be making 'ding-dong' sounds and he happens to be particularly attracted by music. It may appeal to him not in itself at all, but because he's desperately anxious to please the person who is presenting it to him and that in some way he looks at the face and watches the cue and then correspondingly looks at this thing and makes some sort of relationship with it because of the way in which the whole thing is structured.

Cave: The past half-hour for me has been very instructive, although I still think there is a case for a plain man's guide to models. May I say that the best teachers are constantly formulating a particular method to fit the needs of a particular child and they should (I think the best of them do) proceed to assess what kind of effect it has. This seems to be fundamentally the same kind of procedure as that used by the theoretical worker and I'm just wondering why we don't utilise teachers' observations rather more, in other words, what I'm really saying is that when we have an investigation of a particular area which can be formulated by a psychologist about the experimental situation, why don't we, a little more often, involve those who are actually doing the practical work? I think this could invoke the kind of partnership Dr. Serpell was referring to, and which I see as absolutely essential if you are going to get teachers to use their insights to contribute to an accurate process of investigating children's functions. I believe we are looking at this altogether in too abstract a way and we are not involving those who have a very considerable contribution to make.

Serpell: If I might answer that point, two other techniques have been suggested for reconciliation other than the one which I have been talking about, one by Dr. Gunzburg about involvement of the psychologist in decision-taking, in particular in manipulating institutional environments, and the other by yourself, involvement of teachers as partners in research and innovation. I admire both these suggestions and welcome also the idea that research workers should observe first-hand the problems encountered by teachers who are trying in good faith to implement suggestions arising from the research workers' research. All these seem to be very constructive ideas. I am firmly convinced that, if they are pursued vigorously, research can and will yield valuable alternatives to the intuitive approach. To me, Mr. Cunningham's paper stops short of the major area in which the psychology of learning can contribute to education. He has defined on grounds of educational philosophy (a moral philosophy), the goals of education. The means of achieving those goals, particularly in the case of children in SSN schools, is a very difficult technical question to which scientific research is more appropriate than intuition.

Session VI

Learning in the Young Mentally Handicapped Child

The Teaching of Language

P. MITTLER

*Hester Adrian Research Centre for the Study
of Learning Processes in the Mentally Handicapped
University of Manchester*

The gap between research and practice is particularly wide in the sphere of language. This is at once surprising and unfortunate, since language is inseparable from cognitive development, and since language difficulties are almost invariably found in the mentally handicapped. Ironically enough, there has been a rapid growth of research into language in the last twenty years, but this is largely dominated by theoretical considerations, just as earlier work was essentially normative in character. Educationalists have not on the whole initiated a great deal of research themselves, nor been quick to translate the implications of the published research into practice. The purpose of this paper is to indicate a number of ways in which the gap between research and practice might be bridged. In particular, it seems worth while at least to suggest certain frames of reference which might be useful. These will include normative studies and developmental theory, as well as models derived from psychology and linguistics.

Normative Studies

Although normative studies belong to an earlier tradition of child psychology, their potential practical contribution to education should not be ignored. They have become discredited partly because standardised normative tests have been used for educational placement and classification only, and were not seen by teachers or parents as contributing in any direct way to the planning of a programme of education. Criticism has also been directed at normative tests because they failed to provide either the psychologist or the teacher with a detailed profile of a child's relative assets and deficits, and confined themselves to a global estimate of intellectual level in relation to a standard population. It is indeed a curious paradox that the educational and clinical psychologist who claims to be primarily interested in the individual child or patient should have come until recently to place such reliance on instruments which reliably and validly do little more than compare that individual with the general population.

But the value of normative data should not be underestimated. This has provided a wealth of detailed, factual and reliable knowledge on many aspects of development. We know a good deal about the sequence or stages of development, and the characteristics of each stage. It seems reasonable to suppose that the sequence is similar for normal and subnormal children, even though individual discontinuities and distortions will occur. Inhelder (1968) for example has shown that retarded children follow the same sequence of development in respect of Piaget's stages of cognitive development as normal children and there is some evidence that this is also true of language development (Lenneberg, 1967, Mittler, 1972, 1973).

Nevertheless, suprisingly little has been done to apply and exploit developmental norms in an educational setting. Teachers and above all parents could be shown how to help the child towards the next stage of development by structuring play materials, toys, games and activities in the light of a detailed assessment of the stage which their child has reached in different areas of development. This does not necessarily involve specialised assessment by skilled psychologists using time-consuming and recondite tests. Although such assessments would be valuable (if they led to therapeutic intervention) parents and teachers can be helped under guidance to make their own developmental profiles.

Some preliminary work of this kind has recently been attempted in Manchester by members of HARC staff, in conjuction with the North West Society for Mentally Handicapped Children (Cunningham and Jeffree, 1971). The aim of the project was to see if parents of young SSN children could carry out a series of observations and assessments of their own child, and then to plan for the provision of learning and play experiences which might help him to progress to the next stage of development. The workshops were not intended as a research project, but simply as an exploratory service and a learning experience for all concerned. About 100 parents of preschool SSN children took part, and were generally divided into 'working groups' of ten parents. The workshops were run one evening a week for 12 weeks, and a few follow-up sessions were also held.

Detailed child development charts were drawn up, mostly based on items from the better known scales, such as Cattell, Griffiths, Bayley, Denver etc. Items requiring apparatus or specialised testing were eliminated, leaving only those which could be assessed by observations over a period of time. The charts were divided into areas dealing with physical skills (head, legs, arms and hands, general bodily movements), performance (mainly adaptive behaviour and play), social and language skills. Language development was assessed from two points of view: first, a traditional chronological and normative approach, beginning with items such as 'quieted by bell' (1 month) 'vocalises to a smiling or talking adult' (3 months), and progressing through the gradual differentiation of single words (13 months) to items such as 'listens to stories' (22 months), 'follows two or three directions such as 'give the brick to Mummy', 'put it on the table, etc.' (23 months). Supplementing this, however, an attempt was also made to assess the development of different aspects of communication from a criterion or skills point of view. A separate scale was devised in which language development was considered under headings such as vocabulary, communication, sentence structure, comprehension and imitation. Both scales were fairly detailed, and contained a large number of items within each level and at each stage.

Parents appeared to welcome this opportunity to carry out a developmental assessment on their own child, and succeeded in filling in the charts once ambiguities and difficulties had been discussed in the group. The profile approach enabled them to understand the unevenness of development in many cases, both between and within different areas of development. Thus, a young mongol child may be relatively much more advanced in physical than in language development, and although good at imitating gestures may be poor in following instructions or vocalisation. We cannot vouch for the accuracy of parental assessments, since these have not at this stage been compared with those of a skilled and experienced tester, but it was obviously in the parents' interest to observe as objectively as possible, so that the assessments could be accurately and realistically related to the planning of games and activities designed to help the child to reach the next stages in the developmental sequence.

The Parents Workshops were an exploratory exercise which is still in the course of evaluation, but it may not be premature to hope that more systematic use will in future be made of the wealth of normative information that is already available in the child development literature, and that while psychologists should initiate such efforts, parents can be helped to play a much more direct part in their implementation. They certainly seem to respond favourably when they are invited to participate in a programme which is related to the particular needs of their own child, rather than given general advice along the lines of 'Play with your child, take him out to places of interest, and above all keep talking to him'. However, the difficulty of evaluating parental participation in an educational programme should not be minimised. The techniques which are currently available to assess the language of SSN children are unsatisfactory in many ways, and appear in some instances to be insensitive to the language parameters which are of greatest interest (Jeffree and Cashdan, 1971).

The Growth of Single Word Vocabulary

Although normative studies have provided a great deal of information about the *stages* of language development, we still know very little about the *processes* involved, and still less about ways in which one stage leads to the next.

One specific example will be considered in detail: we know that children normally begin to speak in single intelligible words around the beginning of the second year, and that this is followed by a long plateau which lasts from about 12 to 18 or 21 months during which they learn a suprisingly small number of new words. M. K. Smith (1926) found that the number of single words spoken by her group rose from 3 at 12 months to 22 at 18 months, but that the rise between 18 and 21 months was a further 96 words, followed by 154 new words between 21 and 24 months. Although these norms have been criticised for a number of technical reasons, it is generally agreed that they are reasonably reliable for younger ages; in particular the comparitively slow growth of single word vocabulary has also been reported by other workers, though satisfactory explanations are lacking. We might predict on the basis of a simple learning theory model that the child, having begun to name objects and to use single words more or less appropriately, would rapidly develop and extend his skill in exponential fashion, and that regular and enthusiastic reinforcement from the environment would contribute to rapid development. In other words, once the child has started to learn the skill of labelling, and understood that 'things' have names, we might expect him to practice this skill and to learn the names of more and more objects. Instead, we find that his spoken vocabulary increases by only a few words and that very rapid vocabulary growth only occurs some months later.

What happens in the meantime should be of interest to educationalists as well as students of language, since this is a period of rapid cognitive development in other respects. It seems likely that one of the functions of this learning plateau is to ensure that essential aspects of development can take place which will provide the foundation for later linguistic and intellectual development. One explanation commonly advanced for the plateau is in terms of the competing claims of physical development, particularly the skill of walking. It is considered on this view that the child is only equipped to achieve one primary developmental objective at a time, and that language development only begins in earnest when the child has learned to walk. Such a view is implicit in the biological model of language development proposed by Lenneberg (1967). The model is held to apply universally, but has been specifically tested on a population of mongol subjects. He reported that language development was more highly correlated with physical than with mental development, and that the acquisition of linguistic competence depended on the passing of specific physical milestones (Lenneberg *et al.*, 1964).

These and similar findings need not discourage the educator unduly, since physical development may be a necessary but not a sufficient prerequisite for language development. Not only are there innumerable instances of adequate language development in children with gross physical disorders, but both normative studies and linguistic theory emphasise that certain cognitive milestones are essential foundations for language development. One in particular will be elaborated: the development of comprehension skills.

Comprehension

Because students of child language have been more concerned with expressive than receptive skills, very little is known about the processes involved in a child's understanding of language spoken by others. It is particularly difficult in the assessment situation to differentiate between the child's understanding of language and the total communication context within which language normally occurs. We are told, for example, that a nine month old baby normally understands 'No', but this word is normally accompanied by many other non-linguistic cues, such as facial expression, intonation or even a minatory raised finger. At a later stage, the child has to learn to guess the meaning of an utterance by combining what linguistic cues he can derive from the message with what he thinks the speaker is going to say. In other words, comprehension normally involves the ability to use a wide range of non-verbal cues. These cues obviously vary greatly between situations and people, so that the child needs to learn or at least to develop the skills of guessing from context (Mittler, 1971).

It is possible, then, that one of the reasons for the comparitively slow development of expressive language early in the second year is that the child needs to acquire and consolidate receptive skills. He has not only to learn the meaning first of single words and then of longer utterances, but also to become familiar with the wide range of cues which are normally available whenever two or more people are in conversation. What little systematic study has been devoted to this question has usually involved two people who are more or less in a position of equality; nothing is known about communication situations in which only one person is linguistically competent.

Two particular aspects seem relevant from a treatment point of view. In the first place, we might design a systematic and graded programme in which the child is initially given many non-verbal cues by pointing, gesture, eye contact and other redundant information; these cues would then be gradually removed, leaving him at the end of the programme responding to the verbal cues alone, divorced as far as possible from pragmatic expectation or visual or personal cues. A teaching programme of this kind can obviously be criticised on account of artificiality, since communication and comprehension do not normally take place in a vacuum. But it may be justified in the case of linguistically handicapped children because we cannot otherwise differentiate between their understanding of language and their ability to profit from non-linguistic cues; moreover, we know from experimental evidence that they show particular difficulties in incidental learning (Denny, 1964). The programme may need to teach the child to make use of non-verbal cues, firstly by 'fading' them for purposes of assessment as indicated above, but finally by using them as 'prompts' whenever the child finds difficulty in comprehending the verbal message.

A second remedial strategy might be based on teaching the child to emit signals of non-comprehension. In normal conversation between equals, certain social conventions have been evolved which allow the listener to signal non-comprehension to the speaker, who in turn monitors his utterance according to his judgment as to how well he is being understood. Cues emitted by the listener vary widely in explicitness. He may ask for the meaning of a word, for clarification of an idea, for repetition or for slower delivery. This convention is widely accepted when the listener's language of choice is not the same as the speaker's. More subtle signals emitted by the listener may include a slight frown or raising of the eyebrows, or a look of puzzlement or disbelief. Boredom is indicated by a conscious display of lack of interest such as looking or even walking away.

It is possible that mentally handicapped children have not learned how to emit such non-verbal signals of non-comprehension Although no hard data exists on this point, their facial expression seems to vary relatively little in relation to the complexity of the utterance or of the task which they are required to tackle. When a subnormal child fails to carry out a 'simple request' it is often assumed that he has not 'understood'; by this we imply that he is unable to cope with the demands which are being made on his limited intelligence, whereas it is possible that a careful rephrasing of the same request may reveal that it is the syntactic or semantic rather than the cognitive aspects of the instruction that are responsible for his difficulty. In either case, it would be useful to equip the child with a non-verbal signal to indicate that the message has not been understood. Such signs exist in the Paget system which has been widely used with the deaf; modifications are being developed by Levitt (1970) with SSN spastic children. Needless to say, it is not enough to teach the system; the child has also to learn the social conventions governing its use. It is not only normal children but also highly intelligent adults who are often reluctant to admit that they are having comprehension difficulties.

The use of gesture need not be dismissed as a recourse to 'primitive' methods of communication, but should be seen as an important step in a graded teaching programme, to be discarded as soon as the child can dispense with it. It is important for teachers of the subnormal to avoid the controversies between 'oral' and 'manual' methods which have divided teachers of the deaf for so many years (Lewis, 1968), and try to relate teaching techniques to the particular developmental needs of the child rather than to the requirements of fashion or theory. It is also of interest that components of the American Sign Language have been taught to a chimpanzee (Gardner, 1969) who has learned both to understand and to produce signs in quasi-conversational form.

The discussion so far has concentrated on the very earliest stages of language development, since it is these which are frequently the concern of the teacher of at least the younger handicapped child. Particular emphasis has been placed on the development of receptive skills, since these seem to be of a more cognitive nature, and may lend themselves to the design of an appropriate remedial programme based on research findings, and also because it is possible that expressive skills may not develop unless adequate receptive abilities have first been laid down. Certain suggestions for possible remedial strategies have been made, but other examples might be derived from attention theory or from discrimination learning techniques. For example, the child might need to be taught to listen to loud, simple and meaningful sounds which would first be paired with significant events (the rattle of a spoon on a cup to precede food), and then as part of a series of increasingly complex discriminations between different sounds. Such techniques are not uncommonly used by teachers, but they are rarely part of a graded programme, and often begin at too advanced a level. At one point it might be possible to teach a child that reward always follows the quieter of two sounds, or the higher of two notes. It is important not to keep the child as a passive listener, but to try wherever possible to allow him to produce the sounds himself.

The need to teach children to listen and discriminate between sounds as the basis of a language teaching programme has been stressed by a number of workers favouring operant techniques (e.g. Watson, 1970), but more attention needs to be devoted to the actual content of the programmes. In a shaping programme, for example, should we begin with sounds (or words) that are already in the child's repertoire, or should we concentrate on those sounds which we know from normative studies to be the earliest to be formed (e.g. 'm', 'd') or the easiest to produce? This is important in a child who may use only a limited range of sounds from which it may be difficult to move him, especially if they are used in a rigid or stereotyped manner. Operant conditioners have much to learn from speech pathologists in selecting the sounds or words which they wish to elicit. The brief report of Evans and Nelson (1968) represents a useful collaboration between a psychologist and speech therapist, while Bricker is one of the few workers in behaviour modification who is working within the framework of cognitive developmental theory and knowledge (e.g. Bricker and Bricker, 1969, 1970a, 1970b, 1972, 1973).

Language Facilitation Programmes

Developmental and normative research has not on the whole been systematically used in the education of the mentally handicapped. Until recently, the fashion has been to rely on 'exposure' methods to a linguistically rich and stimulating environment, in the hope that the subnormal child would benefit from such environments in the same way as normal children appear to have done in the past. Developmental theory has been invoked to justify methods that rely principally on the provision of stimulating environments; it is argued that workers such as Lenneberg (1967) have shown that since subnormal children go through the same stages of language development as normal children, their difficulties with language should be seen as examples of developmental delay rather than of specific defects. All that is needed, on such a view, is an extension to subnormal children of the kind of 'facilitating and stimulating linguistic' environment that would be considered appropriate for normal children of the same developmental level.

While these methods contain much that is valuable and (no doubt) beneficial, their use does not rest on a particularly adequate rationale (Mittler, 1972); indeed the difficulty experienced by subnormals in incidental learning, (Denny, 1964), in discriminating the relevant from the irrelevant in a learning situation (Zeaman and House, 1963) or in using language as a mediational tool (Luria, 1961, 1963) suggests that more detailed attention needs to be given to designing the content of language training programmes. Although the provision of a stimulating environment is probably an essential first step in any educational programme, it is important to consider more structured approaches to language teaching which should be based on an analysis of the specific assets and deficits of the individual or the group.

Educationalists wishing to experiment with a more structured approach to the teaching of language could with advantage begin to turn both to linguistic and psychological models of language functioning. Similarly, model-builders could consider testing their theories in the classroom or even the child's own home. Only one example will be given in detail, though others can be suggested.

The Acquisition of Two Word Utterances

The previous example of early language development discussed the relatively slow growth of single word vocabulary from about 12-18 months. The reasons for this are far from clear, though psychological explanations have been offered. When we turn to the next important landmark in language—the growth of two word utterances—linguistic models and explanations are perhaps of greater interest and explanatory power. Nevertheless, it has to be admitted that almost nothing is known about the processes that lead to the first true two word utterance, though several theoretical models have been proposed and contested (Braine, 1965; Bever *et al*, 1965). Linguists have described these utterances in terms of the 'pivot-open' distinction, but we do not fully understand the mechanisms involved. Psychologists have now become aware of the cognitive significance of these very early syntactic structures: the child equipped with even a small number of two word utterances can begin to express increasingly complex intentions and meanings (*No dinner, daddy gone, my car, etc.*). He has progressed from the stage of labelling, using mainly nouns, to his first statements of situations and relationships. The appearance of such two word utterances therefore signals a process of profound cognitive significance, comparable in many respects to his acquisition of the concept of permanence of objects.

The linguists' description of the pivot-open structure (Braine, 1963; McNeill, 1966) may or may not be a linguistic universal. We do not know, because only a handful of children have been studied, though preliminary cross cultural studies do suggest striking regularities (Slobin, 1971). Nor do we know whether all or even most early two word utterances fall into the pivot-open pattern. Nevertheless, the pivot-open structure presents a powerful challenge to the educator, since he can try to design a teaching programme to help children who are still firmly at the one word stage to acquire this particular structure. The fact that the pivot-open structure is held by linguists to be part of the Language Acquisition Device (LAD) postulated by Chomsky (1965) and his followers need not inhibit him from trying to help children to acquire it (Bricker, 1972). His success will no more disprove the linguistic theory than his failure would support it, since many other factors are relevant, including the cognitive maturity of the child.

A modest attempt in this direction has just been completed in HARC by Jeffree, Mittler and Wheldall. Two four-year-old mongol children were carefully matched on as many relevant variables as possible, both of them having a small vocabulary of single words. After both had first been taught the appropriate use of ten common nouns from their combined existing repertoire, the experimental child was exposed to structured play situations designed to encourage pivot-open utterances, using 'gone' as a pivot with five of the original ten nouns. At the same time the control child had virtually the same conditions except that his play was relatively unstructured. The experimental subject succeeded in spontaneously generalising the 'gone' construction to the second five words without having been formally taught to do so. The control subject began to use 'gone' soon after his own training sessions began. Although the study involved daily teaching sessions of 15 minutes each over several months, the results did suggest that the structure could be taught, perhaps in future using simpler and quicker methods then are called for in a research design.

Another possible contribution of linguistics to educational practice derives from its emphasis on the syntactic complexity or structure of sentences. This consideration is relevant in relation to the structure of sentences used in tests and instructions. Conventional testing practice is to assume that a child who fails an item is unable to deal with it at a cognitive level. In fact, he might be more successful if the instructions were rephrased in a simpler manner. It is equally relevant to stress the importance of sentence complexity in memory and imitation tasks. Current work by Berry (1971) suggests that imitation may constitute a useful assessment technique, by providing an indication of the level of sentence complexity with which a child can deal when sentence length (and therefore short term memory) are held constant.

Finally, mention should also be made of possible linguistic contributions to the analysis of speech and language samples collected from children either in natural or artificial environments. Although some of these techniques are still rather elaborate, psychologists and teachers are badly in need of methods which will help them to classify the complexity and maturity of children's utterances, particularly when they appear at first sight to be primitive. Such techniques are being developed by Lee (1966), Cowan *et al.* (1967) and Miner (1969).

Conclusions

The gap between educational practice and psychological or linguistic research is wide but not unbridgeable. It arises from divergences of aims, attitudes and methods of work, and from obvious problems of communication which have been fully discussed by other contributors.

But it is also to some extent an accident of professional training and isolation. The training of teachers does not usually provide them either with the means of understanding research or with a very great appreciation of its techniques or problems. Recent surveys by NFER (Cane and Schroeder, 1970) make it clear that they do not respond well to attempts to persuade them to formulate the kind of research which they consider important. Very few teachers have either the wish or the opportunity to participate in research, and this state of affairs is related not only to teacher training but to the astonishingly small proportion of the national expenditure on education which is devoted to educational research. Similarly, psychologists, linguists and other research workers rarely have either the time or the opportunity to get to grips in any real sense with the 'problems of the classrooms', whatever they may be. They design their research studies in the splendid isolation of their institutions, and appear to be more concerned with the niceties of experimental design and the validity of this or that model than with the devotion of slender research resources to the solution of at least a few practical problems.

But all is not as black as it seems. It would be foolish to erect a rigid dichotomy either between the pure and applied researcher, or between research and practice. We are talking here about a continuum rather than a dichotomy. When next to nothing is known about a problem, it may be important to retire to the laboratory and try to conduct some basic research—provided one eventually emerges from the laboratory, either confessing failure or offering at least a tentative idea to be translated into practice. At the beginning of the century psychologists who were interested in human learning beat a strategic retreat to the rat, promising to return when the procedural refinements and other advantages of the animal laboratory had enabled them to understand some of the complex processes involved in learning. Most of them were never seen again, though it is now encouraging to observe a small band of workers in behaviour modification who received their early training in the animal laboratory.

Summary

This paper has suggested that the teaching of language skills to the mentally handicapped or to other linguistically deficient populations can benefit greatly from a number of different but complementary traditions of research and theory. The traditional normative approach to language development has yielded a great deal of knowledge about the stages and sequences of development which has in the past been used for classification and educational placement rather than as a basis for remediation. A detailed assessment of language skills, using both normative and psychometric as well as a criterion approach, can be used not only by psychologists but also by teachers and parents. One example of the involvement of parents in profile assessment is briefly described. But although normative studies have provided useful and as yet unexploited information, they leave many questions unanswered; in particular, they tell us a good deal about the sequence of development, but very little about how one stage leads to another, or the nature of the processes involved. Examples include the relatively slow growth of single word vocabulary after the first few words; a number of psychological explanations are considered, including the parallel growth of receptive skills. Suggestions are made for ways in which mentally handicapped children might be taught to improve receptive abilities by a systematic use of environmental cues, and also by teaching them to signal non-comprehension. It is also suggested that educationalists should not be content with the mere provision of a rich and linguistically stimulating environment, but could usefully consider a more structured approach to language teaching which takes account of psycholinguistic and cognitive models of language development. Examples include teaching two word utterances of the pivot-open type, and the importance attached by linguists to the structural complexity of the sentences spoken both by teacher and child.

ACKNOWLEDGMENTS

I am grateful to Dr. Robert Serpell for his comments on the first draft of this paper.

REFERENCES

Berry, P. (1971). Imitation of language in severe subnormality: a psycholinguistic assessment technique. Paper presented to the XVIIth International Congress of Applied Psychology, Liège, Belgium, July 1971.

Bever, T. G., Fodor, J. A. and Weskel, W. (1965). On the acquisition of syntax: a critique of contextual generalisation. *Psychol. Rev., 72,* 467.

Braine, M. D. S. (1963). The ontogeny of English phrase structure: the first phase. *Language,* 39, 1.

Braine, M. D. S. (1965). On the basis of phase structure: a reply to Bever, Fodor and Weskel. *Psychol. Rev.* 72, 483.

Bricker, W. A. (1972). A systematic approach to language training. In 'Language of the Mentally Retarded' (ed. R. L. Schiefelbusch). Baltimore, Md.: University, Park Press.

Bricker, W. A. and Bricker, D. D. (1970a). Development of receptive vocabulary in severely retarded children. *Amer. J. ment. Defic.* 74, 599.

Bricker, W. A. and Bricker, D. D. (1970b). A program of language training for the severely language handicapped child. *Exceptional Children,* 37, 101.

Chomsky, N. (1965). 'Aspects of the Theory of Syntax'. Cambridge: M.I.T. Press.

Cowan, P., Hoddinot, J., Webber, J. and Klein, J. (1967). Mean length of spoken response as function of stimulus, experimenter and subject. *Child Developm.* 38, 191.

Denny, M.R. (1964). Research in learning and performance. In 'Mental Retardation' (eds H. A. Stevens and R. Heber), pp. 100-142. Chicago: Univ. Chicago Press.

Gardner, R. A. and Gardner, B. T. (1969). Teaching sign language to a chimpanzee. *Science,* 165, 664.

Inhelder, B. (1968). 'Diagnosis of Reasoning in the Mentally Retarded'. New York: J. Day (trs. B. Stephens).

Jeffree, D. M. and Cashdan, A. (1971). Severely subnormal children and their mothers: an experiment in language improvement. *Brit. J. educ. Psychol.* 41, 184.

Lee, L. (1966). Developmental sentence types: a method for comparing normal and deviant syntactic development. *J. Speech hear. Dis.* 31, 311.

Levitt, L. M. (1970). 'A Method of Communication for Non-Speaking Severely Subnormal Children'. London: Spastics Society.

Lewis, M. M. (1968). 'The Education of Deaf Children: the Possible Place of Finger Spelling and Signing'. London: H.M.S.O.

Lenneberg, E. H. (1967). 'Biological Foundations of Language'. New York: Wiley.

Lenneberg, E., Nichols, I. E. and Rosenberger, E. F. (1964). Primitive stages of language development in mongolism. In 'Disorders of Communication', XLII, New York: Assn. Res. Nervous and Mental Diseases.

Luria, A. R. (1961). 'The Role of Speech in the Regulation of Normal and Abnormal Behaviour'. London: Pergamon.

Luria, A. R. (1963). 'The Mentally Retarded Child'. London: Pergamon.

McNeill, D. (1966). Developmental psycholinguistics. In 'The Genesis of Language' (eds F. A. Smith and G. A. Miller). Cambridge, Mass.: M.I.T. Press.

Miner, L. E. (1969). Scoring procedures for the length-complexity index: a preliminary report. *J. Comm. Dis.* 2, 224.

Mittler, P. (1972). Language and mental handicaps. In 'Young Children with Delayed Speech' (eds M. Rutter and J. A. Martin). London: Spastics Society and Heinemann.

Nelson, R. O. and Evans, I. M. (1968). The combination of learning principles and speech therapy techniques in the treatment of non-communicating children. *J. child Psychol. Psychiat.* 9, 111.

Slobin, D. (1971). Universals of grammatical development in children. In 'Advances in Psycholinguistics' (eds Flores d'Arcais and W. Levelt). Amsterdam: North Holland.

Smith, M. K. (1926). Measurements of the size of general English vocabulary through the elementary grades and high school. *Genet. Psychol. Monogrs.* **24,** 311.

Watson, L. S. (1970). Current trends in the assessment and remediation of the handicapped. Paper presented to 2nd International Congress for the Scientific Study of Mental Deficiency, Warsaw.

Zeaman, D. and House, B. (1963). The role of attention in retardate discrimination learning. In 'Handbook of Mental Deficiency' (ed. N. R. Ellis), pp. 159-223. New York: McGraw-Hill.

The Unfinished Child. Effects of Early Home Training on the Mongol Infant

R. BRINKWORTH

General Department, Great Barr Comprehensive School, Birmingham

Before World War II, mongolism was largely a short-lived private tragedy, and though the condition was extensively studied, there probably seemed little point in research aimed at helping the victim's development. Indeed, as Benda (1960) commented, there was even some professional opposition, in America at least, towards work in this direction. However, with the substantial post-war increase in life-expectancy reported by Collman and Stoller (1963), Carter (1958) and others, the position has changed. Since many parents now face a long-term problem, and anxiety for the future of a child who may very well survive them, research has become increasingly urgent, if increased life-expectancy is to be accompanied by any improvement in the quality of that life, in the case of the mongol.

My own interest in the condition having been re-stimulated in 1959 by the discovery of the genetic anomaly by Lejeune, Gautier and Turpin, studies were carried out over the period 1959–1965 that led me to form certain opinions which were put to the test initially on the birth of my own mongol daughter in 1965. From these studies, which will be referred to later, I came to feel that severe mental subnormality in mongolism might not be entirely due to the nuclear fault, but might, in part, result from an interaction between a very immature and ill-prepared organism and an environment which was at worst hostile, and at best unhelpful.

The methods originally devised for my daughter's benefit were based both on theoretical considerations and on a great deal of practical experiment with the child herself. An ordinary trisomic case, she presented considerable problems at first owing to hypotonia and feeding difficulties, and was extremely unresponsive. Her very good progress during her first year, at the end of which she had an independently rated D.Q. of 83, persuaded me to make a wider test of the methods employed, during an advanced Postgraduate course at Birmingham University School of Education in 1966-1967, the results of which were fully reported in a dissertation (Brinkworth, 1967).

With the kind assistance of the Deputy M.O.H. and the paediatricians in a number of Birmingham hospitals, five new mongol babies were reported to me, and contact was made with their parents. Each family received a visit of up to four hours each week, during which advice ,and demonstration were given on the methods I considered generally applicable. These sessions were accompanied by a worksheet (since incorporated in schedules of training for mongol infants, Brinkworth 1967–1971, and Brinkworth and Collins, 1968). Children were initially followed to the age of six months, at which point tests were carried out against controls. Through the hospitals, contact was then made with parents of twelve other mongol infants born from just before the acceptance period for the others, to six months earlier, as described elsewhere (Brinkworth, 1967). Study of the Medical Officer's reports for the previous four years had indicated an average birth-incidence of about 28 for the city, and it was felt that the five experimental cases (born over a 14-week period) and the twelve controls, would form quite a good cross-section of the mongol population in that age group. The small numbers actually born, and the even distribution of the condition among parents of all socio-economic levels provided, in both groups, a comparable spread of parental background, ranging from that of a lorry driver living under very poor conditions to that of a successful business man living in an exclusive area. A selection in order of birth only was made, and this was later felt to be an advantage.

Rationale of the Methods Adopted

Space precludes a full discussion here (see Brinkworth, 1967) but a number of points raised may be of interest.

In the literature of the period 1866-1965, a number of recurrent features had been noted:
1. The bulk of the data on development and intelligence in mongols was based on institutional studies.
2. Medical prognoses suggested a narrow range and a clear cut course in mongolism, while, in fact, other evidence indicated a strikingly wide range of intelligence, particularly in community cases. Such statements as Yannet's (1953) that the course was strikingly uniform within so narrow a range that the diagnosis automatically implied a reasonably accurate prognosis as regards

eventual mental life where shown to be at some variance with the evidence.

3. All the major longitudinal studies showed a regular decline in the mongol's test-intelligence over the early years of life.

The work of Bowlby (1951-1964) and of Spitz and Goldfarb (1943-1949) was cited in support of my contention that the effects of institutionalisation, particularly with the mongol, would be so severe that data from institutional studies would probably give a distorted picture of the 80% or so of mongols who live in the community (Quaytman, 1953; Evans and Carter, 1954). It was further suggested that, as medical prognosis is largely based on such data, an unnecessarily depressing prognosis might eventuate, with the result that parents, already severely shocked by a totally unexpected event which threatened to alter their entire future, might very well abandon or unconsciously neglect their child at the most vital period of its life.

Comments were also made on the degree of prejudice that existed against mongols, and the role of the unfortunate clinical label in arousing misconceptions and prejudices was discussed.

Next the important studies of Centerwall and Centerwall (1960) and of Shipe and Shotwell (1964 and 1965) were cited in support of the view that the child who spends his early years in the community shows a permanent advantage, even if institutionalised later, over the child who was placed earlier. These studies suggested that early environment had an appreciable influence on the development of mongol children, as on others, and that the very low ability of many institutional cases could not be entirely due to the genetic fault alone.

The apparent drop in intelligence over the years was then discussed, but an open mind was kept. It was the opinion of Kirman (personal communication, 1967) that the fall might be an artefact of the tests themselves which cover different cross-sections of intelligence at different ages. However, the reports of Loeffler and Smith (1964), Koch, Share and Graliker (1963) and Zeaman and House (1962) suggested an average fall of over four I.Q. points per annum in early life, and allowance was made for this in assessing raw scores for the older control cases.

Study of the medical literature prior to my daughter's birth had led me to adopt the views of Benda (1949 and 1960) as a provisional working basis, and this still appears to me to have been a good choice, as many subsequent observations on my own child and a large number of other mongol babies have appeared to be predictable from Benda's picture of the mongol's nervous system, circulation, respiration and digestion. In particular, his view that the young baby has a severely underdeveloped nervous system, which conveyed impulses from external stimuli to the brain very indifferently, appeared very logical. It seemed to me to be highly probable that as, in its hypotonic state, the child could not readily acquire the normal amount of experience, this would be unlikely to improve, especially if the shocked parents did not provide the strong stimulation which seemed necessary, unconsciously failed to handle the child sufficiently, and left it for long periods lying on its back staring at a featureless ceiling too far away even to exercise its eye-muscles! Such treatment might very well, I felt, lead to the degeneration through disuse of the brain cells reported by Benda, as a result of inadequate development of the circulatory system in the brain, owing to lack of demand. It was further felt that his picture of the mongol's liver as an inefficient organ, unable to metabolise sugars adequately, liable to store them as fats, and to suffer, itself, from a vicious circle that condemned it to fatty degeneration and the owner to obesity, was probably accurate, and other accounts were cited to support this view.

The children's poor circulation, and the feeding difficulties due to the anatomical faults in the mouth and nose, and to poor swallowing reflexes, were also apparent in the cases I observed.

I felt, however, that many of these troubles could be circumvented, and that a vigorous attack from all sides might help the child's development and possibly forestall the deterioration in the nervous system that seemed otherwise likely.

Reflex tests, such as the Moro, cross-extension, scratch, placing and support tests, were applied to my own child and subsequently to many other mongol babies (with results broadly similar to those recently reported by Cowie (1970). I noted, however, that though the motor nerves appeared to function adequately when the stimulus was strong enough to provoke a reaction, stimuli of normal strength produced little effect. Only stimuli much stronger than those that could be comfortably received by a normal baby appeared to reach the brain, and I came to feel that there must be some defect either in the insulation of the system or in the synapses themselves that attenuated or stopped the nervous impulse. I also noted in some cases that repeated application of a milder stimulus would eventually produce a reaction, as if by an abnormally slow temporal summation. (I was recently intrigued on communicating these views to Lejeune to learn that he had arrived at a similar suspicion from a totally different angle, and was investigating it.)

On this basis, schemes of work were devised, covering, at first, the first six months, and later the first two years of life, with the following main features:

1. Insistence on a low-fat, low-carbohydrate, high protein diet with vitamin supplements, and the substitution of glucose for other sugars, to provide energy and food for the nervous system by a simpler metabolic pathway, and to avoid obesity.
2. Special exercises, first passive and then increasingly active, based principally on the muscle-stretch and tendon reflexes, to keep the brain well-stimulated by proprioceptive and kinaesthetic impulses, which the motionless and hyptonic child could not readily obtain for itself.
3. Strong visual auditory and tactile experience (loud and contrasting sounds, bright light and strongly contrasting colour, and much experience in handling various shapes and textures and in adapting the hand to various shapes were provided).
4. Movement in space, and changes in environment (rocking, swinging, rowing and other exercises to improve balance and proprioception, together with movement of the child to observe its mother's household activities).
5. Maternal handling and affection.
6. Social life and contact with others.
7. Opportunity to benefit from the postural changes available to the normal infant.
8. Provision of aids to independent mobility at the appropriate stage.

A further important step was to place the child, at ages from two months upwards—at first with firm support and in almost reclining position, and then in an increasingly upright posture—in a Baby-Relax chair, which gave a much better view of the environment than the cot, and provided better facilities for play activities.

Results

At six months, in the case of the experimental group, and at ages varying from 29 to 55 weeks in the case of controls, the Griffiths Developmental Scales were used for assessment. As a regular drop of 4.6 I.Q. points per annum was suggested by tables established by Loeffler and Smith (1964), and others previously mentioned, a correction factor was applied in the older cases to permit fair comparison. Great care was also taken not to test control children until they had become used to the tester, and mothers could state that they were behaving in their usual manner (an important precaution, as mongol children are shyer than they seem, and give an extremely poor and unrepresentative account of themselves when tested quickly in unfamiliar surroundings by a stranger).

Scores were rather high for both samples, but this had been expected in view of the relative coarseness of any test scale at its lower end. Means and Standard Deviations were calculated for the experimental and control groups, and results compared statistically. Further comparison was also made with the seven highest scorers among Centerwall and Centerwall's (1960) home-based cases, after the applications of the correction factor for age-weighting referred to earlier.

Griffiths Developmental Tests (Brinkworth, 1967)

Experimental Group

	Locomotor	Personal/ Social	Hearing/ Speech	Eye/Hand	Performance	D.Q.
Mean	85.6	104.6	99.9	113.2	126.8	101.8
S.D.	14.98	15.64	22.56	19.32	28.85	18.45

Control Group

	Locomotor	Personal/ Social	Hearing/ Speech	Eye/Hand	Performance	D.Q.
Mean	70.9	76.0	69.7	81.4	77.8	75.0
S.D.	26.78	20.78	8.43	8.41	19.9	17.21

Fisher's t-test for small uncorrelated samples gave the following results:

	Locomotor	Personal/ Social	Hearing/ Speech	Eye/Hand	Performance	D.Q.
Value of t =	1.01	2.381	2.99	2.705	3.307	2.361
p =	Over 0.2	Under 0.05	Under 0.02	Under 0.05	Under 0.01	Under 0.05

When the scores of Control cases were age-weighted as described, results were as follows (D.Q. only):

	Experimental	Control
Mean	101.8	76.6
	t = 2.25	p = Lower than 0.05

When compared with the seven highest of Centerwall and Centerwall's cases (with age-weighting) results were:

	Experimental	Control
	101.8	82.0
	t = 2.535	p = Lower than 0.05

It was therefore concluded that the hypothesis that mental defect in mongolism was due not only to the genetic defect and the severe underdevelopment resulting from it ante-natally, but also to the interaction between an undeveloped organism and an unhelpful and insufficiently stimulating enviroment, was supported by the results. It should, perhaps, be noted that even in the case of Locomotion, where differences were regarded as statistically insignificant at that point, subsequent observation has shown some long-term advantage. No firm conclusions could be made as to either the permanence of the effects noted, or any extrapolation made to results on I.Q. tests at later ages, in view of the rather weak correlations between early D.Q. and later I.Q. discussed by Illingworth (1966) and of the greater weight given to Speech at later ages, an area in which the mongol has particular difficulties.

It was felt that a definite advantage existed at six months, and that, even if a subsequent decline proved inevitable, the treated children would have much further to fall than the untreated, and ultimate levels might well prove higher. Retesting at one year, did, in fact, show a heavy drop overall in test results during the period in which parents and children were no longer under direct surveillance, and the following results were recorded, (Brinkworth, 1967):

Experimental Group

	Locomotor	Personal/ Social	Hearing/ Speech	Eye/Hand	Performance	D.Q.
Mean	76.45	86.82	82.0	85.45	75.35	81.07
S.D.	7.9	3.7	10.4	6.6	5.5	4.9

Control Group

	Locomotor	Personal/ Social	Hearing/ Speech	Eye/Hand	Performance	D.Q.
Mean	70.9	76.0	69.7	81.4	77.8	75.0
S.D.	26.78	20.78	8.43	8.41	19.9	17.21

Though the gap between the two samples was shown to have narrowed markedly, it should be noted that there was a much greater variation between cases in the Control group, as indicated by the S.D., and that the lower quotient, in Performance, of the Experimental group was partly cancelled out by the smaller Standard Deviation.

On the face of it, it would appear that the results confirm, also, the view expressed by others that mongol children show a decline in test results during their early years. This is, however, only a partial view, as the level of activity and behaviour of the experimental cases did not reflect the drop, but continued to appear very satisfactory both to the parents and to myself, and it was felt to be worthwhile to continue the experiment until the children reached the age of seven—at which their brain's physical development would be largely complete, and testing might be more reliable. Comparisons can however no longer be made on the original basis with the control cases, as I felt morally obliged to offer help to them too, after the criterion test at six months of the experimental group, and many of the controls have also since made quite good progress. In view of the rapid development of the brain in the first year, and especially the first six months of life, and of its inexorable timetable of development which allows of no going back if opportunities are missed (Penfield, 1965) I would expect those who had begun to progress earlier when given special help to retain some advantage permanently. Certainly, observation over the past four years has inclined me to the view that a start at six months is already late, that at nine months much has already been lost, and that after one year the results to be expected (from a start at that point) with these methods, are much reduced.

On completion of the original experiment, I had not intended to continue further than to follow up the original cases to the age of seven years, owing to other heavy commitments. However, the Birmingham paediatricians who supplied the first cases and had observed their subsequent development with satisfaction, have continued regularly to refer new cases for the past four years. Many others have also been referred, both from Britain and abroad, by their own doctors, or, where parents have made the first move, with the consent of their doctors, and at present there are some 225 cases in hand. With assistance of the National Association of Schoolmasters of the Local Authority and of a small Committee a Down's Babies Association was formed in 1970, and during the year, two Centres were run in Birmingham where a large number of the children were seen and assessed, and personal advice was given. Financial problems forced its closure in early 1971, but plans have been made for re-opening. In any event, the intensive work carried out has provided a very large mass of data which awaits analysis, and despite many difficulties, the work has been felt to be worthwhile by both parents and workers.

One thing must be said in conclusion. Among so many parents of all social classes, I have only met one who was unwilling to make the very considerable effort of following the course. Mothers, whether they live in slums or in exclusive quarters have proved equally devoted and energetic once they have a basis on which to work, and even those who had earlier abandoned children in hospital or otherwise rejected them, have accepted their children, and have since achieved much. It is quite obvious, however, that the most vital years of the life of a handicapped child are generally regarded solely as their parents' problem. Medical advice is generally confined to physical illness, as education is, naturally, not considered to be a medical province, while until very recently, educational aid began at five only, by which time, in my view, the mongol will already have lost much of the potential he had at birth. Even at the age of two, it is already late in the development of the brain, whose fastest development takes place much earlier.

There is room both for far more research in this very neglected area of infancy, and for very early professional help and guidance for parents. All too often, mongolism, like some other conditions, is regarded as a static condition, largely uninfluenced in its course by post-natal events. The victim, however, is a living, growing, dynamic organism, whose development, like that of any other creature, must depend on the interaction between the organism itself and its environment.

BIBLIOGRAPHY

Benda, C. E. (1960). 'The Child with Mongolism'. New York: Grune and Stratton.

Brinkworth, R. (1967). 'The Effects of Early Treatment and Training on the Mongoloid Infant'. (Unpublished dissertation, University of Birmingham School of Education.)

Brinkworth, R. (1967-71). Various editions. Pamphlet on 'Care and Training for the Baby with Down's Syndrome'. Londonderry Education Committee. 1967. N.S.M.H.C. Birmingham 1969-70. Down's Babies Association. Birmingham, 1971.

Brinkworth, R. and Collins, J. E. (1968). 'Improving Mongol Babies'. N. Ireland Branch N.S.M.H.C. Belfast, 1968-71 editions.

Bowlby, J. (1964). 'Maternal Care and Mental Health' (10th impression). Geneva: World Health Organisation.

Cowie, V. A. (1970). 'A Study of the Early Development of Mongols'. Institute for Research into Mental Retardation Monograph No, 1. Oxford, Pergamon.

Illingworth, R. S. (1966). 'The Development of the Infant and Young Child'. Chapter 2. Edinburgh: Churchill Livingstone.

REFERENCES

Carter, C. O. (1958). A Life-table for Mongols. *J. ment. Sci. Res.* 2, 64.

Centerwall, S. A. and Centerwall, W. R. (1960). Study of children with mongolism reared in the home compared to those away from home. *Pediatrics* 25, 678-685.

Collman, R. D. and Stoller, A. (1963). A Life-table for Mongols in Victoria, Australia. *J. ment. Defic. Res.* 7, 53.

222

Koch, R., Share, J. and Graliker, B. V. (1963). The Predictability of Gesell Developmental Scales in Mongolism. *J. Pediat.* **62,** 93.

Lejeune, J., Gautier, M. and Turpin, R. (1959). Etudes des chromosomes somatiques de neuf enfants mongoliens. *C.R. Acad. Sci.* 248.

Loeffler, F. and Smith, G. F. (1964). In 'Down's Anomaly' (ed. R. S. Penrose), (1966). London: Churchill.

Penfield, W. (1965). Conditioning the uncommitted cortex for language learning. *Brain, 88, Pt. 4.* 787.

Quaytman, W. (1953). The psychological capabilities of mongoloid children in community clinic. In 'Mongolism—a Symposium' (1953). New York: A.H.R.C.

Shipe, D. and Shotwell, A. M. (1965). Effect of out-of-home-care on mongoloid children—a continuation study. *Amer. J. ment. Defic.* **69,** 649-651.

Yannet, H. (1953). In 'Mongolism—a Symposium' op. cit.

Zeaman, D. and House, B. J. (1962). Mongoloid M. A. is proportional to Log. C.A. *Child Development,* **33,** 481.

SESSION SIX
DISCUSSION

Chairman: Mrs. Margaret D. Cookson

Chairman: I should like to start by making comments about the main aims of the provisions essentially for the pre-school severely handicapped child; the sort of programmes that Mr. Brinkworth,* and to some extent the Hester Adrian Research Centre workshops for parents, have been providing. The first aim of such programmes is to attempt to ameliorate the deficiencies, and the second, to give a positive plan to parents. This is therapeutic and it is definitely needed, and this is probably why the workshops were successful so far as one has been able to assess them; why Mr. Brinkworth has had a considerable following, and why, of course, the Doman Delacato method is gaining in popularity in this country at the moment. I should also like to say that these schemes will peter out unless the first aim, that of amelioration is not satisfied. Programmes must be efficient if they are going to be of any long-term value. I welcomed Mr. Brinkworth's plans for parents, but I don't know whether his programmes are the best sort of programmes. We don't know whether all or any part of the prescribed activities really work; he has not given us very much information here but I have heard him speak about this before when he has made quite striking claims about some of the children that he has dealt with. Even assuming, then, that the relatively high intellectual status of this group is valid, any such advantage could be attributed to a sort of 'Hawthorne Effect'—that is, his interest reinforcing the parent's interest in the child,

* Since Mr. Brinkworth's paper was presented *in absentia,* a brief Appendix to this book summarises his reply to points made in the Discussion.

and not necessarily to any specific part of his programmes. The programmes do meet, to some extent, the second requirement of helping parents, but does their interest last?

Mr. Brinkworth has made a start and I would greatly commend him for doing this, and I am sorry in a sense that it has been left to him to do it. It does indicate a very considerable gap in our Health and Education services for young handicapped children. I hope we shall take this up as a sort of challenge to develop better and properly evaluated schemes for children at this level. I am one of Dr. Mittler's 'wishy-washy developmentalists'. I take 'itsy-bitsies' of research and impressions and observations and try to piece them together to meet the needs of an individual child, and his family, and I think this is extremely important. We can't just get a programme for a child with a defect. We have got to get some sort of a programme which is workable with the teacher that is available, and this teacher is in almost all cases, the parent. A programme has to be devised in the context of the many other commitments of that parent with his own family. It's got to be something that is relatively straightforward and therefore we can't go into as many details as we might wish. It's got to be simplified and workable.

Well, now I should like to comment a little on some of the things Dr. Mittler has said. He has spent a lot of time focusing on the plateau and the gap between the one word and two-word stage in the child, and there are one or two things here that interest me. I think perhaps I'm moving out of the sphere of discussant and particularly out of the sphere of Chairman in raising some of these issues. He asked, for example, whether comprehension comes first. Well, of course, comprehension comes *with*, because a child learns so much about the words he is using by the effect they produce on his environment. If he has heard someone say 'gimmit' and he imitates this and someone turns round and looks astonished and drops the teddy they've walked off with, then he gets some better idea of the meaning of this particular group of sounds. One of my reasons for wanting to focus on the plateau is that if it goes on for 6 months in a normal child, it must go on from 12-18 months in a subnormal child. By the end of this time, if nothing very concrete has happened, both the child and its parent might have got used to a sort of silence and settled down to accept it, and there we stay, so I want to look into the plateau and see what is happening and see what one can therefore encourage, and not say 'well, this is the plateau period,' full stop. I think that we do have research indicating that a baby of 5 or 6 months has produced the range of sounds needed in language. Nevertheless, at 12, 15 and 18 months he's still having difficulty in producing these sounds voluntarily and he's certainly having immense difficulty in combining many of them. A good amount of time, in my observation, seems to be spent in combining and practising and trying to create new sounds during this sort of period, and you see this in 'babble' and you see it in 'jargon.' Another thing necessary for language is, of course, fluency and intonation, and again this seems to be practised through the jargon which a child is using at this stage. In other words, it's not a negative phase and, therefore, one has to encourage parents to take an interest and to encourage the child to experiment with sounds. If he's stuck at 'mama' and 'dada' one has to try and develop some way of extending that child's range of sounds both in terms of length and range. This may involve tickling the child and rolling him on the floor until he produces a noise and then you repeat and encourage it, and there are all sorts of things that one will try and experiment with in a 'wishy-washy' developmentalist kind of way. Another thing which I observed is that we concentrate perhaps on a single word because it's fairly easy to understand, it's fairly concrete, it does seem to happen. I think there are possibly things that we haven't gone into with regard to the extension from single words to more words, and one is that probably the sound comes first and we stick the meaning on to it, that is to say, when baby starts saying 'dada, dada, dada', we say 'yes, there's Daddy!' and we stick a person on to the sound the child has happened to make rather than the other way around. Perhaps the way the words are learned later on is rather different in that you show him the thing and then tell him the sound of it afterwards.

Then, of course, there is Piaget. I think the idea of the concept of permanence of objects would be relevant. At 18 months or so when the child has achieved this, it is said that he will have the mental image on which to stick the verbal label, while before this the image is fluctuating short-term and inconstant. I hope you get my meaning here, it's all very much open to discussion but it might lend some explanation. The last point I want to make is that I suspect that there are many other ways in which a child acquires language and for this I watched my own children with fascination. I think the jargon period is extremely interesting. I watched my youngest at about 16 or 17 months and she was saying something which I observed to recur. It was something like 'Hair—a fa-ya' and I couldn't think what this was, but it seemed to come often enough for me to wonder and think that it must mean something. Then I realised that it was being said in a particular situation, and as her capacity for improved articulation developed, this is over just a matter of 2 or 3 weeks in fact, and her imitation became more precise, I learned that it was 'help—I'm falling' and she was saying it at the top of a little grass bank and then tumbling down and saying 'Help, I'm falling' in imitation of the older children. Then she extended this to many other situations and I began to realise that lots of things I had taken just to be empty jargon in the sense of practise of sounds and rhythm and fluency, probably had content which I was unable to perceive because I couldn't understand it. I think that many situations arise in which a child is using language and we aren't understanding it and therefore probably he is not being reinforced. This learning of language 'on the job' has led me to encourage parents of a child functioning at about the normal 15 month level to try to develop imitation with dolls, and to try to get the child to make the combinations of sounds the mother says to him, when, for example, she tucks him into bed. Combining teaching and play in this way is a more interesting—and normal—method of acquiring language than saying 'table', 'bag', and so on.

A. D. B. Clarke: Can I refer to Mr. Brinkworth's paper? I think this work is extraordinarily gallant and any criticisms I make of it are in the context of a sympathetic attitude towards his exploration. It seems to me that what Mr. Brinkworth has been trying to do is something which normally a small research team should be undertaking. We have mentioned that assessments have not been independent, and in this day and age, this is a very great defect, a defect for which one can't blame him under the circumstances. But I would like to know why on earth he's having to work in this situation, in addition to doing an already extremely responsible and busy job. I would have thought that the local University ought to have offered some assistance to this work because the general rationale is a reasonable one, but it needs to be put to the proper experimental test. There is one area of disagreement, however, which one can't overlook, and this is where Mr. Brinkworth states: 'I would suspect that those who had begun to progress earlier when given special help, to retain some advantage permanently.' I would not; in the *British Journal of Psychiatry* of a few years ago I reviewed this sort of work. All intervention efforts of say, only 6 months or 1 year, are totally hopeless in the long term unless you subsequently reinforce them. Only long-term intervention, and intervention of a particular sort (depending on the population concerned) will have long-term effects. Intervention always seems to have some immediate effects but unless reinforced, these effects fade.

Dybwad: I am very glad of what Professor Clarke said because if any questions are to be raised about this research they should certainly relate to why Mr. Brinkworth was not offered more support in the research he has undertaken. It is a great pity that controls were not more in evidence but the topic deserved many more resources than were available to the author. I want to go further than that because I am now speaking as a sociologist who has looked at the stigma of prejudice and particularly to prejudice of professional people, and it's very interesting that we concentrate on the parents' interest fizzling out instead of saying that the responsible authorities fail to support the parents. For ever and ever you see, just as the educators always insisted, that a child could not learn rather than that the teachers couldn't teach—as we often know was the case—so here we have once again successfully projected the blame on the parents, away from the responsible authorities. I know Mr. Brinkworth, I know Mr. Collins too, and I am keenly aware of the short-comings of such work. I would like to bring to your attention that in the Children's Hospital in Buenos Aires, Lydia Coriat, whom you had on the programme at Warsaw, is carrying out some early intervention with severely handicapped infants of whom a good number are afflicted with Down's syndrome. Unfortunately, she publishes in French and Spanish only, and her command of English is very limited so a language barrier has prevented her very significant findings from being known. I hope that some of you will get to know what she is doing. In terms of early intervention, again we have to refer to somebody like Eloisa de Lorenzo in Montevideo, Uraguay, where under the auspices of a public school—a special school within the public school system of Montevideo—there has been early intervention at the home in terms of stimulation and so on. I just thought I ought to bring this to your attention, but overall, I think the scarcity of any kind of interest in early intervention for the severely handicapped particularly by the medical profession, is really nothing short of phenomenal.

Carr: I think just to get the records straight as far as this country is concerned, perhaps you ought to know there's also quite a large scale intervention programme going on in Sussex run by a retired Medical Officer of Health, Dr. Ludlow, who is running clinics at which mongol babies are receiving stimulation in the same way. They are home-based mongol babies and Dr. Hodgson has been concerned with this. These babies are being compared with others in the same area who are not receiving the same stimulation. I think we can expect some much more firmly-based results to come from this study.

Hodgson: I absolutely agree with your early comments about the parents' efforts, and having worked with handicapped children of all kinds most of my life, I do feel that any kind of stimulation and help is of value and indeed, have tried it, but your comments about interest in early intervention are very unfair and very untrue. It's true that by and large doctors haven't written about it and now go on to explain to us why it hasn't been written about, but my early dealings with mongol children—and I use that instead of the term Down's syndrome—has always been this very programme. I have seen babies from birth and I have sat with the mother and said 'now this is the next stage we are hoping to attain' and in my limited knowledge I have said 'this is how you set about it' and we have done it together and I can say—and I don't want to boast at this moment in time—that two of the children that I dealt with from birth right through school are now at ESN school and doing extremely well, so it's not true to say that there are no intervention programmes. They are not written about and they are not large-scale. Now to go on to Dr. Ludlow's work, it's work in which the Department has been exceedingly interested and funded without any question whatsoever. We were hoping the people would ask for this money. Now in addition to this, intervention programmes for the mongol are going on, there are nurseries for these children in the London area. What is lacking by and large very often is knowledge on what advice to give these parents. Now just to defend the medical position a little bit, it's not defensible in the sense that we should be able to say something. Mongolism is a very very interesting medical problem, but it's exceedingly difficult one because it presents first of all what people have called immaturity or lack of maturation in the central nervous system and it also presents premature ageing. These are the two spheres in medicine about which we know least. We don't understand maturation. It's all right to write about it, but we can't look under a microscope and say 'this is it' and I've been up and down the country and asked this question. In the same we talk about ageing when we can look under the microscope and say these are the pathological demonstrations of ageing but what underlies it, we don't understand. If we take the other subjects mentioned in this paper such as obesity, this is exactly the same problem. We know how to control obesity but what causes it, we don't know.

Ryan: I would like to make a few comments on what Dr. Mittler has said. I think the really important question as regards the subnormal child's language development, as he says, is established fairly well in that a lot of them are very backward. The question is why are they very backward? And this is important both theoretically and from the point of view of any attempt at remediation. So you need to know the causes of the special backwardness. But I do think here that one of theories he refers to, that of Lenneberg, is peculiarly unhelpful in understanding why subnormal children might be backward. Lenneberg's theory of language development is that it is an inevitable unfolding of maturation in which the role of the environment is of minimal importance. And again I did read Dr. Mittler as in some sense approving of that approach, but he then also went on to make a point with which I agree, that at the moment we know very little about the process of development. Lenneberg's position seems to me to imply that it's not important to understand the process of development, whereas I think it is extremely important, and I took Dr. Mittler as saying that in his comments. Dr Mittler did seem to imply that is wasn't so important in the case of normal children to look at the interaction with environment because normal children would develop satisfactorily more or less whatever the language to which they are exposed, whereas this wasn't true with subnormal children. I think the problem here is that we really suffer from the lack of relevant information about how mothers talk to children, and I think it is true to say that current psycholinguistic approaches rather discourage us to do so because of their view of language development and I think Lenneberg might be wrong about this. There are vast individual variations and social class variations in normal children about how fast they develop, but I think the explanations for these are going to be very similar to the explanations one might anyhow explore in the case of the backwardness of subnormal children. And here I am particularly thinking of the kind of interaction that goes on between the developing child and its effective linguistic environment and obviously to begin with the mother is of prime importance. I think we particularly have to concentrate on the kind of processes that Mrs. Cookson mentions, in the case of her own particular child, that a vast amount of interpretation of the child's unintelligent utterances by an attentive, well-motivated mother does go on, and if you look in detail at the speech of mothers and young babies, it is in fact the case the mother's speech is modified when she is speaking to the child, compared with when she is speaking to other adults. It is much more simple, it is clearer, slower, it is more direct and she picks up what the child says, expands it, comments on it, repeats it, things like that. Now my particular hypothesis about the backwardness of subnormal children with respect to language development is that it tends to be very difficult for the mother to do this. It is extremely discouraging for the mother to have to keep on, not for one year perhaps, at the one year stage, but for three or four years, with the child making very little discernible progress. It's not just that the child develops more slowly anyhow, it's that the child does not provide the mother with very effective stimuli for this kind of interpretive process. Now this is purely speculation at the moment, and the information one needs to have is observation of how mothers actually behave towards their children in very naturalistic situations.

Mittler: Well, there are two points from my paper which may have given a wrong impression. The first is the question of theoretical confusion. I certainly don't approve of all the theories, but whether I approve of certain theories or not, is not necessarily going to determine my orientation towards the design of remedial programmes. In other words, I have great doubts about the whole Lenneberg hypothesis but, if I have to take a theoretical position, it would be an interactionist one. That is, we are dealing with an interaction between biological factors of two kinds and the environmental factors among which you've mentioned several but there are umpteen environmental factors of which obviously you've only been able to mention a few. There are many others that we haven't looked at. The two kinds of biological factors are first those that affect all normal children and have to do with physical maturation about which, as Dr. Hodgson says, we know precious little. The second we know even less about and that is the specific kinds of biological impairment which are likely to be present in the mentally handicapped, particularly in mongol children, but some of them are highly precise and they have to do with the anatomy of speech production, to do with the relationship of the tongue to the palate and so forth and here we do have some specific problems in mongolism. The example of interaction that I want to use is one that Dr. Ryan herself has really suggested in her discussion of the role of mothers, and that is that we have a circular process here. Let's assume we have a mongol child who is talking jargon for a very much longer time than would be the case in a normal child. He is trying to communicate. His utterances are totally unintelligible, and this produces certain effects on the mother. Some of them get discouraged and stop speaking to their child, others implement their own kind of language training programme in a very systematic way, without any guidance from experts or 'wishy-washy developmentalists'. Now, Miss Jeffree in the Hester Adrian Centre was exploring this question before she actually started working with us, and she is still going on in this area. One of the findings emerging from her present research work is that both mothers, and to a certain extent teachers also, tend to address language to the child which has certain formal properties, which could probably be described by a very simple grammar. One of these is that the kind of way they structure their questions is such as to elicit only single word responses. We constantly say to children, 'what's that?' 'what colour is it?' 'do you like it?' It's the skilled teacher who knows how to talk to children in such a way as to practically force them to use a two-word or a three-word utterance. Mothers of subnormal children, even when they are of high intelligence, don't seem terribly good at this. This is one thing. A second point about the same kind of data is that the words, the signle words which are squeezed out of children, tend to be nouns so that we have classrooms organised in such a way that we label things. I said last night that we put the word 'window' on the window. These are all nouns and nouns have a certain function in the development of language that mustn't be minimised, but verbs have an even more important function slightly later, as I'm sure you agree, in development. Verbs signify actions, actions make one think of Luria, the interaction between activity and verbalisation. At the moment, we are trying to design a study which is designed to increase the ratio of verbs to nouns in children who have already started to talk. Some work on this in the single child has already been published. So my reply to your second point about our need to know more about how mothers talk and teachers talk to children is a whole-hearted affirmative, but I would say that some work, quite apart from our own, has already been started on this. Finally, on the question of social class differences, I am very glad that you've brought this up because I find it a fascinating question having done a bit of work on normal four year olds in relation to social class differences and found vast differences—almost no overlap between three social classes, and more in some aspects of language than others. I was very interested in Dr. Carr's negative findings of no social class differences (quoted in your paper, Dr. Ryan) between middle class and working class subnormals. And you don't find it either and I don't think anyone else has ever found it, the few people who have addressed themselves to this question. You put a certain interpretation on this, I'd be interested to hear Dr. Carr's. I'm going to play devil's advocate to say something I don't really believe, that Lenneberg would say that this finding suggests (I stressed that I wouldn't really agree with it) that it is possible to argue on a Lenneberg-type language acquisition device hypothesis, that the reason why there are no social class differences between working class and middle class mongols, is that they are all relatively impermeable to the sorts of environmental influences which affect normal children. To some extent, I have twin data to support this kind of assertion, twins are less accessible to environmental stimulation from their upper middle class parents than normal non-twins are. It seems to me that some children are more accessible and others are less accessible, is partly also a function of factors which have been mentioned from time to time, namely personality factors to do with inhibition-excitation, but I think this is at least an hypothesis and we mustn't reject the Lenneberg hypothesis merely because its maturational and unfashionable.

Ryan: I think we should just take a look at the alternative interpretation which is that having a subnormal child may, in itself, be such a potent stimulus that it may completely disrupt all the usual patterns of behaviour in social class differences, so that we just don't find these correlations, that is to say, it might alter the effective environment of the child rather than the child not being responsive to the usual sort of environment.

Herriot: To take a situation, if the cat wees upon my kitchen floor then I have certain expectations about the utterance that my wife is about to make: it's apt to be a request or a command and it's apt to refer to the mop and the bucket. In other words, most of the theoretical analysis of language hasn't taken into account the non-verbal context in which the utterance is made. This seems to me to have remedial implications because it may well be that in the normal communication situation, the person who is trying to understand language uses so many non-verbal cues that he doesn't have to listen to the language much at all, and therefore if one is trying to get people to listen to the speech and understand it, then one is going to have to follow the same process as has been recommended in discrimination learning, that is, to fade away the other cues that are salient and being used by the person but aren't the ones that you are interested in treating. So in the end you might have all these cues removed and just the utterance to be comprehended, or alternatively, in terms of speaking, you might make the speaker have a barrier between him and the listener so that the only thing the speaker had to use was his voice. He couldn't point, he couldn't gesture and he couldn't wave something around.

Serpell: This is actually advocated in Dr. Mittler's paper and it is very creditable that he does suggest reducing the amount of non-verbal support for utterances as a technique.

Mittler: Yes, we all live in each others' theoretical models, you know. The non-verbal factors in comprehension is something, I think, that Dr. Herriot has developed very powerfully and I am indebted for this since I do think it has these remedial implications. But there are, I suggested, three remediation programmes on comprehension which I discuss and I was hoping people would say what was wrong with them.

Serpell: It seems to me that the Lenneberg position, which is, after all one of the best known theoretical positions, does have possible remedial implications and it is something which other data which you cited in your introduction also could lead one to believe, and also data from discrimination learning experiments, using language as an attempt to promote attention, could point towards. You mentioned (I think this is Marinossen's study) that on the Illinois Psycholinguistic tests profile there is less than parity in SSN children on the one test which is in fact non-verbal, in fact you've only got the paradoxical assertions that these are quite good at non-verbal language. Well, if one takes this quite literally, it does suggest the possibility that rather than work at remediation of language as such, one should be looking at substitutions, as of course is tried in some schools of deaf children using sign languages. Here I would like to pick up Mrs. Cookson's point about the possible significance of jargon. Another research worker at the Hester

Adrian Centre, Mr. Dempster, has told me from his observations—I don't think he has documentation of this yet—that there appears to be a remarkably effective secret code amongst mongoloid children who have lived together in the same institutions, to such an extent that he feels like defining them as subcultural group with its own language. I don't have the data for this, but it does bear discussion in very broad terms, wherever we identify the very major deficit in a particular category of children. There are two alternatives, one is to meet it headlong and try and make up for it by improving the process that seems to de deficient, and the other is to try and circumvent it and substitute some alternative. If I could add to that a comment on your reference to the use of normative developmental data as a guide to parents. It seems that there is a considerable danger here that, if we use the strategy that you advocate, of working in remediation towards the goal of the next stage of development, as defined from normative studies, we may be overlooking the possibility of short-cutting the traditional developmental sequence observed in normal children with a view to achieving minimal progress towards goals which might be defined *a priori* from the child's needs for social confidence at the age at which he is going to leave the educational environment. I think that Dr. Gunzburg's criteria for defining what one's aims might be are very often in conflict with the sorts of aims which arise from looking at a developmental sequence.

Chairman: May I intervene here? Would you say that it was perhaps better to select certain words and possibly phrases which would be the most important to concentrate on, similar to a social sight vocabulary in reading? And to develop these rather than to concentrate on developing a whole range of language in a less specific way?

Serpell: That is exactly what I mean.

Mittler: It is quite a dilemma. If you watch behaviour therapists at work as we've had occasion to do both in Hull and Manchester recently, one is struck by the way in which they ignore what knowledge we have about the development of speech which every first year speech therapy student knows. The ordinary behaviour therapist is quite uninterested in the difficulty and the relative developmental order of the sounds that he is squeezing out of the child. But there is a body of knowledge that certain consonants come before others, for example. Now the dilemma is this, if a child is hardly making any sounds at all and you want to shape him to produce certain sounds, are you going to use sounds which you know from your developmental theory are likely to be the easiest or are you going to try and shape the sound which is a close approximation to a key word in the environment, like mum or milk or whatever reinforcement that he wants. Everybody has to make a decision on this. It seems to me that behaviour therapists don't even consider the nature of language or speech they are trying to produce, and I think we can do better than that.

Chairman: Can I again intervene here? I've used a speech therapist to help me put in some sort of order the kind of sounds that I want the children to start to produce. On the other hand I would say that there probably isn't very much difference between those sounds that a child makes most easily like 'mum' and 'dad' and the ones which we want him to make first. It's not accidental that 'mummy' has one of the easiest sounds to produce and so does 'daddy'. Certainly, I think that this is extremely important and it's quite ridiculous that we start to try and develop sounds and combinations of sounds which may be very much more difficult than we psychologists appreciate.

Kiernan: I think there's a danger here in the use of developmental schedules in that these may or may not reflect the actual process which you are trying to potentiate and simply to develop in a child an ability to produce a correlate of a process that you are concerned with maybe through some other means may not be of any value to the child and could presumably, theoretically at any rate, be deleterious to the progress of the child.

Mittler: Sorry, I don't quite follow that, could you expand the point?

Kiernan: What I'm simply saying is that if you consider the possible alternative outcomes from using developmental schedules, you might or might not be training the child to do something, or training a process, which is something that you wanted trained. You may, and I think that the discussion of behaviour actions in getting children to produce sounds which are highly complex could come in here; you may in fact do something which is, as I say deleterious, to the progress of the child, since you risk the production of sound becoming aversive which might lead to a reduction in the child's output. I don't know if Dr. Herriot's model would allow, if you like, distortions of development to be developed through intervention techniques. This seems to be a possibility for which the best analogy would be the type of development which I understand might occur with a physically handicapped child if his physical disabilities are not assisted in the appropriate way by a properly trained physiotherapist.

Hodgson: I was actually going to ask you this about your programme for the parents, whether this was mainly concerned with language or did it also involve physical development.

Mittler: It involved all aspects of development. The interest of some of the people was rather more in language than other things and these parents, it is probably true to say, had children to whom it was particularly relevant, but if you look at the charts you will see that it is a profile approach being adopted and one aspect we call performance, which is really another way of describing play and adaptive behaviour, was just as important I would say, as language. But can I bring Mr. Cunningham in on this because he was more involved in this on a day-to-day basis.

Cunningham: Yes. The point of our objective was never to train or to give the parents a particular programme for specific problems of their child. Our objective was to try to give parents what I call a model for approaching the learning situation, regardless of task. In other words we were training them to observe, to train them in techniques of analysis, in a small sense in the principles of reinforcement, how you evaluate outcome, and how this becomes cycled. We're trying to internalise this model so that the parents could use it tomorrow, and, we hope, in 20 years time. In other words, to an extent we were trying to train the parents in the initial stages of being teachers because we felt if we did it the other way around we would go in, we would analyse their child's problems, we would need to be there every day saying when he does this, you do that. Then as soon as we move away the parents would not know what to do next. If you give them the principles to develop their own programme, whether they achieve it or not, they may be better off. We use developmental norms to give parents a baseline against which to start making their observations. We also tell them that children are all different, which is a principle of teaching, so don't expect the child necessarily to do this. Make your own decisions here. However, use it to start from, to give us something positive to work from. In fact, parents will come back and say, we didn't go on to that stage, or they'll come back and say the difference between the two stages that you've got is so wide there's nothing there for me in the middle. The developmental chart for a teacher which is going to solve very, very practical problems almost becomes irrelevant once you've got off the initial process on which you started.

Hodgson: But you have made one very important point you see, that the parents can come back and you can say you cannot get from this stage to that without an intermediary one. You know, a very simple one. I've seen people trying to teach a child to walk who has no hip control and I've seen this over and over again. Well, you've got to, somebody has got to be in a position to say and I'm sorry, but you've got your little bit in between, and this is why I'm asking you to consider the other aspects of development because you know, speech and language remediation are dependent on this research.

Cunningham: The answer I think here is in what you say to the parent, if you want your objectives to achieve this piece of behaviour and you fail, then don't change your behaviour, but examine the techniques you were using, then ask yourself if your analysis of the problem is correct (you can use different terms for this, depending upon the parent again as it's an individual problem) and in that situation, we would hope that the parent will come back and say that 'it didn't work that way, so I tried this and I thought that perhaps I'd better start again because his head wasn't right,' and you're giving them your prescriptive approach when they come back like this. So objectives, you see, start from that angle and because they start from that angle, what we end up with is this. I don't know if that explains anything.

Hodgson: Yes, very clearly. I just want to say I find this very interesting because this is where I see the value of the multi-disciplinary team. I've always maintained that doctors don't make very good teachers and this is unfortunate when we are advising parents. We tend to see only the next stage, this is what you aim at, whereas you are trying to devise a method whereby the parents themselves can reason about it and experiment themselves. This is very valuable.

Cunningham: Dr. Mittler blushed and said you know this is all charm. This was policy you see, we didn't want to see a child because we didn't want to solve his problems, we wanted the parents to do it. Most of us, once we see the child and parent, we begin to solve the parents' problem immediately by wanting to help the child, and, in this case, our learner was the parent not the child, so we weren't too interested in the child except through the experiences of the parent, again this is compared with objectives.

Chairman: I would like to say here it seems to me to be an exceedingly interesting, valuable approach and I'm fascinated to hear about it. I'm glad to hear a comment that the parent can come back to you and discuss the matter if the level is too high. It's important that the step can then be broken down together because if the parent has no prospect of reaching the next step within two years then he gets no reinforcement whatever and therefore he must be given a series, or helped to find or pinpoint, a series of sub-stages which will give him reinforcement because he can feel he is going up the ladder.

Cunningham: That reinforcement maintains his behaviour. There is the important principle of constant evaluation, once a parent has got that and does it and can observe, you've set into motion almost a self-perpetuating system and it's my belief that that becomes permanent, I hope it does. And you can, with a bit of luck, set the parent off and you don't have to keep going back every two years to support him.

Serpell: May I ask the people who have spoken about this type of programme which, as I recall, was designed almost entirely for parents of pre-school subnormal children, whether they would advocate, and in particular Dr. Mittler, the same definition of objectives in terms of developmental sequences for children at a later chronological age who are roughly still at the same apparent verbal age? Perhaps I might just develop the implications of the alternatives which I suggested, very briefly, in a practical situation. You suggested that theoretically from the literature we might conclude that the pivot-open stage is an essential method of making a transition from one-word to two-word utterances. Now if we have, let us say, a twelve or thirteen-year-old child who is still at the stage of making only one word utterances and we are concerned with this child's ability when he leaves the junior training centre to operate in a social environment with a reasonable degree of autonomy, it seems to me that we are faced with certain alternatives about our choice of things which we may have to work on for anything up to six months with the child to get him to master it; we may conclude from the theoretical position outlined by Dr. Mittler that we should take one or two of his apparently preferred one-word utterances and try and establish these as the pivots and build up the rest of his vocabulary into the open category and hope this will build up a two-word utterance. Now in doing this, it does seem to me that our priority ought to be guided by the kind of situation in which we hope the child will operate when he leaves the school and I would like to draw into this net not only the language but also the non-verbal communication scientist. It sounds to be shocking, but it is perfectly okay if he is able to point to the item he wants in shops and say 'How much?' and if he thinks that 'How much?' is one word and if this doesn't fit with Chomsky's theory of grammar, it doesn't matter a hoot!

Mittler: Well, Dr. Serpell raises a very important question about which there can be no generalisations, but if I have to answer I would say that there is no *prima facie* reason why a training programme which is applicable to a three-year-old child or a four-year-old child should not be tried on a twelve- or sixteen-year-old child provided, and this is a very strong proviso, that it is developmental, and that it is not used to keep the child at one stage too long. Its seems to me that the main purpose of training programmes which are not continuing is to make the therapist or the parent an autonomous person who is able to continue. Now my criticism of much of what goes on in the school is precisely that it is too static and the nature of the environment in the schools is often such as to perpetuate an immature level of development in relation to language. I think this is unnecessary and I would be quite happy, provided the child could talk, if he said 'want milk,' 'want soap-powder,' 'want this, no want something else', because I would hope from my developmental theory that this would be a stage that he could get through relatively quickly. Having got there, he could use non-verbal means as well, but the non-verbal aspects that we have already discussed are critical and can be systematically used, I think in a treatment programme.

Chairman: Thank you very much. If I can make a final point there about the danger of parents' attention fizzling out, I don't in any sense wish to imply criticism of the parent. I agree with you entirely that this is primarily due to the ineffectual nature of advice, or failures at certain points in the sort of programmes and the kind of information and help that the parents are being given.

APPENDIX–A REPLY
R. Brinkworth

I am grateful to Professor Clarke for the opportunity to add this note on the foregoing Discussion and thank him and Mrs. Cookson for their kind remarks.

The type of work outlined in my paper does indeed require a research team, but when I embarked upon it few would have considered it worthwhile, though the work of Dr. Ludlow and that projected recently by Mrs. Bidder of the University of Wales does, I believe, meet that requirement. Most previous literature, unfortunately, merely describes the development of the unaided mongol.

My own experiment did have the serious defect of a lack of confirmatory evidence. It was, in fact, arranged that my supervisor should retest the children, but either through pressure of work, or because the dissertation was completed after I had left the University, this was not done.

However, my own child who has Down's syndrome was tested independently at 13 months by Dr. Brian Kirman and Miss Jean Robertson from Queen Mary's Hospital for Children, Carshalton, with results virtually identical with my own. More recently, two subsequent cases have been independently assessed, by Dr. Ludlow and Mrs. Bidder respectively, again with results concordant with my own statements. The paediatricians, too, who supplied the original cases, have followed them up, and though I do not possess their data, the fact that they have continued to send further cases for the past five years may argue that they feel something is to be gained by the approach.

Of the five experimental cases, four were recently assigned to Educationally Subnormal Schools, though one was subsequently transferred to a Centre. He was the weakest of the original cases and his family's particular difficulties were referred to in the original dissertation. The fifth child has been recommended for E.S.N. School, but has not yet entered.

Of the seven controls, who were aided from the age of 7 to 13 months only, one has died, one is in a Centre, two are in E.S.N. schools, and I am awaiting up-to-date reports on the others, one of whom is also, I believe, in an E.S.N. School, as is my own mongol child.

Only a small number of subsequent cases are yet of school age, but of those who are, all have so far been admitted either to E.S.N. schools or, in a few cases, to ordinary Infant Schools, though I would not expect them to remain there after seven years of age. Obviously, a proportion of the total may be expected to need Severely Subnormal (S.S.N.) provision, as the range of variation in mongols is very wide indeed, but test results on many of the older infants indicate that quite a satisfactory number may reach E.S.N. admission standards; a few in fact are doing remarkably well. Reported mortality has also been significantly low, though I may not, of course, have a full return.

I was most interested in Professor Clarke's comment on the limited effect of very early treatment alone, and cannot dispute this, or substantiate my earlier suspicion, as the children have been helped continuously throughout their lives so far.

Professor Dybwad (whom I have not met, though I sent details of my work to Dr. Rosemary Dybwad in Germany just before the Warsaw International Conference) feared, with Dr. Cookson, that parents' interest might tend to peter out. I am glad to say that this has not proved to be the case so far. The vast majority of parents have maintained a faithful contact over a period of years—either by correspondence, or during visits to my Centre or by my own visits to their homes—and have remained very enthusiastic. Last year alone, I wrote no fewer than 172 detailed letters to parents, and our recent A.G.M. of my small Association was attended by 120 parents and 51 children, half of them mongols. As many had travelled long distances from all over Britain, this may indicate that they were rather highly motivated by their children's progress.

You might also, perhaps, concede that as my work, that of my colleague, Miss Madge Duffin, and our Committee is entirely voluntary and carried out under great pressure, we would hardly have continued for so long, to our own personal disadvantage had we not had continuing evidence that the effort was well worth the sacrifice. We hope to continue at least until others more competent than ourselves are prepared to take up the challenge. No-one indeed can alter a genetic condition, but much can be done for the child himself, I am convinced, provided that help is given in early infancy when it is most needed and most effective.

Final Discussion

Chairman: Professor A. D. B. Clarke

Editors' Note: The Final Discussion was originally planned as an opportunity to draw together various aspects of the Study Group which seemed of particular importance. Quite early on, however, several participants suggested that time was needed to raise important issues which did not arise specifically from any of the invited papers. It seemed to us that these requests in themselves testified to the value of having meetings of this kind, with a wide representation of professional and administrative disciplines. In the event, we were sorry that the time available for this discussion was rather limited. Nevertheless, so many different issues were mentioned by participants, that it seemed desirable that the transcript should be annotated in such a way that the reader would not be bewildered by the several rather abrupt changes of subject. We have therefore inserted headings either before a contribution, or during a contribution, to indicate the subject which the speaker is introducing.

Chairman: A small group has met to produce an agenda for this session. First of all, I felt that perhaps early on in the discussion we might raise the question of what might have been the strength of our discussions and, equally important, what have been their weaknesses.

Dr. Hodgson was concerned about the title of this Study Group. She felt that the papers are in their general implications a good deal wider than the title and she has suggested that maybe the book might bear a different title.

Then Dr. Mittler considered that we had not been sufficiently explicit for educationists in discussing structured programmes versus non-structured programmes and, incidentally, a point here for those who are not research workers, and I think it ought to be underlined, the Hester Adrian Centre people, and indeed many other research workers, are really experienced in practical matters and do indeed go into schools and sit and observe and know what the teachers have to deal with; they are very familiar with these problems. So far as that Centre is concerned, we must not see them as sitting from an Olympian height watching at a distance.

Professor Dybwad raised the very pertinent question of why there is a lag between the adoption of research findings as part of policy. What cultural social factors, what resistance to change, what inadequacy on the part of research workers in putting over their ideas are responsible for the usual time lag?

Dr. Gunzburg raised the problem that there are large numbers of very vital issues upon which work is not done. How far do we ram these down the throats of research workers asking them to do something, how far do we leave it to research workers to choose their area to study? Anyway, what should really be the areas to study? Do we need a 'consumer council' for research projects coming from applied fields? Indeed, is the Institute under which this Study Group is currently meeting, able to help more by acting as a 'clearing house', and by clearing house I think members meant putting out even more literature than it does, directed to teachers or others, pointing out the implications of this or that study? There are, of course, very obvious financial constraints.

Then Mr. Cave reiterated his earlier point that there is a gap between laboratory-type studies and what they seek and studies in which practitioners in the field are interested. Can this gap be closed?

Ann Clarke raised the question of whether there should be a unit of some sort, the prime function of which was to deal with immediate short-term practical problems as opposed to the longer term problems on which, for example, among other things, the Hester Adrian Centre was involved.

Finally, Dr. Gunzburg touched upon something which was raised in his paper explicitly: 'are behavioural scientists ready at this point in time to move away from making advisory noises off-stage to coming onto the centre of the stage with others in a multi-disciplinary managerial type of situation?'

These, then, were our thoughts and I will be glad to learn what you think of them. There has, throughout all the discussions, been a 'recency effect' in that the last paper to be presented has had a little more discussion than the earlier paper. Perhaps, therefore, I could come back to the beginning of my list, which is to remind you about the title and other general points concerning the strengths and weaknesses of our discussions.

Consumers' Council

Schiphorst: I was wondering about the suggestion concerning a Consumers' Council, I think this would have enormous value. It would help to get participation from the teachers. I think it would also assist those who fund research, and thirdly, it would help grant applications in the sense that certain areas of work would be encouraged.

Kiernan: As someone who has direct and continuing contact with consumers, it seems to me that one alternative to a Consumers' Council is to try, both through Departments of Psychology and other agencies, to involve post-graduate students much more in the day-to-day problems experienced in training centres and so on. Too much of the research coming from Departments of Psychology, even in this area, arises from someone imposing an idea from 'outside' on to a situation. Agreed, the Consumers' Council could possibly help to overcome this but this assumes—and I don't wish to be sectarian—this assumes that the consumers know where their problems lie and I would have thought that as psychologists, we might possibly advise them a little on this and therefore provide a better solution. In this case, one would require that the psychologist worked very closely with the consumer, even to the extent of perhaps six months in a hospital, before formulating the research project.

Cave: I think that the gist of Dr. Kiernan's remarks is that the researcher and the consumer should really always be part of a continuing process. When a researcher is commissioned in the area it could lead to feedback quickly to the consumers who would be expected in turn to do something about it. Now this may in fact lead to other research or it may lead to a re-definition of the problem. It seems to me that perhaps this re-defining by a Consumers' Council will ensure that research findings are closely related and really have some practical application.

Chairman: There seems to be some agreement that there is a need for such a body. Can we shorten this part of the discussion by saying that we will take note of this. I think it would be a courtesy in the first stage to refer it is a specific suggestion to the Research Committee of the Institute. It could be entirely novel in the field of mental retardation.

Holden: I don't know if this is really relevant but there is envisaged a new Council which will act as a developmental body to cover the whole field of the social services which is in fact in the process of being set up.

Chairman: I don't know at what stage this might occur?

Holden: The Training Council is being consulted about it. We've made our views known from time to time but they could be made right away. It hasn't actually been initiated but it would be set up under our Secretary of State. It would be an independent body but the sponsorship would come from the Department.

Chairman: I think, therefore, it would be sensible for this suggestion to go to the Institute and perhaps, through Mrs. Holden and anyone else here who has some line of communication, to this newly born infant.

Ryan: May I say something about this suggestion? As I understand it, it is to set up a body to produce research which is more efficiently geared to immediate practical needs. I absolutely agree that this is one thing we need, but I don't think it should be taken to imply that it is the only thing for which research is required. I think maybe it's important to discuss other functions.

Chairman: Let us then underline the fact that applied research is obviously not the only sort of research and indeed it would be disastrous if it were.

Ryan: Well, I must say I am getting increasingly confused about what is pure and what is applied and whether it's really a very useful distinction in psychology.

Mittler: Can we put it another way? It would be highly undesirable if the only research to be supported by the grant-giving bodies were research that had been in some sense vetted or even initiated from this body. I see such a Council as having two functions. First of all, the ones Dr. Ryan has mentioned and the second would be the one discussed earlier, namely, that it would have to contain some kind of highly trained Secretariat whose job it was to communicate any research that they thought was important. So I see this body issuing streams of pamphlets rather like the Schools Council does now for normal children on new developments in the teaching of number, reading, and language to children who don't talk, and so forth but this would be costly and if it's not done well and professionally, then it's not worth doing at all.

Serpell: Might I suggest rather that the Council might cut down on the number of pamphlets and so some of the other types of implementation which have been suggested in this Study Group. It would appear that pamphlets and publications are the top priority in the forms of communication used by academic research workers and from the need for this Meeting and the problems that seem to have come from it, it appears that it is not a particularly effective way. I would have thought there might even be a case for forbidding more than one pamphlet a year!

Chairman: Coming back to your point of immediate needs, I don't think this is the only function of—with all respect to Dr. Ryan—applied research. There may be very long-term applied needs such as the requirement for residential accommodation in 1984.

Mittler: Can I just mention the fourth function of this particular body? Mr. Cave has already mentioned it but I think it needs to be underlined, that on the model of the Schools Council this body could also get teacher involvement in the actual execution of certain ideas and projects as in the example of the teaching of mathematics in the primary schools.

Title of Study Group*

Chairman: Well, I think we have cleared that as far as we can at the moment. The next thing on my list is the title. Perhaps I should begin by saying that the title was suggested by me in an idle moment at the end of a meeting years and years ago, without much thought and I've regarded it ever since as a sort of projection device with the power to interpret it in any way you like. I think my motive was that apparently research was becoming more and more rarified and that at some stage society ought to begin to ask the question 'what's in it for us?' i.e. 'us', the consumer.

Chairman: I would have thought of 'Behavioural Research and Mental Retardation.'

Mittler: How about the other way round—'Mental Retardation and Behavioural Research'?

Chairman: Is there anything further on this point? If there are no comments on that, can we discuss the omissions from the deliberations of this Study Group and amplify those matters which we have discussed?

OMISSIONS FROM, AND AMPLIFICATIONS OF,
THE MAIN DISCUSSIONS

Categories of Subnormality and their Labels

Cooper: I have felt there has been an enormous gap in the discussion. Dr. Morris did raise one or two points which were quickly glossed over. The emphasis has been right the way through on the individual sub-normal child and his defects and what we should do about them. I realise that this is obviously for psychologists and educators a very important aspect of research in mental retardation but there seems to be a whole area which I think should be considered, namely, the old business of the categories of mental retardation which exist in our society. We have not in this Study Group questioned at all the existence of these categories and their definitions, we have completely accepted them and all the discussion has gone on within these categories as if they had a kind of fixed absolute existence. Very few assumptions have been questioned here. For instance, the model of mental retardation with its emphasis on the psychological defects has not really been specially questioned, except once and we did not go into detail and the problems were not taken up. No one has discussed the selection criteria

* The Study Group met under the title of 'The Application of Fundamental Research in the Behavioural Sciences to Practical Problems in Mental Retardation.'

for which psychologists (who make up about 50% of the Study Group participants), are in fact responsible. We have not examined the processes by which children get assigned to one category of retardation or another. We have not even questioned whether these processes are valid or not. I am suggesting that this is the only sort of thing that should be done but I feel that we should be doing more of this. I feel that we are smugly assuming that our definitions are correct and I think that certainly in the field of special education we are going to have to do some research on the educators. While Mr. Cave feels strongly that participation is important with teachers, I think we are going to have to study teachers' behaviour in situations with subnormal children and psychologists and clinicians, and the administrators because it is their behaviour that very often reinforces particular sorts of behaviour which may then become extreme. You, as psychologists, seem certain that they have some kind of existence in themselves and come solely from the child. The Unit in which I work is in fact trying to redress the balance a little and look at the question of subnormality from this point of view. We have spent a year working with teachers simply as one way of getting into the whole business of the interaction between the retarded child and the wider environment. We have no figures or results yet but the teachers seem to be very pleased to be regarded as the subjects of research. They feel that they may be able to learn something about themselves in relation to handicapped children and therefore learn more about the business of educating such children. I think it is just a question of saying again that it is the total context of the mentally retarded that we must examine and I think this is a phrase that has been used of which we should be aware. We have not been concerned here with the politics of stupidity and it is a concept that I find very useful and I think it is something which should be brought to our attention a little more.

Chairman: We are very grateful for those comments; they are very useful.

Teacher Training

Borkwood: I feel that we should have followed up on Mr. Cave's paper and said more about the actual training of the teachers. If teachers are to do work which is worthwhile for your researchers, that is to do something in the practical field applying research work practically, then the teachers themselves must have more training in practical teaching. I am very concerned about teachers that come out of college today. On the whole, they are academically excellent, but as teachers, they don't know where to begin, they are lost and I feel that unless this is rectified then they are not going to use the material you have given them.

Curzon: I was going to make a point similar to those made by Mrs. Cooper and Mrs. Borkwood. It is teachers who are going to use the material. I think it is simply not in teacher training to make a practical teacher but there is a need to teach the teachers to use the materials. This is very important and there is very little of this, as far as I can see, in teacher training. I also tried to say something about the training of the instructor or the teacher of the adult and I think here we might have followed this up just a little more.

Kiernan: Might I come in to add a third dimension to this particular problem in the training of nurses in subnormality hospitals and also, I believe, in the training of parents? The technology of this type of operation, as far as I can see, is in its infancy even in the United States where it is much further advanced than it is over here. It is my impression that with those who are attempting to influence and evaluate the effectiveness of their influence, and I say this advisedly, that they discovered that at first they feel they can do lots and lots of different things. The more they try and check to find out what they actually want of a parent or actually want of the nurse, the more they discover that their technology is inadequate. I think that as far as this meeting is concerned we are a bit too previous to try and discuss this but this problem is an urgent one which lies at the very heart of the whole of this particular issue.

Support for Research

Ryan: I would like to bring up another issue which I think is fundamental to various things we have been discussing. How do we evaluate the effects of research and who decides how much money to give to research? One thing which seems to me very striking is the discrepancy between the services which are provided at large in our country for the subnormal and the money which is given to research on the subnormal. There are lots of terribly basic matters of social policy and things concerning finance for hospitals that we do not need any more knowledge to implement, we just need some more money. I think if one of our justifications for doing research at all is that we wish to help the mentally subnormal, we have to work out some way of evaluating whether it is more efficient to try and put money into helping the subnormal by doing research, including pure research, as against putting that money more directly into providing better staff, more humane institutions, more teachers, all of which we are in a position to know would be a good thing. I think it is terribly difficult but I wondered if some of those from the Civil Service could perhaps shed some light on the way in which these relative priorities get decided, if they ever do get decided, and if anyone has any ideas on how we can actually evaluate the importance of the research that we are doing.

Mittler: Before any answer on this is given, I would like to put another point of view on this question raised by Dr. Ryan from the consumer. To a certain extent, these decisions are taken as an act of conscious policy. It is rather like the argument that if only the money that went on the development of space rocketry were devoted to the social services just think what we would do for the social services. Professor Tizard has gone on record as saying that about 50% of the problems posed by the educationally subnormal could be put on one side if the money spent on armaments and defence were redevoted to this purpose. Well, this may or may not be true, but in fact nobody ever takes decisions in that kind of way and it is unrealistic to support it, but we do have some factual information. For example, of all the money that is spent on education, the proportion devoted to educational research of all kinds is 0.01% and, before I came here, I tried to get comparative figures from other countries but so far, have been unsuccessful in so doing. But I read a report in which a Department of Education & Science spokesman, when questioned about this by a Parliamentary Committee, stated that the reason why so little money was spent on research was that there were not sufficient research workers of good enough calibre to justify this. The same argument was used by the Medical Research Council in the days when they were criticised in Parliament, and elsewhere for the fact that at one stage only 2.2% of all its research budget was devoted to any questions concerned with psychiatric illness or mental handicap. I think the figures have now doubled to 4.4% but the relative proportions remain still very small. The third thing is that in the last two or three years there has been a very severe and quite conscious and deliberate cut-back by the Government on the amount of money devoted to post-graduate students and this, of course, is an attack on research in universities and also, the budget of the Social Science Research Council has been slashed. I am surprised that when we were talking about the faults underlying research there was not more concern about this question. The Government has already decided that research has a low priority. This is not directed specifically at research into mental retardation, it is directed at research in the social and educational subjects. Now the effect of this is obviously to put constraints on the kind of grant applications we make. If we want to do a piece of what might have been called 'fundamental' research, then we would think twice for we would assume that in the current climate of stringencies, we would be very unlikely to get support. Therefore this is driving us to do work which has an applied setting. This may be a good thing because we want our research to be of practical significance. On the other hand, it does mean that certain basic questions are not going to be answered and we shall rush headlong into applications perhaps before we are sometimes ready to do them.

Dybwad: Mr. Chairman, these comments could have equally been made about the present state of affairs in the United States.

Holden: Fundamentally, the decisions are political decisions in that we vote for the Government that we get. Usually both parties make some statements as to what their policies are going to be if they are returned and those about to work in certain fields know, or have a pretty good guess, as to the outcome if an election swings one way rather than to the other. Believe me, all Government departments fight for as much as they can get. No Government department voluntarily and willingly gives up any share of the 'national cake' but the decisions on what should be the share—and it is done with forward planning for several years ahead—for each of the various services are made by our political masters, acting on the advice of Civil Servants. But the decisions are ultimately political and it was a political decision which has restricted the amount of money for the various research Councils. Now within a department—and I can only speak for the Department of Health—the priorities within that department are, of course, again at the behest of the Minister. For many, many years it has been well known that within the total health services, mental health had a very low priority. The amount of money which hospitals spent was extremely small and local authority services were very, very low down on the priority list. This again is a reflection of the political situation at the local level, in that most Local Authority Councils are not very interested in spending money on mental health. They will build old people's homes, they will build schools, they will build new Town Halls, they will build swimming baths, they do not want to build a hostel for mentally ill people. But the outcome of the last few years, the scandals which were revealed by a series of misfortunes in the hospitals for the mentally handicapped, has led to a very substantial interest in mental health. The hospital authorities in the health service are being told that they must do certain things within a certain time in order to upgrade the hospitals, and, if I may just say something on Dr. Ryan's point, I do not think personally that we are really absolutely sure of the best way to spend the money we have got and it is very questionable how far the money should be spent on upgrading the hospitals if, in the long run, one does not feel that the hospital is the right place in which to keep the mentally subnormal. You see that you are in a dilemma, you have got a lot of inadequate hospitals but in the long run, you do not really want the people living there and how far must you spend money on upgrading which is only going to be for a short term? Also on research, we have got money within the Department of Health for research and that money has again been directed more towards mental handicap.

Mittler: I do not want to give the impression that the situation has not vastly improved, nevertheless, we are still all the victims of financial stringencies and the official political attitude to post-graduate research is over the whole spectrum of education and social sciences broadly unfavourable. Within that, we happen at the moment, to be going through rather a positive period in the field of mental handicap.

Schiphorst: Many people applying for a research grant have to state their case and really sell the idea and if there were something like a Consumers' Council, this would be far more practical for people in the field and this is what this 'high on the priority list' involves.

Cave: I think one would be wrong to read into Dr. Mittler's remarks any active hostility by Government Departments towards research. This really is not so. It is a question that Mrs. Holden put quite clearly of where you put your resources and it's a difficult matter to decide whether money should be allocated to educational research or into Ministry provision for the under-privileged areas. This is the kind of decision which is facing politicians continually. A second point concerns where the decision about research is taken. In our particular case, we have, I think, a very high-powered advisory committee appointed by the Secretary of State and they have a research sub-committee which contains quite a number of people very well-known in the field of research. This body provides advice and information.

Chairman: Any comments on this? I think this connects rather closely with Professor Dybwad's original suggestion that we might discuss both this and other matters in terms of the lag in the application of research findings.

Dybwad: Well, I thought about the original formulation of the question of applying research in the behavioural sciences to practical problems. We have heard comments about the lag, a lack of properly constructed programmes, the lag in development of early intervention services, and so on. Reference has been made to an analysis of what was published in research journals; may I suggest it would be profitable to do an analysis of text-books? They are more important in the training of a new generation of teachers, doctors and others. Is the latest research included in them?

Models and Rôles

Another matter which we have not discussed sufficiently is the question of models and rôles. We have all in our time talked about the distortion of the medical models of subnormality, but I want to say 'God help us if this will simply be supplanted by a psychological model, or, as it appears now, a social services model.' I think we must be constantly examining our model, its possible abuse, its limitations and its political significance. I think sociology has a contribution to make in terms of social policy and particularly social change and reasons for resistance to change. There is a stigma attached to being labelled 'subnormal', which may extend to families—too often people regard this as an unalterable state of affairs. They say 'let us adjust to it, try to live with it' instead of questioning whether it is necessary at all.

Now to turn our attention to rôles. Mr. Cave asked today whether we should not have more interplay between the psychological research and the teaching profession; I think that rôle theory can account for the fact that this has not happened very often. The rôle in which the professional person sees himself, and sees himself as a member of one profession, as opposed to another profession, is important. Then we have the consumer, the citizen who needs mental health services or the parent who needs special education for his child, and once again we have the question of defining deviance and the possibility that a deviant person fulfils a rôle. It is quite remarkable to see the reaction of professional people when you tell them that a very subnormal person can find his way through the London subways, and they are reminded that yesterday they themselves got lost there.

Another factor in resistance to change is the total denial that certain problems exist. You just say—'it isn't true that our service is inadequate; all subnormal people are provided for.' You carefully do not look into the existing situation and hope that reality will not catch up with you. So we have system maintenance which often is related to rôle theory. The academic world is a good example: this is a system that insists on maintenance itself and woe betide anyone who tries to threaten it. In some universities, for example, communication between the Departments of Psychology and Education is impossible. System maintenance demands no communication. You just keep out research findings which in any way threaten the system in which you are operating.

Ethics of Research

A matter which we have not as yet discussed, and which is of increasing importance, is the ethics of research in subnormality. There have already been sufficiently horrible incidents brought to our attention for us to be vigilant of the research worker who may be carried away by the great contribution he hopes to make and overlook the consequences of his research procedures for the subjects of his experiments. I believe, too, that the advances in human genetics and the possibility of genetic engineering is going to raise a large number of ethical problems which must be discussed.

Finally, there are questions to be asked of the sociologists on researchers. We need to look at those who conduct research and at the methods they employ. Who does research, for what reasons, under what circumstances and where? We must also ask why certain research is not being done. There is danger that if we go on expanding, building on research already undertaken, that we may simply overlook some important problems and forget to query why certain research is not undertaken.

Classification and Labelling of Deviances

Chairman: Let us pause for breath and digest that very interesting set of comments. One very important matter emerged out of comments made by Professor Dybwad and Mrs. Cooper. Both have outlined a number of very important topics we have not discussed. Not because we did not know about them nor that we did not want to discuss them but simply because time has been too short and we have had to have a circumscribed set of discussions relating rather to the areas with which this Study Group is involved. For example, we have not discussed the politics of stupidity, we have some writings on this; or the question of the rationale behind the classification of the mentally retarded, we have discussed this, as Professor Dybwad and I know, in detail in the World Health Organisation; the processes whereby a child gets labelled and the effects of that label, this again has been discussed.

Serpell: I would like to ask the question, this approach which has been outlined by Mrs. Cooper and Professor Dybwad; the significance of the rôle of the subnormal in society as a factor defining our approach to the subnormal seems to me to raise certain problems which are very closely tied into what we have been discussing and which haven't really been spelled out. I would like to ask one or both of them to comment on this, in particular the question to which Mr. Cunningham's paper was largely devoted, namely the question of the aims of education. It does seem to me, particularly from Dr. Gunzburg's work, that there is a general feeling that the aims of education are social competence. Now if in fact there is a somewhat arbitrary definition by society of the rôle of the adult subnormal in society, this must reflect on what we are doing when we tailor the education of the child towards achieving this presumably somewhat arbitrarily defined role. I would myself be inclined to feel that the subnormal does a great deal of the defining of himself as deviant, that he is a different case from the maladjusted person or the criminal where society is somewhat more punitive towards him, but I sense from Professor Dybwad and Mrs. Cooper, and also Dr. Morris' comments, that this is something about which not everybody agrees.

Dybwad: A Danish colleague of mine once said that he was so eminent in the diagnostic skills that he could diagnose retarded adolescent boys from 300 feet away. If he saw coming down the street, an adolescent person clad in little children's clothes with a funny cap on his head, he was quite sure that that would be safe to diagnose mental retardation, and you can be sure that he did not buy his clothes. Nor is it a choice by the young ladies and the young girls (I know this point has been made often enough), who run around in slovenly, purposely slovenly, clothes, at the insistence of the mother as a reaction they have learned from eminent professional people, be they psychologists, physicians or educators who said that the greatest problem is that you must protect your child and she does not become a sex problem and so on. The examples are very numerous, that in contrast to other children, the mentally handicapped are treated differently to their normal peers, often to their detriment. To this day it is difficult for parents of retarded children to get eye-glasses because the doctor will say 'why bother?' and so he runs around with the reaction of a person who has poor vision and then people say: 'obviously he is a handicapped person.'

Cooper: I would like to comment on the notion of the subnormal producing behaviour that reinforces the definition of him. I think it is perfectly true, I think that labelling theory accepts this that if a person is defined they, in turn, like that definition and then behave in such a way to reinforce it. The behaviour of the subnormal may in some cases be the behaviour that is reinforced by his own position but I do not quite understand how you see this as different from criminal behaviour of any other more classically accepted forms of deviant behaviour.

Serpell: I think I failed to make it clear here that I was not subscribing to labelling theory, I was suggesting that the labels are originally applied for good reasons in most cases, and in the case of severely subnormal children, that the child reacts to the label by reinforcing it. But may I, rather than provoking this controversy, ask whether you could comment on how you see the implications of this for the sort of principles outlined in Mr. Cunningham's paper. Do you accept that there is, in fact, a different adult rôle which we should set ourselves as the objective in education for a child who has been classified as severely subnormal? I am taking an extreme case, not an educationally subnormal child; a severely handicapped child.

Aims of Education for the Mentally Subnormal

Cooper: A different rôle in what, different from what?

Serpell: Different from the type of rôle which the educationist sets himself for the normal child in normal education. This seems to me to be the major task of Dr. Gunzburg's work and I see it as very important in defining what we should be working at in research for the educationally subnormal. If we have totally different goals in mind then we must be doing different things. It would appear that you might question this in different schools.

Dybwad: Take, for instance, the blind. There are widely different provisions made for them in different countries. I was shocked to find in Spain that the only rehabilitation effort for blind people is that they can sell tickets for the lottery on the street corners. In blindness, the image has certainly been radically changed in England and other countries; one of the difficulties is that we are trying to make predictions in an era of change where the mentally retarded will be in society. It really was a genius of Stanley P. Davies during a single life time to change the title of his book 'Social Control of the Mentally Defective' to 'The Mentally Retarded in Society.' That he has special and different needs, I would not deny, but I have seen no proof that severely subnormal persons are a race set apart. I know that at the moment they are struggling against heavy odds, but the movement is upward, and so far whenever we have given them a chance, they have been able to move up. We have had no catastrophe as yet, no country has said 'oh, we were all wrong, we must push him down again.'

Gunzburg: I do not think I really meant to imply that we want different goals for the mentally subnormal. I really felt we ought to try to define what sort of rôles he can play in society, what sort of modest rôles and go for these particular ones. With normal people, with normal children, you have to provide for everything. For our mentally subnormal we need not do this, but we know that for certain areas they have got a chance to function really well and for that we will prepare them. Is that acceptable? It is not different goals but different contexts of their education.

A. M. Clarke: Let me say I would like to repeat a point which Dr. Serpell made this morning and I think it bears repetition. It is that although we may accept that the severely subnormal person is quantitatively different from the normal person, his needs are qualitatively different and I think quite honestly that this is one of the more important things which have been discussed, and I believe agreed upon, at this Study Group. It needs to be given to teachers as a concept to guide their rôle in helping the mentally handicapped child through childhood, through adolescence, to attain the social competence which, in a limited extent, we desire for him in adult life.

Curzon: It has already been said, but I want to raise it again. Unwittingly we may be as specialists and as separatists and different professions building up a further isolation from which we are trying to move. It is probably all right for subnormal children, but there is some sign of further isolation of this group of people within society at an older age and I do think this needs spelling out and it does need some looking into so that we can avoid this. If we are not careful we might even make matters worse for them than they were before.

Mittler: We were all obviously going for basically the same point, but while the goals and objectives might be agreed and might even be agreed by the politicians, in fact the realities of the situation are ultimately political, as Mrs. Holden has very rightly pointed out, and these realities seem to me to be essentially expressed in terms of negative discrimination against the subnormal. The whole movement of Community Care is a complete sham unless you provide in the community the resources to optimise potential of development.

What has happened is that the politicians and the administrators have asked themselves what sort of services and what sort of buildings do we need to provide for adult mentally subnormal people and the answers have been expressed largely in terms of sheltered workshops and adult training centres, which is fine, although it is clear from our discussions that we have not begun to define what the objectives of these premises ought to be. We have not really started to provide community resources for these people. Although there were sceptical looks around the room, it is perfectly true, and medical conferences have confirmed this, that many people who are subnormal fail to get the sorts of services which they would get if they were not mentally subnormal. Dossiers could be made up where doctors had written 'not suitable for spectacles, too low-grade mentally for a hearing aid, unsuitable for speech therapy," and the whole movement of Community Care is designed to allow mentally subnormal people to have access to services in exactly the same way as if they were perfectly normal.

At the moment, I feel that all we have really provided are buildings, a few trained staff, a great many untrained staff, but very little policy about the next steps. We have got some training but the main area where we have not done anything is in terms of positive detailed constructive help for families. I do not just mean parents here, but families. It has taken many, many years to get a disability allowance even considered by the Government; I believe this is quite common in many other countries. There is now a 'constant attendance allowance' which has been put through this year for people who are completely physically incapacitated. Why has it taken so long to do this? If anybody here has a mentally subnormal child next year and a completely helpless child, they will get that allowance but there is still a differentiation between a disability caused by an industrial injury or a war injury and the disability that is caused by a congenital handicap and this is merely symbolic, it is a reflection of society's priorities in this matter and attempts made by various charitable organizations, by institutions, by parents' societies, to get this changed, have on the whole, been very unsuccessful in this country.

Cunningham: I think the curriculum which you end up with depends upon the objectives, and the objectives in education depend upon what you see the child ought to be in the future. Now 50 years ago is this country we were very clear because we knew what the child would be, we said what society would let him be. He would be working-class or whatever it was and he should fit in to wherever we fit him in society. The modern concept for most children is that—well the sky's the limit—of course it is a ridiculous concept, I think in some ways because we have a system which depends upon 80% failure because we do not have 11 plus exams and yet we tell them all the time 'if you don't pass academic exams, it's your fault, because the sky's the limit.' Similarly, I am very worried because when I am trying to think of the curriculum I will give to the handicapped child, I can see the skills that he needs perhaps in these things, but what I cannot judge is what society will allow him to be, in 20 years time or 10 years time. It is a sociological problem.

Recently, someone said to me at another conference, that they were working with the blind and they can train blind people in dozens of ways, but in fact, they can only get them a small number of jobs and it occurs to me that this has direct effect upon what you are going to teach that child in the curriculum. If in 20 years time we do not want them to work because of labour problems or unemployment, our curriculum now is going to be terribly different, or should be changing, and people developing curricula for the severely subnormal have got to use the same principles as with the normal. I know we have had these discussions, but I think it is a part of the Study Group which we have allowed to slide until this moment.

Chairman: In that connection one of my few regrets about this Study Group is that there were not tape recorders at the bar, because some of the most significant discussions on this particular point occurred there.

Cave: Could I just add to this something which disturbs me even more deeply? It seems to me that if we are going to tailor our educational objectives to what society is going to decide the child should do, we have got a priority for maintaining the *status quo*. I should have thought that in the last 20 years we have had ample demonstration of what children can do today being rather more than what they could do then. It is obviously stupid to think of the 'sky as the limit' but, on the other hand, it is equally stupid to think that all we have got so far is the ceiling. There is one other thing that we have not discussed; this is the presumption that we know where a child can get to and therefore we structure a programme in order to enable him to get there. If we take this as partial knowledge which we need to revise continually, and then when we reach one goal, we are prepared to construct our curriculum to attain the next, fair enough. However, if, in fact, we are using our objective in, say social training, then it seems to me that this aspect of it we have discussed at some length; and we have also talked at even greater length about objectives in cognitive functioning but I see these as only two aspects. But we do know that some comparatively quite severely mentally handicapped adults have considerable creative abilities and so far, we have barely mentioned this and it has not received mention in the curriculum. I think that when we are talking about our aims and objectives, we must be much more flexible, and I do not think we can really talk about either our curriculum or even the means of achieving objectives, unless we are a bit clearer than we are at the moment what the objectives are.

Gunzburg: Mr. Cave, you gave a very good suggestion just now for research. If we could have a comparative study of a certain percentage of the blind people in this country, in France, Germany, Sweden and in the United States with their comparative occupational status, it would be very interesting because we would find that the greatest discrepancies are that the number of blind lawyers, blind attorneys is steadily increasing; people are managing, they are moving into all sorts of unusual professions, they are able to function and I think that I would underline this. I do not think we can expect a law firm to say '10 years from now we will have a plan, a place for a blind attorney, will you start training one?' I think we need to train the manpower and just hope that through social influence we can get them into places, so I would agree with you fully that if we do not want a *status quo* we simply have to open up the training rationally, moving upward.

Cave: You quote this differently and you have done this yourself,

Professor Clarke, in your own writing, but we know quite well that
what now were formerly ESN (educationally subnormal) people, the
old type, in fact often cease to be mentally handicapped. There may
come a stage when in fact they are not really mentally handicapped in
the sense that they were 10 years earlier.

Gunzburg: I am not quite sure whether I disagree completely on this
but let us look at it really as a practical situation. What you all seem to
say is 'let's be fair to the child, let's not put an artificial ceiling on him.
Let him be creative and so on.' In practical terms, we have only so
many hours per week, we have got only so many years for teaching and
so on, and he is a slow learner, he takes an awful long time to learn
anything. Are we fair in the long run to such a child, who will be an
adult, letting him be creative, paint wonderful pictures and so on but
not teaching him to become acceptable to society? I think we have to
start thinking in terms of how he can be best absorbed in normal life
and what is needed for that, and if creative activities and finger painting
are going to be of any use to him as an adult. I know this is
narrow-minded, but I have got youngsters coming to me who can read
the Bible from beginning to end, very wonderful indeed, but they
cannot add their pennies together! Someone has put his educational
skills to the wrong priority and again I think we have got to make quite
sure what we can do within the available time with available staff and
with available facilities.

A. M. Clarke: May I comment on this? Although I have spent much of
my life saying there is more to the mentally handicapped than anybody
knows and we do not yet know what the limits are, I would venture to
suggest that without the sort of curriculum that we have talked about
and carefully avoided defining—probably quite rightly—the danger is
not that we will limit the potential, but rather we will prevent him from
fulfilling it in the sense of becoming an independent adult. Without
clearly defined goals and carefully devised curricula, the mentally
handicapped is not going to be able to be independent and socially
acceptable, he is going to be a deviant all his life and society is going to
reinforce this social deviant image that he has. That I think is the
greater danger of the two.

Need for Discussion of Curricula

Cookson: Can I just say that there is so much of this problem of
curriculum that I would have liked to see a whole period of discussion
devoted just to this, with people who are also more involved in the
practical side of the education of the severely subnormal child than any
of us here.

Lambert: I suppose I am the main person in Hull responsible for trying to advise on how we run the training centres, so I have got several comments to make from the consumer angle. I have kept quiet so far, but I would welcome something very much along the lines of, say, Luke Watson's manual, some curriculum guides, but I am very much aware that I have got to go away and digest what to me is quite a lot of high-powered stuff and interpret it and then try and make some use of it in our training centre or in our new special school. Therefore, I would hope that at a future meeting there will be a consensus of opinion which will produce usable curricula. Whether the ceiling of the curriculum is too low for the particular type of child we are dealing with or whether the ceiling is too high, can best be judged by the teacher.

Chairman: Can I just come back on one point 'the teacher is the best person to judge.' I think a trained teacher who has even a 'wishy-washy' developmental outlook, to use that hallowed phrase, may well be in a position to judge but I would think that for many teachers, expectancies are such that they would be extremely bad judges of where they can take their charges. They would underestimate what can be attained and remember, we are talking about the service where about two-thirds have had no training whatsoever. The other one-third have had training of different vintages and of different degrees of relevance to current thinking. So the one point I would be worried about in your otherwise excellent statement is whether the teacher can be a good judge. Anyone who is up-to-date with the literature knows that the most common error in this whole field is an error of underestimation by experts as well as by non-experts.

Lambert: If I may persuade you to come back, this is where I see the rôle of the educational psychologist in the training centres, to make sure the teacher pushes the child without pushing him too far.

Failure of Institutions

Atkins: May I say I think there is a fantastic gap between what is being said here and what is actually happening. What shall we do, what's the best thing? There are not only the 'maypole dancers' and the 'sweat shops', there are also the sleeping beauties and they are in the hospitals and Pauline Morris' book has demonstrated just how many there are. Need we really worry about potential and capacity as long as something is being done for these people? Yes, I am sure we should, but this is an ideal situation we are talking about. Lots of mentally handicapped people just sit all day long, staring out of the window. They haven't got their own property, there isn't enough room between the beds. Please can I ask what can we do about this? Why are not Professor and Dr. Clarke's words and research being put into practice? Why has the problem been left lying so long and books like that of Dr. Morris* can still be written proving that nothing is being done? As I say, if you dance them around a maypole, they are doing something; they are probably learning something and they are certainly not sliding backwards. If you have them in a 'sweat shop' you have got an objective. Neither of these situations is ideal, but something is being done, somebody's caring, somebody's watching what's happening and somebody is going to come along and criticise, but if you are sitting in a smelly, grey serge suit and with no one to talk to except someone who is even dimmer than you are, then you know nothing's happening, you are just sliding backwards. What can we do? I would have thought that everyone would come here as shattered as I was by that book. Perhaps everyone is, but it hasn't really been raised, not to any point, but what can be done?

Chairman: Some of us were shattered long before that book!

Gunzburg: May I make a comment and answer to Mrs. Atkins? A few months ago, we were in Dublin† where I had a shattering experience, because I had never heard, from presumably responsible people, such a denial of reality in the institutions in the United Kingdom as we were able to hear there. The people simply denied the allegations all the way through—there is no real problem, we need a little bit more of this, a little bit more of that and everything will be fine! I felt that there was a total failure on the part of some speakers to acknowledge the problems that exist and may I say, we have this not just in the United Kingdom, but in many other countries.

Operant Learning

Kiernan: I would like to try to comment on Mrs. Atkins' remarks and also to point out one lack in the programme. I am sure Professor Clarke agrees there was a deficiency in the programme in that the operant work or behaviour modification has not been directly discussed at these meetings. The first point is that this research has obviously been amongst the most important developments, of maybe, the last hundred years in the field of mental retardation. In the United States it has been extremely influential and through the work of people like Bijou, Baer, Luke Watson and others, has brought out very substantial changes in

---

* Morris, P. (1969). 'Put Away: a Sociological Study of Institutions for the Mentally Retarded'. London: Routledge & Kegan Paul.

† 'Action for the Retarded' Conference, Dublin, 1971 (WFMH and MSMHC).

practice in subnormality hospitals. In this country there really is, as of now, a very small amount of work being done in the operant field and personally I feel that the position in Britain is one which is particularly delicate at the moment. Professor Dybwad has mentioned the problems, the ethical problems, to which behaviour modification can give rise, and I think those people who are working in this area are acutely aware of these problems. This, together with academic considerations, lead them to a position where, on the one hand, they feel very enthusiastic and very committed about this work but on the other, feel extremely cautious and, in my own case, extremely anxious. The work must be put in train in a well-monitored and precise manner so that we do not run into the position encountered in some parts of the United States and also in Denmark where, largely through ignorance, techniques usually involving negative reinforcement, are used indiscriminately, giving rise to public outcry and then leading to, in many cases, a legal ruling such that operant techniques may not be used again.

Now apart from the fact that Skinner has always been fairly firm in his opposition to the use of negative reinforcement, I think that the strong tradition in the operant field which has come over to this country is one whereby it is always seen as much more beneficial strategy to try and develop new behaviour rather than to stamp out behaviour which, although it may be deviant, is none-the-less behaviour which is well-established. So this, in fact, is the ethic of the operant movement and it is an ethic which I am perfectly certain is being perpetuated in this country.

Now after that general statement, let me go on to a further point which I would like to tie back into a lot of what has been said, and particularly what Dr. Clarke and Mrs. Atkins have said. I do not want particularly to try and argue this now but I think one might suggest that operant techniques represent form, without content. The techniques are there, the techniques are available, but the operant work as a whole does not tell you *what* you should train. This means that the individual skilled in operant work has at his disposal the means whereby he can train behaviour of whatever type he wishes. This I think is particularly important because it means one can, if one wants to, devise the behaviours which you should train for any system you like. Provided the desired behaviour can be explicitly enough stated, then there is no reason at all why an operant technique shouldn't be applied. Although I hesitate to suggest this, they could be used in the development of, for example, an Oedipus complex! On a more serious level, operant techniques do offer a means whereby—and again I am going on American experience—using relatively unskilled staff, you can

train or educate patients in subnormality hospitals, in training centres
and so on, in a variety of different ways. Beyond this, however, there is
a common misconception that these techniques are only applicable
where the behaviour to be trained is fairly narrow, very restricted.
There is a study done in the United States, the author of which is
Nancy Peterson, who trained creativity by operant methods. She did
this by analysing the features of behaviour which was said in the
classroom situation to show creativity. She said 'O.K., we'll take this
group of kids, we'll train them to behave like this' and she did. Now
you can argue about whether this is real creativity but the fact of the
matter was that those children's behaviour changed and in such a way
that made their behaviour indistinguishable from that of children in the
classrooms who were originally deemed creative. Now I would like to
go beyond this to make a couple of positive curriculum suggestions
which might be conceived as being implemented some time in the
distant future but I will comment on that again Mrs. Curzon, I'll not
leave that one like that. In the distant future one might see these as part
of every retarded person's curriculum.

One feature which has been pointed out about the behaviour of the
retarded is that he is lacking in the ability to show spontaneous
learning. Now I will just hypothesise that if one could analyse
adequately what we meant by spontaneous learning then it would be
worth attempting a training programme to make the individual
spontaneous in his learning. In parallel, if the individual's attention is
defective, then let's try and train him. This has of course been done in
many studies in the United States and, although there's a great deal to
be learned still, there's a great deal of advancement been made in that
direction. One might argue that what's needed from the operant
conditioner is a programme for training the retardate in strategies of
problem-solving. Why should we just train him to solve particular small
problems? Is it beyond our wit to discover how you train generalised
problem-solving? Certainly with ordinary industrial workers there has
been a transition from training them in particular job skills to training
them in generalised job skills and surely the same thing could be done
with the mentally retarded? Now this brings me to my final point, in
actual fact to Mrs. Curzon. I think that the operant theory left to itself
could generate *the* type of developmental theory, or *a* type of
developmental theory. What I'm suggesting is the idea that one should
pick up notions from other theories and build them into operant
techniques deduced from techniques to train hypothetical, beneficial,
changes. This is not strict operant work but I am in entire sympathy
with what Mrs. Curzon said and most of the operant people whom I
know in this country are in complete sympathy with her when she said

the problem is the problem of *now*. What I, as someone committed fairly heavily to operant work, would like to see, is a greater attempt made on the part of other colleagues in the field to place in a more explicit and behavioural manner, the type of behaviour which they say is critical. If they produce the behaviour, specified behaviours, then I am sure that within the next few years many people will come forward to attempt remediation, amelioration through operant techniques, using the type of notions which many such workers are throwing out.

Chairman: Thank you very much. Well, I think I really ought to close at this point. It remains for me merely to thank a number of people for this Study Group; first of all the Institute for Research into Mental Retardation for initiating it and sponsoring it and particularly Miss Elizabeth Osborn, the Secretary and Librarian, for all her detailed work. Secondly, I must thank the Department of Education and Science which have given us a grant for the basic expenses. This was absolutely essential and extremely helpful. Thirdly, we are grateful to the authors for their papers; fourthly, I am indebted to three of my long-suffering secretaries who have done a good deal of work on all this, and indeed to the technical department of the University of Hull for organising the tape-recording, and last but not least, to you yourselves for having come to this Study Group and for making it a successful one.

Overview

A. M. CLARKE and A. D. B. CLARKE

In this final chapter we propose to indicate, with suitable cross-references, some of the main themes which occurred in the 48 hours over which this Study Group extended. Before so doing, two important points should be emphasised. First, the mixture of different professions, ranging from civil servants to research workers, course tutors and teachers, all of whom were concerned with very similar problems, proved immensely useful and enabled what was probably a unique interchange of views to take place. Second, a good deal of the discussion was concerned not so much with what is right about research in the area of mentally retarded behaviour as with what is wrong and with what is lacking. A particularly vigorous critique of some psychological research is to be found in Dr. Ryan's paper. Some of the same points are made by Clarke and Clarke in their overview of problems. It would be a pity, however, if the soul-searching which was a feature of some of the discussions were to give the impression of overall doubt and pessimism. In fact, both experimental and correlational methods have produced a great deal of 'hard' knowledge about the mentally retarded and the close agreement on most issues among the participants bears testimony to this fact. We know, for example, a lot about the natural history of mild mental retardation, about spontaneous improvement and of successful prospective intervention programmes. Much impeccable evidence exists on the parameters of retarded learning, on retention and on learning transfer. We know that the retarded are bad spontaneous learners and that trial one on any new task is unlikely to predict responsiveness to formal learning or training opportunities; we have much information about the necessary technology for teaching the handicapped (see Mr. Cunningham's paper). We know the actuarial prospects for children of the mildly and moderately retarded whether adopted or brought up by their parents. We know much about the causes of institutional retardation and its remediation; we know something about the relation of staffing structure and type of care. We know why many current methods of training and caring for the retarded are inadequate and we know a good

263

deal about alternatives. In short, there is a mass of relevant and good evidence on a variety of practical problems. But no-one in the field can feel complacent about research and our sometimes destructive criticisms must be viewed in this light.

Thus, the symposium was in effect *about* research and researching, not a catalogue of good research which would be relevant. An attempt to allude to some major research findings which have practical implications is made in 'What are the Problems?' However, probably the single most important recent research development in the behavioural sciences, with implications for severe subnormality, is in the area of *'operant learning'*. The fact that there was no session devoted to it indicates that we were not attempting to spell out the practical applications of certain research findings. Inevitably, however, several references were made by various participants to this important subject, particularly in Sessions 1 and 7.

Since the terms *'behavioural scientist'* and *'behavioural research'* are not without ambiguity, an attempt was made to define these concepts in Session 2 (p. 70). The reader will, however, develop a more elaborated idea of the concerns of the behavioural sciences by following the whole text.

An important distinction is made in Dr. Morris' paper between research which is directed to the resolution of a contemporary social problem, which cannot be free of the values of that society; and the discovery and verification of principles and limited general laws of social behaviour and factors determining it, which can and should be value-free.

Clarke and Clarke, in connection with their review of some research in both areas mentioned by Dr. Morris, add a further distinction which is of importance to citizens and administrators: namely the difference between facts established by careful research, and value judgements sometimes based on those facts, sometimes made in ignorance of the facts, or even in defiance of the facts.

Dr. Morris alludes in her paper to a question to be asked of the politician and administrator, namely how they define a specific form of deviance: by what criteria do they decide that a person should be *labelled as deviant?* This may seem to some readers at first glance a strange question, particularly nowadays when deprivation of liberty is less an accompaniment of a deviant label than heretofore, and also since some of the more severely retarded label themselves as deviant, indicated by Dr. Serpell in Session 7 (p. 251). However, Mrs. Cooper felt that the categories used in mental retardation, and their definitions had not been sufficiently considered (p. 243). Furthermore, some participants, and notably Professor Dybwad (p. 251) and Dr. Mittler

(p. 253) pointed to the fact that even in a beneficent welfare state, by labelling a person in a particular way, he may be deprived of certain benefits which might otherwise accrue, and thus the process of labelling and the criteria for labelling are of great importance. The threshold of community tolerance for specific forms of behaviour varies from across generations and across communities. This problem is, of course, of greatest relevance to the mildly subnormal. It will become apparent to the reader that our symposium was, by mutual consent, rather strongly biased towards the problems of the more severely subnormal.

Since the major concern of our two-day discussion was research, we will attempt first to give an overview of the several themes raised in this connection.

Research Strategy

An important issue for the participants was the question of *pure and applied research* in mental retardation, with some general consensus that this dichotomy is not particularly useful, although many scientists still appear to employ it. Dr. Kiernan, in introducing Session 1, makes a valuable contribution to clearing up some of the confusion, and Dr. Mittler (p. 36 argues against the dichotomy, while Dr. Ryan (Session 7, p. 242) suggests that the distinction is not useful in psychology.

A distinction was, however, implicitly accepted between strategically adequate and inadequate research; some criticisms of experimental strategies, as already noted, appear in the two papers for Session 1, and the whole of Session 5 was devoted to this topic in considering Dr. Herriot's paper on psychological models and Dr. Serpell's contribution on attention theory.

Dr. Gunzburg (Session 1, p. 41) doubts the value of a good deal of laboratory research in psychology and suggests (Session 7, p. 240) that there are large numbers of important problems to which research workers are not addressing themselves. This latter point is relevant to the question of choice of problem and the rôle that funding organisations play in determining the nature and quality of scientific work.

Funding of Research

This matter was first raised by Dr. Morris in her paper for Session 2 and discussed at some length following Dr. Mittler's contribution (p. 71) on the subject. A further consideration of the problem was introduced by Dr. Ryan in Session 7 (p. 245) with important statements from Mrs. Holden and Mr. Cave.

Translation of Research Findings and the Rôle of the Consumer

Closely linked with the questions raised above, and having particular relevance to the problem raised by Dr. Gunzburg, was the issue of whether practitioners and administrators ought to have a bigger say than at present in the kinds of problems research workers are invited (and supported) to undertake. The possibility of creating a Consumers' Council was discussed in Session 7 (pp. 240-242). The question of how best the behavioural scientist can contribute to an evaluation of a new service or a new method of teaching the mentally subnormal, together with some of the limitations, is discussed rather fully in Session 2 (p. 73-75). A relationship between the teacher and the research psychologist as potential partners was suggested by Mr. Cave (Session 5, p. 194) and elaborated by Dr. Serpell. An interesting development in this connection was reported by Mrs. Cooper (Session 1, p. 43) towards the end of a long discussion of how best the psychologist can help the teacher of the mentally handicapped child (pp. 37-45). During this part of the Study Group various views were expressed on communication with teachers, the rôle of clinical and educational psychologists and the question of which journals teachers are likely to read in order to keep abreast of new knowledge in their field. For an important statement on this problem the reader is referred to Mr. Cave's paper (p. 87). In Session 2, Mrs. Borkwood, a practising teacher, once again urged collaboration between the research worker and the educationist (p. 80). In Session 7 Professor Dybwad, however, alluded to the sad facts of professional jealousy and resistance to acknowledging information from a rival discipline (p. 249).

Although several speakers urged the importance of knowledge for its own sake in this field as in any other, there was general agreement that in mental retardation the chief impetus to research tends to be prevention or amelioration of the condition. Thus a major theme of the symposium was a discussion of how to teach the severely handicapped, how to help their parents and how to educate their teachers.

The Mentally Subnormal Child as a Handicapped Person

As already indicated in the Preface, one matter fundamental to this, was the discussion of whether the severely subnormal should be viewed predominantly in relation to his Mental Age or as a handicapped person in relation to his Chronological Age. Criticisms of using the M.A. match in psychological research were elaborated in the two papers introducing Session 1. The relevance of knowledge of normal young children and educational methods suitable for them to teachers of the severely subnormal was discussed at length in connection with Mr. Cave's paper (Session 3). He pointed to the heterogeneity of subnormal children (p. 110); A. M. Clarke (p. 107) outlined some outstanding characteristics which the mentally handicapped have in common, namely their slowness at learning and their relative lack of ability to discover things spontaneously, to learn for themselves.

The Goals of Education for the Mentally Handicapped

Participants expressed their strong approval of accepting all mentally subnormal children as part of the general educational system, but pointed out that the differences between them and normal children are such as to make necessary special curricula and special techniques of teaching. Dr. Kiernan (p. 110) was among those who expressed the view that, for handicapped children, a goal needs to be defined in terms of certain essential skills needed for social adjustment. Mr. Cave (p. 110) suggested that there are dangers in such an approach. Dr. Gunzburg in his paper defines the goal as 'normalisation'.

Mr. Cunningham's paper for Session 4 touches on a number of important matters in this connection, elaborated by Mrs. Curzon in her opening remarks to this session, and again (p. 131) in connection with Mr. Morley's paper on industrial training. The problem is implicit in many statements made throughout the Study Group, and was raised by Dr. Serpell in the final session, provoking a long discussion to which the reader is particularly referred (pp. 252-256).

Techniques for Teaching the Mentally Handicapped

This was another strong theme underlying much of the discussion throughout. Indeed the very first contribution to the symposium (Session 1, p. 32) was by Mrs. Cookson in connection with the statement made in the Clarkes' paper that a structured learning situation is essential for subnormal children who lack the ability to learn spontaneously. Mrs. Cookson obliged us by defining a teaching situation which no psychologist would want to see employed; thereafter several statements particularly in Sessions 4, 5 and 6 made clear a consensus, on the part of the psychologists concerned with research into learning, that structuring the learning situation is essential to overcome the subnormal child's handicaps. Nevertheless, in the final session Dr. Mittler was quoted as feeling that we had not been sufficiently explicit for educationists on this matter, which probably deserves a whole symposium of its own.

The Subnormal Child's Interaction with the Social Environment

Linked with the question of structuring, the urgent problem of the nature of the interaction between the subnormal child and his parents, teachers and others in various social contexts was raised on several occasions, initially in connection with Dr. Ryan's paper for Session 1. Dr. Carr outlined some of her findings on mother/infant interaction (p. 34), while Mrs. Cookson, in introducing Session 6, outlined an important process in the language development of normal children, which Dr. Ryan (p. 227) later suggested may be seriously impaired in the relationship between a subnormal child and his parent. Dr. Mittler followed with a long statement on biological and social factors in language development, and methods whereby the subnormal can be enabled to develop language. Dr. Herriot (p. 231) suggests a method of structuring a social situation in such a way as to force a person to use his voice rather than other methods of communication. Dr. Gunzburg's paper includes a wealth of thought-provoking suggestions as to how the physical and social environment can be manipulated to encourage learning and personal development.

Advice to Parents

This matter was the subject of Mr. Brinkworth's paper to Session 6, and discussed by Mrs. Cookson in her introduction. Dr. Hodgson (p. 226) contributed to the discussion early in the session, and later (p. 233) introduced a question concerning the programme for parents which is being developed at the Hester Adrian Centre.

The Behavioural Scientist in Hospitals for the Subnormal

Dr. Gunzburg's paper to Session 2 was largely devoted to the rôle of the psychologist in institutional management, although much of what he had to say would be equally applicable to any educational unit in the community. Mrs. Harbinson, in introducing the session and again on p. 78) discusses some of the difficulties to be overcome in putting his proposals into effect, with particular reference to the necessity for reorientation of staff rôles. Dr. Kiernan (p. 78) gives from his personal experience a vivid example of such a difficulty, and later during this important discussion Dr. Hodgson (p. 82) drew attention, with an illustration, to the need for sensible collaboration over a very wide range of professional workers. In Session 7 (p. 257) Mrs. Atkins introduced a brief discussion of some of the unfortunate aspects of mental subnormality hospitals.

The Responsibilities of the Behavioural Scientist

Finally, at various points during the symposium, speakers touched upon two issues: the psychologist's obligation to hold himself responsible for his prescriptions, and his ethical responsibilities. Dr. Kiernan in his concluding introductory remarks to Session 1 (p. 32) introduces the subject; Dr. Gunzburg (p. 39) complains that psychologists often recommend action which they are not in a position to implement; Dr. Mittler gives as an ideal example the operant movement in which the psychologist assumes that he will make an assessment as a necessary first step to a remedial programme. As already noted, much of Session 2 was devoted to a discussion of the psychologist's rôle as part of a managerial team, and here Dr. Gunzburg spoke of the danger of the psychologist perceiving the mentally handicapped as interesting material for laboratory experiments rather than as a human being who needs certain specialised help. In Session 7 (p. 249) Professor Dybwad raised the question of the ethics of research in subnormality, while later Dr. Kiernan (p. 259) expressed some of the problems which confront those who learn effectively to use the potentially powerful techniques of operant conditioning, and some of the widespread misapprehensions concerning these methods, which can be as useful in stimulating creative behaviour in normal children as they are in eradicating destructive behaviour in the severely retarded, or helping them to social adjustment.

As noted earlier, this Study Group was primarily concerned with the application of research to practical problems in the field of mental retardation, and at the beginning of this Overview we exemplified some of the areas where already very detailed knowledge exists. This concern for better services for the mentally handicapped proved to be topical and, with the publication in 1971 of the Rothschild Report, and the subsequent White Paper, *Framework for Government Research and Development* (Cmnd. 5046, H.M.S.O.) in July, 1972, Government Departments have been encouraged to be more sensitive to the use of the powerful methodology of science for clarifying issues of policy and practice. It is our expectation that the behavioural sciences will have an important function here both in the objective evaluation of preventive and ameliorative schemes for the handicapped, and in suggesting new and better approaches to their problems.

List of Participants

J. Appell, BA, Dip.Psych.

Senior Clinical Psychologist, London Borough of Croydon and Warlingham Park Hospital, Surrey

Joanna Atkins, Dip.T.C.T.M.H.

Teacher of the Mentally Handicapped, Hull

M. Bagot, MA, BSc(Econ)

Chief Inspector of Schools, City and County of Kingston upon Hull

Nan Borkwood, Dip.Ed., HCh

Head Teacher, Special School, Bleach Green, Co. Durham *and* formerly Lecturer, Durham College of Technology

R. Brinkworth, BA, DCP

Head of General Department, Great Barr Comprehensive School, *and* Director, Down's Babies Centre, Quinton, Birmingham

Janet Carr, BA, PhD

Lecturer in Psychology, Institute of Psychiatry, University of London, *and* Hilda Lewis House, The Bethlem Royal and Maudsley Hospitals, Shirley

C. W. E. Cave, H.M.I.

Department of Education and Science, London

A. D. B. Clarke, PhD (*Chairman*)

Professor of Psychology, University of Hull

Ann M. Clarke, PhD

Honorary Research Fellow, Department of Psychology, University of Hull

271

Margaret D. Cookson, BA	Advisory Officer responsible for Severely Handicapped Children, Staffordshire Education Authority
Elizabeth S. Cooper, BA	Scientific Research Officer, MRC Unit for the Study of Environmental Factors in Mental and Physical Illness, London
C. C. Cunningham, BSc	Robert Bailey Research Fellow, Hester Adrian Research Centre for the Study of Learning Processes in the Mentally Handicapped, University of Manchester
Jeanne M. Currie, BSc, Dip.Ed.Psych.	County Educational Psychologist, Durham County Education Committee, *and* Hon. Secretary, Association of Educational Psychologists, Durham
Winifred M. Curzon, H.M.I.	Department of Education and Science, London
Christine E. Doyle, BA	Research Student, Department of Psychology, University of Hull
Gunnar Dybwad, JD	Professor of Human Development, The Florence Heller School for Advanced Studies in Social Welfare, Brandeis University, Waltham, Mass. U.S.A.
H. C. Gunzburg, MA, PhD, FBPsS	Director of Psychological Services for Subnormal Hospitals, Birmingham area
Sonja G. Harbinson, BA	Professional Adviser, Training Council for Teachers of the Mentally Handicapped, Department of Health and Social Security, London

Miriam J. Harris, BA	Secretary, Psychology Committee, Social Science Research Council, London
Gail Hawks, MSc	Senior Psychologist, Queen Mary's Hospital for Children, Carshalton
P. Herriot, BA, MEd, PhD	Lecturer, Hester Adrian Research Centre for the Study of Learning Processes in the Mentally Handicapped, University of Manchester

Maureen J. Hodgson, MB, BS, MRCS, LRCP, DCH
Medical Officer, Department of Health and Social Security, London

Sheila M. Holden, BA	Secretary, Training Council for Teachers of the Mentally Handicapped, Department of Health and Social Security, London
C. C. Kiernan, BA, PhD	Senior Lecturer, Centre for Advanced Study and Research *and* Department of Child Development, Institute of Education, University of London
A. L. Lambert, BSc, Dip.Psych.	Senior Educational Psychologist, Education Department, Kingston upon Hull
P. J. Mittler, MA, PhD	Director, Hester Adrian Research Centre for the Study of Learning Processes in the Mentally Handicapped, University of Manchester
K. G. Morley, DMA, AMBIM	Assistant Director of Social Services, London Borough of Croydon

Pauline Morris, PhD

Research Director, Legal Advice Research Unit, The Nuffield Foundation, London

A. D. Murray, HNC, AMBIM

Principal Assistant, Day Care Division, Social Services Department London Borough of Croydon

Joanna Ryan, MA, PhD

Research Psychologist, Unit for Research on the Medical Applications of Psychology, University of Cambridge

B. F. C. M. Schiphorst, Dip.T.C.T.M.H.

Social Work Services Officer, Department of Health and Social Security, Newcastle upon Tyne

R. Serpell, BA, DPhil

Senior Research Fellow, Hester Adrian Research Centre for the Study of Learning Process in the Mentally Handicapped, University of Manchester

Index